What People Ar... About *Women Circling the Earth* . . .

"Of the constellation of literature on this subject, Beverly's contribution is a bright shining star. It speaks to the reasons why many woman are seeking to circle now. With practical wisdom and spiritual guidance, she illuminates for all of us ways to circle together and, equally important, to link with other circles so that women together can encircle their lives and this Earth with their love."

Carol Proudfoot-Edgar
poet, shamanic path walker, tender of Sacred Circles

"*Women Circling the Earth* speaks from the heart to the heart. This book illuminates the spirit of the circle in a way that brings it within the reach of any who wish to move their lives in that direction. It is a rich source of information, resources and inspiration for both women and men. In this book I felt loving intent and an honoring of the many sources of wisdom about circle."

Kay Pranis
restorative justice planner
Minnesota Department of Corrections

"I love this book. It spurred me to action in both my personal and professional life. Beverly did a remarkable job of reminding us who do this work that circle is the way to transformation. I tend to forget this when I am right in the middle of it. It takes a book like this to put it all together."

Ellie Mercer
ordained clergywoman
United Church of Christ

"An idea often sprouts in widely separate places. Then someone comes along and sees the pattern. In *Women Circling the Earth* Beverly Engel brings great synthesis and clarity to the sacred practice of circles."

Cindy Spring
coauthor, *Wisdom Circles*

Women Circling THE Earth

A Guide to Fostering Community, Healing and Empowerment

BEVERLY ENGEL

Health Communications, Inc.
Deerfield Beach, Florida

www.hci-online.com

Circles Devoted to Individual Healing reprinted by permission of Ailo Gaup.

Library of Congress Cataloging-in-Publication Data

Engel, Beverly.
   Women circling the earth : a guide to fostering community, healing, and empowerment / Beverly Engel.
     p.   cm.
   Includes bibliographical references and index.
   ISBN 1-55874-775-9 (trade paper)
   1. Women—Psychology. 2. Women—Social networks. I. Title.
HQ1206.E53 2000
305.4—DC21

                      00-027611

©2000 Beverly Engel

ISBN 1-55874-755-9

Publisher: Health Communications, Inc.
               3201 S.W. 15th Street
               Deerfield Beach, FL 33442-8190

Cover design by Larissa Hise
Cover illustration by Gail Lapins
Inside book design by Lawna Patterson Oldfield

This book is dedicated to
Christina Baldwin, Sedonia Cahill,
Carol Proudfoot-Edgar, Cindy Spring,
Sandra Ingerman, Kay Pranis and
all the women who are circling the Earth
with their wisdom, grace and
generous spirits.

And to the life and memory of
Sedonia Cahill—may the circle be unbroken.

"She was a bright walking star.
We shall walk within the illumination
she will continue to cast."

Carol Proudfoot-Edgar

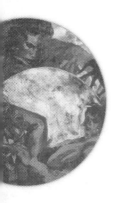

CONTENTS

ACKNOWLEDGMENTS

Firstirst and foremost, I wish to express my heartfelt gratitude to all the leaders of the women's circle movement who gave so freely of their time and generously shared their wisdom—Christina Baldwin, Sedonia Cahill, Carol Proudfoot-Edgar, Cindy Spring, Sandra Ingerman and Kay Pranis. Without their contributions, both in terms of their willingness to be interviewed and the wealth of information I gleaned from reading their wonderful books, this book could not have been written.

I am especially grateful for the generosity of Christina Baldwin and Sedonia Cahill. This book would have been impossible to write without their help. Christina gave freely of her time, resources and bountiful wisdom. I quoted liberally from her book, *Calling the Circle: The First and Future Culture*, and she referred me to both Mary K. Sandford and Ellie Mercer. Sedonia's book, *The*

Ceremonial Circle, offered a wealth of information and was the source for much of what I wrote about ritual and ceremony.

I consider both Christina and Sedonia the "mothers" of the current circle movement. Their dedication to transforming the Earth and her inhabitants, and to spreading the word of the circle, seems to be boundless.

I want to give a special thanks to Carol Proudfoot-Edgar who not only painstakingly completed my questionnaire but wrote answers that were truly inspiring.

I am also deeply indebted to all the women who helped add depth to this book—who have made circling an important aspect of their lives and who generously agreed to share their experiences so that other women could learn the value of meeting in circle—Mary Elizabeth Thunder, Mary K. Sandford, Ellie Mercer, Patricia Waters, Julie Steinbach, LaWanna Durbin and Angie Ober.

Gail Lapins, an artist I've long admired for her dynamic, evocative paintings, graciously donated the art for the cover of the book. I am deeply grateful.

I could think of no other art or artist I would rather have represent this book. Not only does this particular painting convey the meaning and message of the book but the artist is herself a woman circling the Earth with her wisdom, grace and generous spirit.

My deepest gratitude goes to LaWanna Durbin, for her

willingness to pass on her wisdom and for being an example of someone who walks her talk, to my two circle buddies, Mo and Marianne for walking along side of me as we explored, and laughed; and to the wonderful women of the Cambria circles.

Finally a special thank you to all those at HCI who worked hard on the book: Christine Belleris and Allison Janse for their fine editing and "behind the scenes" help, Kim Weiss for helping to get the word out about the book, Lawna Patterson Oldfield for her inside book design and Larissa Hise for the beautiful book cover design.

INTRODUCTION

I am the woman who holds up the sky.
The rainbow runs through my eyes.
The sun makes a path to my womb.
My thoughts are in the shape of clouds.
But my words are yet to come.

POEM OF THE UTE INDIANS

I am not the first person to write about circles and I certainly won't be the last. Starhawk wrote about circles in 1982, and Sedonia Cahill and Joshua Halpern introduced many people to circles in their 1990 book *The Ceremonial Circle*. In 1994 Christina Baldwin, in her groundbreaking book, *Calling the Circle: The First and Future Culture*, introduced many to the idea that through circling we have the power to change our culture and the way we relate to one another.

Nor do I consider myself an "expert" on circles, although I've had many profound experiences in circle and have been part of one form of circle or another for many years. What I bring to this book is a deep belief in circles as vehicles for personal, community and global transformation, and an equally strong belief that women currently play, and are meant to continue to play, a significant role in this transformation.

I was called to write this book for reasons I still cannot fully explain. The primary messages of the book—that women must be the ones to lead the way in making the changes that will save humanity and Mother Earth, and that this change will come one circle at a time—came to me as an epiphany. The title and original structure of the book revealed themselves to me without any conscious thought or planning on my part.

Like a circle, this book has taken on a life of its own. Just as we need structure to begin a circle, I needed an original structure to begin the preliminary work. But, just as most circles become outpourings of spontaneous emotion and insight, so too has this book evolved. While the original structure remained intact, many other elements changed over time.

Along the way I learned many lessons, the most important being to trust the flow. Even though I was originally excited about writing the book (enough to sell Health Communications on the idea), there have been several periods when I resisted writing it. Because I was given no deadline, I kept delaying the writing. At times I became upset with myself about this because I normally do not procrastinate when writing a book. I am usually eager to begin writing, and I normally stay very involved throughout the writing process. Not so with *Women Circling the Earth*. Once I got my original ideas down on paper, I put off doing the necessary research and contacting those I felt would be instrumental in helping me add breadth and authority to the book. Since this was the first book I've written where I relied heavily on research and interviews with experts in the field, rather than on my own expertise and experiences, I rationalized that this was the cause of my procrastination.

Interestingly, as much as I agonized over the fact that I wasn't getting the book completed, another voice inside me kept saying, "Give it time, let it unfold." This helped me take a deep breath and relax for a while. I was learning through my spiritual practices not to push the river but to trust that life will unfold in its own time.

Eventually I came to realize that it wasn't resistance to the research or the interviews that was causing me to write so slowly. It was a lack of courage and conviction. My original ideas—that the women's circle movement was the new women's movement for the millennium, and it was up to women to change the world—were met with some resistance from a few of the women I first interviewed.

Because I respected these women, their resistance caused me to lose confidence in my ideas, especially since it was so difficult for me to trace their origin.

It seemed there were still some lessons I needed to learn—about circles, about the world and about myself—before I could return to my original vision and complete the book. One such lesson was that if you trust your inner knowing, your inner wisdom, you will find your answers and your path. Ironically, this is one of the lessons stressed in women's circles.

As time went by and I kept adding more and more material to the book, I came to realize that the book was too "big" and too important to rush. I came to see the fact that I had no deadline as a wonderful gift. The book could move along at its own pace. I could add what was important and take away what was not, like crafting a finely honed instrument.

Unconsciously, I was also waiting for the right time for the book to be published. This is the right time. The energy is right; people are more open to circling than at any other time in recent history. As we enter the new millennium, more and more people are recognizing the need for community and the need to return to ritual for sustenance, spiritual direction and enlightenment. *Women Circling the Earth* shows how we can strengthen both our social and spiritual ties through circle.

Many people are also interested in discovering ways to

have a positive impact on the world. Circling can literally change the world, one circle at a time.

And now, when argument and confrontation have replaced discussion and understanding, we desperately need a more positive way of resolving our conflicts and settling our differences. Circles, with their focus on speaking and listening from the heart, listening without judgment, not only tolerating but welcoming different perspectives on an issue and working toward consensus, offer a simple but profound way to resolve conflicts.

Equally important at this time in our history, more and more women (and men) are coming to the realization that we need women's energy and the feminine values of connection, compassion and cooperation to turn this world around.

As a psychotherapist for over twenty-five years, I may seem like an unlikely person to write about women's circles, particularly spiritual circles. But more and more often, spirituality and psychology are being intricately interwoven, forming a new school of thought altogether. No place demonstrates this new way of thinking more profoundly than do women's circles, which often have as much power to heal the human psyche as some forms of psychotherapy.

This does not mean that I believe that circles can take the place of psychotherapy or recovery programs for people who have serious problems. But for those who have already worked on these issues in therapy or Twelve-Step programs (which, by the way, are excellent examples of circles) and wish to continue their growth, meeting in circle, especially if that circle is structured in a positive way, can do as much as or more than the average group counseling experience.

Personal growth is a continuum, and hopefully we are all continuing to grow and change. My interest in women's circles is what I consider a natural outgrowth of the group work I did for so many years with survivors of childhood abuse. Just as there is still a need for survivor groups, especially during the early stages of recovery, there is also a need for the kinds of circles I write about in this book.

Part One of the book introduces you to women's circles and the women's circle movement. I share some of the history and symbology of the circle and explain its power.

Part Two offers an overview of the various ways circle can be utilized: to provide a much needed sense of community; to manifest healing; to achieve consensus and create change; and to help people reconnect with the sacred.

Part Three offers suggestions on how to create your own circle. I begin by presenting an overview of the various types of women's circles that now exist so you can decide which type of circle best serves your purposes. This section includes a listing of the elements needed to create a circle, as well as suggestions for structuring your circle.

Part Four discusses how women are circling the Earth with their ideas, traveling around the Earth to learn and share their wisdom, and bringing important information from other countries back home. I interview major leaders and role models in the growing circle movement to get their input about the power of circle, to better understand the circle's role in saving the world and its inhabitants, and to learn what these leaders' individual goals are. I then show you how to become part of the circle movement and how to make circling an integral part of your life. You will learn how to translate what you practice and learn in circles into your daily life, and how circling principles can become a spiritual practice.

Several years ago I had a dream so real that for several hours afterward it felt as if it had actually happened, a dream so poignant that the feeling of joy it elicited stayed with me for days. In the dream I had traveled to a place not too far away, a land that seemed very familiar. Once there I was delighted to discover that a group of women had been waiting for me. These wonderful, wise and caring women welcomed me into their fold, and I felt privileged to be with them. They were the women I had always dreamed of being with, the women I knew waited for me somewhere. I was filled with joy now that I had finally found them. These women were my home.

I believe that within every woman lies this same dream and that we are all longing to come home to our circle of women. We all have a circle of women waiting for us somewhere—or a circle waiting to be created. My highest hope for each of you reading this book is that you find your circle, that you find your way home.

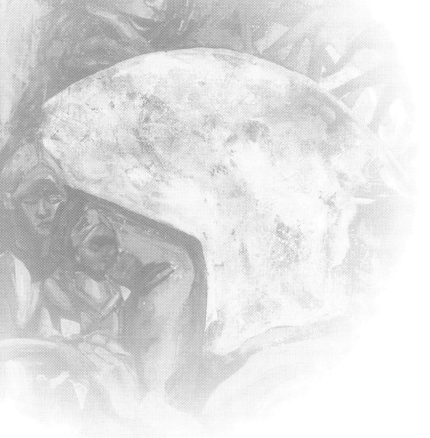

PART ONE

The Quiet Power of Women's Circles

ONE

The Quiet Power of Women's Circles

A woman is the full circle.
Within her is the power to create, nurture,
and transform. A woman knows that nothing can
come to fruition without light. Let us call upon
woman's voice and woman's heart to guide us
in this age of planetary transformation.

DIANE MARIECHILD

This book is about women meeting in circles for the purpose of creating community, and about how the circle can inspire and empower women to develop creative solutions to individual, community and world problems. The book is also about how the ancient practice of circling is being recaptured, revitalized and fast becoming the new social movement for the millennium.

Women Circling the Earth celebrates the incredible power and healing that can be created when women meet in circles, and the transformation that can occur when we speak from the heart and listen to one another with open hearts and open minds. It is about the spiritual reawakening that women can experience when they quiet their minds, open their hearts and listen for their inner wisdom to guide them.

Women Circling the Earth is also about the women who are modeling the circle and the circle way of life and, by so doing, are inspiring others all over the world to join the circle.

Finally, it is about how by joining the circle and living your life by circle principles you can become one of the women circling the earth who takes the circle's message and healing to everyone—men, women and children.

Until recently, the primitive practice of gathering in circles—perhaps the oldest and most powerful form for creating community, teaching and healing—was nearly lost to modern cultures. But today people are finally coming home to the circle and coming home to themselves.

People all over the United States, Canada, South America, Europe, Asia, the Soviet Union, Australia and Africa are meeting together in small circles, speaking from the heart, listening openly to one another, reaching consensus, practicing ancient rituals, drumming and singing songs together. Some of these people have never before felt the power a circle can radiate; others have been meeting in circles their entire lives, just as their elders did.

Meeting in circle began to be the new social, spiritual and political forum for the 1990s, and it will most certainly be a primary forum for hearkening in the new millennium. Circles have taken the place of support groups and consciousness-raising groups as more and more people discover the power of circling to effect change and quench the hunger for soul and sacredness. The circle as a format is being introduced into every aspect of society, from grammar schools to universities, from churches to the criminal justice system.

In this book you'll learn what the circle is, what purposes it can serve, how it is being utilized by various groups of people, and perhaps most important, how you can become involved in circles yourself.

What Is a Circle?

Is a circle like a support group? A consciousness-raising group? A town meeting? No, it is far more than those things. A circle is not just a gathering of people who sit in a circle on the floor or a meeting where the chairs are arranged in a circle. As Christina Baldwin stated in her groundbreaking book *Calling the Circle: The First and Future Culture*, it is a way of thinking and doing things that is radically different from the way we normally think and act. At the same time it is a return to our original form of community, a return to an ancient process of communion. In council circles, such as PeerSpirit, Wisdom and Peacemaking Circles, it is a return to a form of consultation that literally shaped the course of humanity. In ceremonial, healing, sacred and shamanic circles, it is a return to the use of ritual and ceremony, and the creation of powerful healing energy.

Circles are similar to support groups in that they can offer much needed support to those who are struggling with various issues. But the circle offers a unique format that provides even more.

Circles provide simple yet powerful tools to help teach people how to communicate more honestly and openly. They foster cooperation and understanding, help implement creative solutions, bridge differences and encourage reconciliation. Circles are an excellent forum for organizing and planning strategies, and are often used successfully for settling disputes and reaching consensus on issues about which there is much disagreement. Circles are especially effective in helping those who come from diverse backgrounds, or who hold extremely different views, to learn to listen to one another without judgment.

In circles, advice giving is discouraged, as is cross talk. Instead, circle members pass a talking piece or talking stick around the circle. When someone is holding the talking piece this signals to others that it is this person's turn to speak and that everyone's focus needs to be on the speaker. When it is someone else's turn to talk, others are encouraged to focus all their attention on what this person is saying, as opposed to thinking about how they wish to respond. And everyone is encouraged to open their hearts and minds, and listen without judgment to what the speaker has to say.

There are many types of circles—PeerSpirit Circles, Wisdom Circles, simplicity circles, Peacemaking Circles, Empowerment Circles, crone circles, drumming circles— but all share the same values and basic structure. All circles are built around the following six elements, which I will describe in detail later in the book:

- Intention
- Sacredness
- Commitment
- Equality
- Heart Consciousness
- Gratitude

Why Women's Circles?

While there are men's circles and circles with both men and women, this book is about women's circles. Meeting in closed circles is particularly powerful for women because circles eliminate the sense of hierarchy, are protective and express a human sense of the wholeness of life—the roundness of birth, the embryo curled up in a circle, the pregnant belly, the full breast.

Although both men and women met in circles in ancient times, women seem to be most comfortable with this form of community.

Circling seems to come more naturally to women, perhaps because we are more accustomed to functioning without a hierarchy, and are more open to those who have different perspectives and divergent points of view.

Women resonate to the concept of the circle because it stresses the beliefs that we are all equal and that we are all parts of the whole. In a circle each person's face can be seen, each person's voice can be heard and valued. All points on a circle are equidistant from its center. In fact, it is the circle's definition and function to distribute energy equally.

Perhaps another reason why women take to the circle more readily than men is that women tend to think in complex, *circular* patterns rather than in a linear progression, as males do. Traditionally, thinking has been considered a male province, and women's thought processes have been devalued and downgraded. But while women's thinking can be characterized as different from men's, it is not less than men's and this is made abundantly clear when women meet in circle.

Some of those who have written about circles write to both a male and female audience. But I identify the circle movement as a women's movement. I do this for several reasons. First of all, most of the people who are circling are women; by most estimates, circles are comprised of as much as 85 percent women. Although there are men who circle, women far outnumber the men, and more women are making circling a way of life.

Second, the current circle movement originated as a women's movement and is fueled by feminine energy. Those men who are a part of the circling movement have recognized this and have been willing to step into this energy and learn from it.

This is not to say that men are not or cannot be a part of the circle movement. Those men who are open to their feminine sides and are willing to trade the power of leadership for the power of cooperation are welcome.

Third, women are the moving force behind teaching circling principles and bringing circling to all peoples of the world.

Most of the leaders of the circle movement are women— Starhawk, Christina Baldwin, Sedonia Cahill, Kay Pranis, Berma Bushie, Cindy Spring and Carol Proudfoot-Edgar.

Last, but certainly not least, the circle is significant to women because it has always been one of the primary feminine signs (as opposed to the line, cross or phallic shaft representing masculine spirit). According to Barbara Walker in *The Women's Dictionary of Symbols and Sacred Objects*, early matrifocal villages had round hearths, round houses, round fences and defensive shapes. The circle was associated with the idea of a protected or con-secrated space, the center of the motherland, a ceremonial space where all participants were equal. Worship circles like the Hindu *chakra* and the Arabic *halka* were those in which female influence was prevalent.

The modern world needs a sense of wholeness, of the essential unity of all peoples, creatures and nature on this earth. According to Barbara Walker, we need to restore the idea of the great round, before our linear, "power-over" mind-set destroys not only the concept of life, but even the fact of life altogether. We do not have many places from which to begin. The women's circle is most certainly one of them.

The title of this book, *Women Circling the Earth,* is meant to evoke many images: the circle as symbol of the feminine; meeting in circles as a source of power and support; the power of the circle to enlighten the people of the Earth; and circle as a way to save the Earth. My vision is for all women to see themselves as part of a whole, part of a giant circle of women holding hands as they encircle the globe.

I, and many of the women you will hear from in this book, believe it is up to women to save the Earth, to teach the world the truth about compassion and empathy, and to repair the damage of war, poverty and ecological ruin. Men may still rule the worlds of finance and politics, but women rule the world of the heart and soul. Many people, like myself, believe that the salvation of our planet lies in the hands and hearts of its women.

The Western world has been built upon masculine mastery, and this mastery has brought us to a powerful place in the evolution of humankind. But to move forward, we must call on the healing powers of the feminine.

Feminine qualities and values—such as a need for connection with others, and a willingness to compromise and negotiate in order to meet everyone's needs—that women bring to the world and to men in particular are what give this world its humanity, and its true strength and meaning.

Until recently the male way of being has been more highly valued, and females have been seen as deficient. But women's tendency to focus outward, and our seemingly inexhaustible fascination with and concern for others and their needs, are what make women such good mothers, mates and friends, and make our world a more caring, compassionate place.

Our current and enduring sex-role stereotypes reflect a conception of adulthood that is *out of balance*, that favors the separateness of the individual over connection to others. But by beginning to understand the different ways females and males think and act, we come to realize that what has been labeled "female passivity" is sometimes the female's need to seek a solution that is most inclusive of everyone's needs. Or, as Carol Gilligan has stated in her groundbreaking book. *In a Different Voice,* "as an act of care rather than the restraint of aggression." (Some researchers even believe that females are biologically wired to avoid anger and to instead work toward peaceful solutions to problems.)

This "ethic of care" as Gilligan refers to it is only one of the many things women can teach men. Here are others:

- An awareness of the connection between people
- A belief in communication as the best mode of non-violent conflict resolution
- A network of relationship versus a hierarchical ordering
- Self-delineation through connection versus self-definition through separation
- A responsibility to others as well as to oneself

Carol Gilligan and others urge us to begin to define "adulthood" and "normalcy" based on the inclusion of the psychology of women. Using this model, versus the separation model already in existence, would have a profound impact on both men and women. For males, "development would entail coming to see the other as equal to the self and the discovery that equality provides a way of making connections safe." For females, "development would follow the inclusion of herself in an expanding network of connection and the discovery that separation can be protective and need not entail isolation."

Circles can create the "expanding network of connection" to which Gilligan refers. This is exactly the experience that Andrea, one of the women I interviewed for the book, shared with me about her circle:

> *Through my circle experience I've learned to value the feminine spirit and feminine values. I was raised in a very misogynistic family where a female's opinions and ideas weren't valued and where men were perceived as superior to women. Because of this I grew up negativing my own thinking, and feeling and believing that the male point of view was always more accurate.*
>
> *But in my circle I learned that the female point of view, while often different from that of males, is no less valid. We may not think and act as logically, but we tend to think with more feeling and in deeper ways. We tend to consider the consequences of our behavior more than men, especially how our actions will affect others. I like this about women. I appreciate our caring and our compassion.*
>
> *My circle experience has been so healing for me. The love, support and respect I've received from these wonderful women has helped heal the damage of growing up in such a female-hating environment, and has helped me to love and respect myself. I'm no longer afraid to speak my mind, even to men. And if a man puts me down or negates what I've said, I have the strength and self-respect to stand my ground. I'll forever be grateful for this experience.*

Men need women to teach them about equality, compromise and cooperation—attitudes and behaviors that do not come naturally to men. They need the skills that women and circle can teach them about how to relate to others in a more respectful, meaningful way and how to achieve true understanding with others. They need to learn the feminine values I call the three Cs—connection, cooperation and compassion—to balance out the typical male values I call the three As—autonomy, aggression and action.

In *The Redemption of the Feminine Erotic Soul*, Jungian psychologist Rachel Hillel states that her research reveals that we need feminine lunar consciousness with its diffuse awareness and instinctual knowledge of balance. To survive sanely, we need its wisdom of the heart, its deep roots into the mysteries of soul and body, and its irrational access to the creative process.

We have reached a time in our spiritual development as a planet when we once again have begun to value family, community and the sacredness of nature; cooperation and harmony over noisy protest or forced allegiance; quiet contemplation over rapid, disruptive change. These are the values and mind-set most often associated with the feminine rather than the masculine, and these are the cornerstones of circle philosophy.

The Purpose of This Book

Women Circling the Earth has three purposes. The first is to introduce more women to the concept of the circle as a vehicle for emotional and spiritual healing, for building community and consensus, and for offering support and validation to those already meeting in circle. The book describes the types of circles that exist, explains how they function and shows you how to start one of your own. Unlike other books on the subject I do not advocate any particular type of circle. I believe there is a circle structure that is right for each woman, and women need to know what is available in order to make this decision. To this end I present a broad overview of the various types of circles along with the benefits of each. My hope is that every woman reading this book will feel inspired to either join an existing circle or create one of her own.

Second, *Women Circling the Earth* is about how women are producing change on a worldwide level, and are literally and figuratively "circling the Earth" with their vision, wisdom, grace and noncompetitive spirits. They are traveling around the Earth, meeting with indigenous peoples, congregating at international conferences and bringing information back home.

It is my belief that this is how the world will change— one circle at a time, encircling the Earth. The power of women meeting together in small circles is phenomenal. In these circles individual women come to know the quiet power of deep connection, the strength of oneness with a group and with self.

The power of women circling the Earth truly has a ripple effect. Just as it happens when you throw a pebble into the water—one small circle becomes a larger one, which in turn becomes a still larger one—each small women's circle has a subtle yet profound effect on the immediate environment.

Each person within a circle is changed in innumerable ways—some visibly, others less obviously, but none insignificantly. In turn, each person has an effect on her environment, such as beginning to treat others differently or radiating a different type of energy.

Sometimes the effect a circle has on an individual is explainable; other times it is more of an enigma. On an obvious level we can say that because a woman feels supported and empowered by the nurturing environment of a circle, she is motivated to produce change in her life. But not all changes can be so readily explained. Some women have experienced emotional and physical healing, often in startling and profound ways. In healing, shamanic, drumming and artists' circles, women have transcended severe emotional, physical and sexual trauma in far less time and in more dramatic ways than are normally achieved in conventional psychotherapy.

Third, I wish to introduce you to the women's circle movement in the hopes that you will feel inspired to join us in our attempts to transform the world. The women's circle movement is quietly and strongly moving along, but it lacks definition and direction. My hope is that this book will be both the hub from which other ideas about circle can emerge and the spark that ignites the movement and gives it momentum. The women's circle movement could go on quietly without *Women Circling the Earth*, but perhaps because of the book many women will feel validated and encouraged, and many more will join the circle's ranks.

Throughout the book you will hear from the leaders of the women's circle movement. Many feel as I do that it is up to women to initiate and carry out the important changes needed to save our planet and its people. Others are less certain about this, but they agree that women lead the way in circling and make up the majority of those who are meeting in circle.

You will also be introduced to women who are participating in circles. They share their perspectives on the importance of circles in general and how circle has affected their lives. These are women whose daily actions and attitudes are dedicated to making the world a better place. For example, every year in the little town of Cambria, California, a woman has thirty to forty women over to her house for a winter solstice celebration. She tells a story, often based on a feminine myth, and creates a ritual that exemplifies the myth. Then she gives each woman a gift—often created by her own hands—that symbolizes the story and ritual, such as a stone with a hand-painted spiral on it, which was the offering the first year I attended. Then she leads the women in songs and encourages them to look around the room and acknowledge all the wonderful women in their presence. She asks only that the women remember the night and give back to one another throughout the year.

Although it may not appear as if anything dramatic occurs on this evening, each woman is affected in some way, whether it is just feeling less isolated or more connected to others.

Who Will Benefit the Most from the Book and from Circling?

Most women reading *Women Circling the Earth* will benefit from it no matter what their social, financial, political or religious background. But those who hunger for community with other women and for a deeper connection with others will benefit the most. As we become more and more alienated from one another, as we women lose touch with our similarities and our need to connect with one another, we feel more empty and alone all the time. Women need one another. We need the energy of other women to wash over us and fill us up. We need the sense of acceptance and belonging that only other women can give us.

Mary K. Sandford, associate dean, College of Arts and Sciences at the University of North Carolina at Greensboro, shared with me her first experience with circle, which she described as "a life-changing event":

> *I consider my first experience in circle as one of the defining moments in my life. I first met Christina Baldwin and Ann Linnea, the creators of PeerSpirit circles, at a retreat center when I was on holiday. They showed the video* Goddess Remembered *(directed by Donna Read), which is a very powerful video to show to a group of women.*
>
> *Throughout the workshop I saw the power of the form, and I began to understand its benefits. I immediately started thinking about how I could utilize it in the academic environment.*
>
> *I discovered the power of people being able to speak their truth openly and have this witnessed by others. The power of someone sitting in witness without making suggestions, giving advice. We are all on our own journey, but there is a tendency in this culture to tell people what to do—instead of allowing them to make their own connections.*
>
> *When we use the talking piece people begin to focus on what the speaker is saying; we begin to listen to one another. When we speak with intent we begin to speak our truth as opposed to what we are "supposed to say."*
>
> *But I also benefited on a more personal level. I discovered what a safe space was for the first time. And I came to appreciate a connection with other women that I had not felt before. Although I had always thought of myself as a feminist, in circle I was able to feel a heart connection with other*

*women that I had never felt before. I gained a better under-
standing of other women.*

Those who have been searching for a community in which to grow spiritually will also find what they have been looking for in the form of the circle. The same is true for those who have been longing to find a way to apply personal consciousness toward healing the world.

Those women who have difficulties trusting other women, and who are plagued by feelings of envy and competitiveness toward other women, will find that the circle engenders trust between members. It offers a way to experience the kind of true intimacy that can arise out of a long-lasting commitment. In addition, many problems related to our ability to connect and bond with one another, such as fear of intimacy, lack of trust, defensiveness, egocentrism and being overly critical and judgmental, are regularly dealt with in circles.

Those who distrust psychotherapists and have issues with authority in general will find meeting in circle particularly beneficial, since most circles are leaderless or have rotating leadership.

In addition, circles are particularly attractive to and beneficial for those women who are themselves teachers, healers or therapists, since our roles tend to separate and isolate us from others. Because everyone in a circle is equal, circles offer the unique opportunity to melt into a group and not have to carry the burden or the privilege of leadership. This enables us to become more vulnerable and to reconnect with our basic humanity.

Recently I attended a professional workshop on group process. The workshop was to be an experiential one, giving therapists a chance to receive support, since we are usually the ones giving support to others. Unfortunately, as I had predicted, most people did not feel safe enough to freely open up and share. Even though we had a leader, he offered no structure or rules, thereby adding to our reluctance (therapists are known to be defensive and protective of themselves, far more comfortable in the "leader" role or the "caregiver role" than in the role of client.) Sadly, it wasn't until the end of the weekend workshop that we were finally able to begin to talk about our deep feelings of isolation and our hunger for connection. Had the workshop been conducted as a circle, with circle rules and principles, I am certain we would have had an entirely different experience, one that was far more fulfilling.

While many women may still need individual and group psychotherapy to heal from such traumatic events as childhood neglect and abuse, and current abusive relationships such as domestic violence, circles focused on healing and empowerment can be powerful tools in any woman's recovery process.

Those involved in studying and worshipping the goddesses will discover that the women's circle movement has much in common with the women's spirituality movement. As Layne Redmond, in her book *When the Drummers Were Women*, writes:

> *Many women believe that locked in that history [Goddesses] is an ancient wisdom transmitted by long-vanished sages and benevolent deities that may speak to the problems of contemporary life, such as how to live individually with a sense of spiritual connectedness and belonging each day, and, most important, how to live with one another and share a sense of community and purpose.*

Those involved in studying and practicing the rituals of Native Americans will be particularly interested in this book. Many Native American beliefs and practices are rapidly becoming an integral part of American society, and this is partly because of the numbers of medicine circles now in existence. The circle represents complete harmony and balance. Today, many Native American people are speaking again the words that tell us about their ancient wisdom. The message is not, "Become like an Indian," nor is there a desire to convert people to Native American religion. Instead they are saying, "Let us join hands, each as we are, to rebuild the sacred circle of the Earth. Let us honor the traditions of all our peoples. Let us know that there is one truth, and all our roots have come from the great tree."

The History of the Circle

Many believe that the practice of meeting in circle more than likely originated when our ancestors first captured the spark of fire and began to carry the embers along with them from site to site. It made sense to put the fire in the center in order to keep everyone safe and warm. Sitting in a circle allowed space for everyone to face the flame, thus illuminating each person's face and causing each to be recognized as a part of the tribe.

In time the circle became the primary social, political and spiritual structure as evidenced in paintings, carvings, petroglyphs, runes, crafts and, later, architecture. We see the remnants of circle-based cultures among indigenous peoples all around the world. For example, the Inuits of the Arctic still meet in circle as do most Native American tribes.

Carl Jung, a visionary psychiatrist in the time of Freud, noted that all humans share a number of images that seem to originate from a common source deep within the psyche. He called this source "the collective unconscious." Jung believed that over the course of millions of years the brain evolved and now represents the very history of which it is the result. Naturally, it carries with it the traces of that history, exactly as the body does. According to Jung, "The deepest we can reach into our exploration of the unconscious mind is the layer where man [woman] is no longer a distinct individual, but where his [her] mind widens out and merges into the mind of mankind [humankind]—where we are all one."

As Christina Baldwin notes in *Calling the Circle:*

One of the symbols that led Jung to contemplate this point of oneness was the recurring imagery of the circle. The circle, often in the form of the Sun Wheel (a pie cut in eight equal pieces), is represented in different cultures as the Medicine Wheel, the Wheel of Law and Life, the Wheel of the Year and the Catherine Wheel. Jung traced the image of the circle back to the Paleolithic and Mesolithic periods, when wheels were carved and painted as a sacred symbol, thousands of years before the wheel was invented as an actual tool. Based on this research, Jung saw the wheel as a primary symbol, one of the mythic motifs springing from the collective unconscious.

So it seems the circle has resided within us since the dawn of time, and is a form familiar to us at a deeply resonant level. Over and over again, when this mythic resonance is activated, people experience a sense of "having been here before" as they enter the circle. Sometimes we are buoyed up by this familiarity and proceed with confidence: "I know how to do this . . . I know how to behave here." Sometimes we are shaken by how even a vestige of circle carries profound impact.

Indeed, ancient stone carvings and other archeological evidence support this belief that the circle is one of humankind's oldest and most elemental symbols. We see evidence of the importance of the circle in archeological discoveries around the globe. The aborigines of Australia paint sacred spirals on cave walls and on their bodies. The native tribes of the American plains constructed tepees and set them in circles, and some African peoples still build circular villages. In all these cultures, the circle is the common element.

Therefore, if we hold within our cells the memory of a time when we were all part of a cohesive culture that was structured around the circle, where the family was part of community and not an isolated unit, where life, with all its joys and sorrows, was celebrated in communal gatherings, when we form a circle we trigger this memory and reclaim our innate knowledge of circle. As Christina Baldwin says, "We are not different from our ancestors; they are still here, coded inside us. They are—I thoroughly believe—cheering us on."

The Teachings of the Circle

After decades of focusing on our individual selves and our own needs, on "doing our own thing," we are now experiencing a longing for connectedness with others, for community, for ways of extending our sense of self and joining with the Circle of Life.

Meeting in circles can and does teach us such important

lessons as learning to be less judgmental and more compassionate, forgiving and loving to one another. It can teach us to respect ourselves, others and Mother Earth.

Once we have learned the lessons of the circle we need to pass the information along to others. Our men need us to show them a different way of communicating and connecting with us and with one another, and a different way of conducting business. Our children need us to act as role models, showing them a new way of relating to one another. This will, in turn, create a whole new generation of people who are truly open to seeing one another, hearing one another and connecting with one another on a more empathetic level. As the circle continues, more and more people will be brought in, fewer and fewer will be on the outside. This will be both a small step and a giant step toward world peace.

As you read this book, allow yourself to be drawn into the circle. Allow yourself to feel your connection with all women and all humanity. Allow yourself to be healed of your feelings of alienation from others and from yourself. Feel the hope that lies in all of us: the hope for meaningful connection with others, the hope for understanding and compassion, the hope for a deeper spiritual awakening. As you are inspired by the words of other women who have discovered the circle, know that you too can inspire others. Opportunities to enlarge the circle are all around you. Give the gift of the circle to someone you love.

TWO

Changing the World, One Circle at a Time— The Women's Circle Movement

*The dramatic action that we need
to create a way of life on Earth that really
works will be taken not through personal, social,
or political action, but through
spiritual action.*

BROOKE MEDICINE EAGLE
BUFFALO WOMAN COMES SINGING

*We will remember, together,
that the honor of the people lies in the
moccasin tracks of the women. We will see that
if the pride and virtue of our women are lost,
the spring will come, but the buffalo trails will turn
to grass. We will come to understand that no
people can be defeated as long as their women's*

> *hearts are strong. We will know that*
> *when the women's hearts turn to dust,*
> *the people perish . . .*

> SCOUT CLOUD LEE
> *THE CIRCLE IS SACRED*

There is a quiet revolution occurring all over the world. But there are no marches or protests, no speeches or strikes. Instead there are quiet gatherings held in living rooms, backyards and community centers. We usually do not read about these gatherings in the newspapers or hear about them on the news. Word on when and where the meetings will be held is spread by word-of-mouth, by small mailings or in small presses. People meet weekly or monthly, annually and biannually.

Sometimes the people discuss and plan, other times they sing and drum. Sometimes they meet to work on a common goal, other times they meet to discuss their differences. Sometimes they meet to offer one another support, and other times to support a cause or a group of people. They are Christians, Jews, Buddhists, Hindus, Muslims and pagans. They represent all political and ideological points of view.

Who are these people? They are members of the new women's movement. Even though they don't hold marches, speeches or bra-burnings, they are a powerful presence in our culture, quietly changing not only the way women are perceived and treated, but how *all human beings are perceived and treated.*

The History of Women's Circles

Women have always met in circles. Throughout history women around the world have come together in circles to worship and pray, to explore their relationship to the sacred, to share personal stories, to celebrate and to experience ritual together.

For centuries, indigenous tribes have had separate circles for women and men. While we know very little about these secret circles, we do know they exist. For example, aboriginal women of Australia have circles and ceremonies of their own to honor their "femaleness" and to mark the different stages of their lives (menstruation, defloration, pregnancy and childbirth) by gathering together and performing certain rituals and songs.

As we became more "civilized," women met in sewing circles, afternoon teas, and garden and book clubs for the purposes of sharing, learning and celebrating. While these circles may appear on the surface to be insignificant or even frivolous, in many instances it was the only opportunity women had to share their deepest feelings with other people.

In the book and later the film *How to Make an American Quilt,* we see how a highly ritualized, though informal, gathering becomes the vehicle as well as the metaphor for the intense personal narratives of the quilters. In addition to the focus on biographical stories, the occasion incorporates many other elements associated with women's circles and rituals, such as the fact that the participants sit in a circle, and that leadership and dominance fluctuate among members.

Throughout Western history, bridal and baby showers have always been more than just parties or gift-giving occasions. They are rites of passage into marriage and motherhood.

During the 1960s and '70s, women met together in assertiveness-training and consciousness-raising groups, often choosing to sit in circle. They met to express their outrage and pain about being seen as second-class citizens, to tell their stories of abuse, harassment and mistreatment by men in a predominately male society. They met to organize, to insist on their rights, to tear down the establishment. They met to provide support for one another in their attempts to stand up to unfairness and domination.

In the 1980s, women met in circle to tell the stories of their abusive childhoods, to rid themselves of the shame and guilt of sexual abuse, to express their rage at having been raped, used, or mistreated at the hands of men. In the '80s and early '90s, women also came together to heal from codependency, to offer support for one another as they healed from their pain and to empower one another to leave their victimhood behind.

Today women are meeting together again. While some still need to tell their stories of abuse and mistreatment by men, many have done this work and choose to move on. Today women need to meet together not only because we must educate ourselves and lift one another's consciousness, and not only for the purpose of identifying our problems and gaining strength from knowing we are not alone with them. Women also need to meet for the purpose of expanding our awareness, reconnecting with our depth and our souls, and finding out how to be authentic, nonjudgmental and honest with ourselves and others. We have evolved, and so the form of our meetings and groups has evolved along with us.

The first women's circles to take their current form were created by such visionaries as Starhawk, Christina Baldwin and Sedonia Cahill, who were influenced by such diverse traditions as the symbol of the goddess as a sustaining divine presence, Native American spirituality and the Quaker religion.

The Connection Between the Women's Spirituality Movement and the Women's Circle Movement

The women's spirituality movement was one of the many seeds from which the women's circle movement evolved. It was comprised of those who were fed up with or deeply wounded by traditional religions, as well as those who believed that change needed to occur within the system, and at its core was the symbol of the goddess as the archetypal divine feminine.

The women's circle movement has much in common with the women's spirituality movement. Both movements share the goal of empowering women, and many of those who meet in circle have a strong belief in goddess-based religions. But there are also differences. The women's circle movement is far broader and more encompassing than the women's spirituality movement, and its goals are somewhat different.

For example, those who make up the women's circle movement come from all religious backgrounds and represent a variety of belief systems. Some do worship the goddesses, but just as many practice Christianity, Judaism, Buddhism and other religions. Many practice Native American and/or shamanic spirituality, and some do not have a connection or affiliation with any religion at all. And while ritual is a part of all circles, in circles such as Wisdom Circles, ritual plays a far lesser role than in most women's spirituality circles.

While the women's circle movement believes in the empowerment of women, it also stands for the empowerment of everyone. At the core of the movement is the belief that we can make the world a better place by our individual actions and by the positive energy we raise in circle.

The Need for a
New Women's Movement

Many believe we need a new women's movement because a majority of women today do not see traditional feminism as relevant to their lives. Several writers have voiced their concern that the feminist movement is failing to address the most pressing needs of contemporary American women. For example, Emory professor Elizabeth Fox-Genovese states in her book, *Feminism Is Not the Story of My Life: How Today's Feminist Elite Has Lost Touch with the Real Concerns of Women*, that feminism has two primary shortcomings: The movement's platform tends to advance the interests of economically privileged women, ignoring the poor; and it seeks to devalue maternal bonds that many women continue to see as central to their identities. The author argues that feminist indifference to the unique concerns of women as mothers has made motherhood an increasingly difficult role for women to assume.

The women's circle movement embraces all women, from every walk of life, from all over the world. It is not divided along class lines, economic lines or any other lines. It is not divided between radical and conservative, lesbian and straight, black and white. It includes all women looking for safe and affirming community. It includes both politically attuned feminists and the apolitical; women disillusioned with traditional religion and those still steeped in it; nonreligious women looking for a meaningful spiritual experience and Christian feminists; New Age feminists and nonfeminist New Age seekers; and feminist and nonfeminist Wiccans. In addition, it includes such divergent groups as those reclaiming the ancient worship of the goddess, those practicing shamanic spirituality or Native American traditions, and those practicing paganism.

The women's circle movement celebrates motherhood as a creative process, a loving and learning experience, and a way to change the world. For example, it affirms the vital role of women in teaching children about native languages, cultures and spirituality.

It also celebrates and values the wisdom and experiences of our elders, particularly that of our crones. It realizes that they hold our history in their stories, in their traditions and rituals, and in their hearts.

Although Western society tends to devalue the contributions of the aged, we hold our elder women in high regard. Older women often have the crucial task of teaching younger women the ethics, rituals and lore of the circle, and rituals are often organized and conducted by elder women. Many circles create ceremonies to mark a woman's passage into cronehood and designate special status to crones in order to combat the social disdain, loss of self-esteem and loneliness experienced by older women, as well as to confirm the wisdom and guidance they can contribute.

As Scout Cloud Lee wrote in the introduction to her book *The Circle Is Sacred:* "We will again see that the welfare of our young and our elders is of paramount importance, for therein is held all wisdom and our future."

The women's circle movement is less about political action and more about individual action and responsibility. Therefore, we do not have to protest or plead for understanding, improvements or handouts. Instead, we believe we deserve a certain quality of life and have certain rights and we act accordingly.

Another difference between the women's circle movement and the women's liberation movement is that we do not ask anything of men except that they treat us with the respect we deserve. We will work with them for a common cause, will exchange knowledge with them, but we will no longer be dependent on men for change.

The women's circle movement is less about helping women only and more about helping the poor, the sick, the misunderstood. It is as dedicated to helping the environment and saving endangered species as it is to protecting women from job discrimination and sexual harassment.

To summarize, the women's circle movement tends to be different from the women's liberation movement in the following ways:

- There is more of a celebration of motherhood and a newfound respect for the important role mothers play in our society.
- The women's circle movement is more spiritual than political.
- We do not wish to alienate men but to bring them into the circle by teaching them a new way of relating to others and the world.
- The goal is less that of becoming more like men than in fulfilling our potential as women.
- The movement is based on empowerment versus victimization, and is a celebration of our strengths versus our weaknesses.
- It is based on quiet action versus noisy political protest.
- The women's circle movement is more positive. It is full of hope versus gloom and doom. It is based on love instead of hate.

The Spiritual Perspective

Another reason for our need for a new women's movement is our deep hunger for the sacred. The women's circle movement has a decidedly spiritual aspect, unlike the traditional feminist movement—which is far more political than spiritual. While traditional feminism gave us a sense of connectedness and empowerment from a political perspective, the women's circle movement provides us connectedness and empowerment from a spiritual perspective. While the feminist movement helped us to feed ourselves and our children, the women's circle movement helps us feed our souls.

Even though the feminist movement and the women's circle movement are different in some aspects, they are not mutually exclusive. In fact, they share some commonalities. Spirituality has become a part of many feminist communities, and spiritual strengthening is part of a general desire to empower women. Feminist insights, writings and theory often inform many of the rituals and ceremonies conducted in circles and inspire women to work for change. Many women's circles are intentionally feminist since their convictions lead them beyond religious meaning into the politics of justice.

In addition, some of the authors writing today about circles and the circle movement, such as Starhawk and Christina Baldwin, write from a feminist perspective.

But clearly, not all participants of women's circles, even in the West, identify themselves as feminist. Many simply rejoice in the freedom, camaraderie and power they experience from meeting in circles and do not identify with feminist beliefs or practices. Moreover, those women who meet for the purpose of worship in non-Western religions generally do not place feminist issues at the heart of their worship.

Separatism

While feminism's separatist ideology often stemmed from anger toward men, the women's circle movement's separatism (if it truly can be called this) stems not from anger but from love, not from political ideology but from its spiritual roots and beliefs.

Those in the women's circle movement do not choose to have separate circles from men because we hate them. Rather, we have our own circles because we love ourselves, we want to honor and develop our feminine powers, and we feel that the world needs our compassion, tolerance for diversity and knowledge of community building.

Our beliefs, as diverse as Jungian philosophy, Native American spirituality, shamanic religions and goddess spirituality, all point to this being a time in history when women need to remain separate for their spiritual growth and for the spiritual growth of the planet.

For example, many Jungians point out that the rapid social and psychological changes we are experiencing at the beginning of the new millennium relate synchronistically to an apparent archetypal shift as we move from Pisces to Aquarius. Jung believed that the new archetype will pose a problem with the union of opposites, and will challenge and stretch our ability to contain female and male, good and evil, light and dark.

This confirms what Native Americans believe is occurring. There has been a great deal of Native American prophesy that in the end days the sexes will divide even further. Women will congregate with women, men with men. I believe that spiritually-minded people intuitively understand this need, and that is why more and more people are gravitating to the concept of separate circles for men and women. Many people believe this time has already come, as evidenced by the men's movement led by such leaders as Robert Bly and Warren Farrell, and by the increase in women's spiritual groups and healing circles.

Carol Proudfoot-Edgar, a shaman and leader of women's circles and vision quests, shared with me why she believes women's circles are important from a spiritual perspective:

Women carry particular regenerative powers through all the cycles of our lives. This is not a feminist statement but a matter of spiritual biology: the mystical union of our female bodies with Spirit. For thousands of years this was honored and manifested in the way early cultures valued the female of any species. This is not a matter of women versus men, but of honoring our ways of being and our ways of knowing. Through reclamation of our own selves we are then clearer in our relationships with other women, with men, and with Earth herself.

In a journey two years ago I asked one of my Spirit teachers, "Why are women's circles so important?" I was shown

*how men carry the power of fission (taking apart, separating)
and women the power of fusion (bringing together, joining).
Both are powers in creation, in evolution. I was told it is time
now to strengthen the powers of fusion—knowing how all is
joined and joining. In women's circles we can return ourselves to wholeness, and fuse together the "ways" that ensure
a planet that we and our descendants know as our earthly
home, and not feel orphaned in an alien land.*

*At this time in our history, both as individual women and
as participants in the collective whole, being in circle can
teach us how to further our knowing that we are one people
and how to experience the development of community-based
or spiritual values.*

These views were shared by many of the women I interviewed for this book, including the shamanic practitioner, LaWanna Durbin:

Beverly: Is it true that you believe that we are entering a great
time of transition and that during these times, women and men
will be separated, possibly for the purpose of focusing on separate issues?

LaWanna: Yes, these are transitional times leading us toward
a greater knowledge of equality consciousness, where we
understand that all people are equal because we are made of
the same essence or spirit. A vision I had some ten years ago
showed me these times would be characterized by separation:
separation between men and women, between children and
their parents, separation between the generations. This is very

sad to think about, and to see happen. It is due to the stresses of these times, where all things are reaching toward an evolutionary peak, including the energies of separation itself. But we are also unifying, and this is what is most important. Sometimes we have to separate out in order to get clear, to know our soul, to learn our destiny. Each part—each individual man and men collectively, each individual woman and women collectively—has to move toward becoming authentically what it is and toward unity within itself in order to fulfill its responsibility to the whole. So knowing oneself as a separate soul or separate gender-soul is important, but the bigger picture is about coming together, about unity. Through the process of authenticating the individual, separate soul-self, we access the knowledge that everything on the planet is of one essence or spirit.

Beverly: Many cultures and disciplines speak of this time as one of major change (astrological predictions, etc.).

LaWanna: Yes, I would call this period a time of "spiritual renaissance," with an emphasis on mysticism, a time when we are respiritualizing the Earth. The Earth has always been spiritual, of course, but we as a planetary people are in the process of consciously reclaiming the knowledge of life's spiritual dimensions.

Beverly: Do you feel as I do that women's circles play an important role in creating major changes in the world? Do you feel that some of the most important changes are those being created by women?

LaWanna: There are significant differences between women and men energetically, in terms of how their energy fields are configured. Male energy is conglomerated in the lower part of their bodies, whereas the energies of females, in general, is frequently conglomerated in the upper part of the body. For this reason, men as a whole are more anchored to the Earth plane, which implies a more sure-footedness and ease in manifesting the material successes in life. Women, as a whole, are more "skyed" than grounded. The top half of the body, where their energy tends to mass, includes the voice (truth), second sight and crown center, which connects the cosmos. For this reason, women as a group may more likely and more regularly be recipients of transpersonal information and guidance than men are as a group, but we may also have difficulty bringing our superb awarenesses down to Earth. Because of these differences in energy configuration, and other reasons as well, men and women need each other. The heart, midpoint between the upper and lower bodies, is the middle ground, the most important point of connection between the two. But women also need each other, and to be with one another in circle, strenthening our common visions and intentions for a healthier, happier and holier world.

Beverly: And so the circle can serve to both attract information and to ground women?

LaWanna: Yes.

Those who practice goddess spirituality also believe that this time in history is women's time. They believe that the feminine divine is reemerging from centuries of repression at a time when we are desperately in need of inspiration, community and courage.

And finally, still another reason why women choose to have separate circles from men is that after years of attempting to secure power, equality and a place in the masculine, power-driven environments in which we find ourselves, we women, too, have become disconnected from our emotions, senses and intuition. We have come to realize that we need a place where we can strengthen and regain these feminine powers.

While it may seem paradoxical that women, who have been fighting for the right to be equal to men, to work side by side with them, would want to segregate themselves into women's circles, the fact is that many women long for a feminine haven where feminine values and ways of being are not just tolerated but embraced.

Although there can be some benefits from meeting in circles composed of both men and women, this changes the circle. It only takes one man to completely change the energy in any circle. One male can totally dominate a circle within minutes, just by exerting his energy and speaking his truths. This is partly because many women are still willing to give their power to men and partly because most men, even those who are more conscious, still have a need to dominate.

Women need a space where they can begin to trust their feelings and instincts once again. They don't need to defend themselves against those who wish to talk them out of their feelings and instincts. Nor do women need to be constantly negated by the masculine tendency to be logical and rational.

As Ellie Mercer, an ordained minister with the United Church of Christ, explained to me:

My sisters and I grew up on the campus of the oldest boys' boarding school in the country. My father, and later, my mother were on the faculty there. I was surrounded by boys and was seldom around other girls until I was sent to a girls' boarding school at the age of fourteen. Even there, I wasn't around women who spoke the truth about their lives. I learned all the rules that made life work at these institutions, but I didn't learn the truth of my own heart or the words of my own voice.

It was only late in life, when I first became part of circles, that I felt free to listen to women who were not male-identified as they spoke the stories and truths of their lives. Through their courage, I discovered the courage and strength to find my own words and tell my own story. It is in these circles that I often find the "work of the spirit" because these circles focus on celebrating one's essential nature. For me, that is spiritual work—offering ourselves as we are—not as someone else wants us to be.

The following interview reflects the feelings and thoughts of yet another woman involved in the circle movement, Sandra Ingerman, who teaches workshops worldwide on shamanism. While Sandra also conducts circles that include both sexes, she feels as I do that there is a particular significance to women meeting in circle at this time in our history, and that women have a special role in healing the Earth and its peoples.

READER/CUSTOMER CARE SURVEY

If you are enjoying this book, please help us serve you better and meet your changing needs by taking a few minutes to complete this survey. Please fold it and drop it in the mail.

As a special **"Thank You"** we'll send you news about new books and a valuable **Gift Certificate!**

PLEASE PRINT   C8C

NAME:_____

ADDRESS: _____

_____

TELEPHONE NUMBER: _____

FAX NUMBER: _____

E-MAIL: _____

WEBSITE: _____

(1) Gender: 1)_____Female 2)_____Male

(2) Age:
1)_____12 or under   5)_____30-39
2)_____13-15   6)_____40-49
3)_____16-19   7)_____50-59
4)_____20-29   8)_____60+

(3) Your Children's Age(s):
Check all that apply.
1)_____6 or Under   3)_____11-14
2)_____7-10   4)_____15-18

(7) Marital Status:
1)_____Married
2)_____Single
3)_____Divorced/Wid.

(8) Was this book
1)_____Purchased for yourself?
2)_____Received as a gift?

(9) How many books do you read a month?
1)_____1   3)_____3
2)_____2   4)_____4+

(10) How did you find out about this book?
Please check ONE.
1)_____Personal Recommendation
2)_____Store Display
3)_____TV/Radio Program
4)_____Bestseller List
5)_____Website
6)_____Advertisement/Article or Book Review
7)_____Catalog or mailing
8)_____Other_____

(11) What FIVE subject areas do you enjoy reading about most?
Rank: 1 (favorite) through 5 (least favorite)
A)_____ Self Development
B)_____ New Age/Alternative Healing
C)_____ Storytelling
D)_____Spirituality/Inspiration
E)_____ Family and Relationships
F)_____ Health and Nutrition
G)_____ Recovery
H)_____Business/Professional
I) _____ Entertainment
J) _____ Teen Issues
K)_____Pets

(16) Where do you purchase most of your books?
Check the top TWO locations.
A)_____ General Bookstore
B)_____ Religious Bookstore
C)_____ Warehouse/Price Club
D)_____ Discount or Other Retail Store
E)_____ Website
F)_____ Book Club/Mail Order

(18) Did you enjoy the stories in this book?
1)_____Almost All
2)_____Few
3)_____Some

(19) What type of magazine do you SUBSCRIBE to?
Check up to FIVE subscription categories.
A)_____ General Inspiration
B)_____ Religious/Devotional
C)_____ Business/Professional
D)_____ World News/Current Events
E)_____ Entertainment
F)_____ Homemaking, Cooking, Crafts
G)_____ Women's Issues
H)_____ Other (please specify) _____

(24) Please indicate your income level
1)_____Student/Retired-fixed income
2)_____Under $25,000
3)_____$25,000-$50,000
4)_____$50,001-$75,000
5)_____$75,001-$100,000
6)_____Over $100,000

FOLD HERE

((25) Do you attend seminars?

1)_____Yes   2)_____No

(26) If you answered yes, what type?

Check all that apply.

1)_____Business/Financial

2)_____Motivational

3)_____Religious/Spiritual

4)_____Job-related

5)_____Family/Relationship issues

(31) Are you:

1) A Parent?_____

2) A Grandparent?_____

Additional comments you would like to make:

_____

_____

_____

_____

Thank You!!

HCI

The Life Issues Publisher

N-CS   C8C

Interview with Sandra Ingerman

Sandra Ingerman is the leading practitioner of soul retrieval and is the Educational Director of the International Faculty of the Foundation of Shamanic Studies, directed by Michael Harner. One of the leaders of the women's circle movement, she is also the author of *Soul Retrieval: Mending the Fragmented Self*, *Welcome Home: Following Your Soul's Journey Home* and *A Fall to Grace*.

Beverly: Do you feel that women's circles play a significant role in helping to heal the Earth and to bring about changes in our consciousness?

Sandra: I really do. My own personal opinion is that the next step in the healing of our planet is going to come through women. I'm not a staunch feminist, but I don't see that most men are in a place—or the male energy is in a place—to really heal right now. I cannot believe that there's a woman on Earth who could go inside herself and tap into her female energy and say it's okay that there are so many children who are starving. I cannot believe that if women were really able to come together in a circle and ask themselves, "Is it okay that there are children who are starving and have no place to live on the planet today?" that they wouldn't work toward changing the situation.

But what happened through time is that women have become so disconnected from each other. I actually think that they've been pitted against each other in a very competitive way to get a man, to have safety and security in their life. In prisons, one way that they keep the prisoners from overthrowing the authorities is to separate people by different racial groups. Then they pit them against each other so they're so busy fighting with each other that they have no strength left to overthrow the authorities.

I think that in some way that is what's happened to women over time. Women have actually come to a place where they see each other as enemies.

Also, women got into a place where they began trying to be like men, trying to get into the business world, trying to create the same careers and career advancements that men have. I'm not saying that there's anything wrong with that, but I do believe that a different kind of energy is needed on the planet right now, and it does not involve the male dynamic energy. I think what really needs to happen is that we open up to the feminine nurturing sides of ourselves. I think that women have lost their power to a great extent. And this is the time for women to connect to each other and come together and see what has happened through history: how women have been pitted against each other; how it's not about competing for security but about learning about mothering, nurturing energy; how circles of women can start to create change by inspiring women not to put up with abusive behavior anymore, whether it's abusive behavior towards themselves or towards the children of the planet. But it's all too much for one woman to do. There is no way for women individually to create the kind of change that is needed right now. It would just be taking on too much. That is why it is important for women to come together in groups. Every time a women's circle is formed, consciousness is changed by the women in those circles. They're inspired by the other women in the circle, they're held in love by the other women in the circle— and that gives them the strength to go out and start to create some of the needed change on the planet.

Beverly: Do you feel there is a benefit in having separate circles for women and men?

Sandra: Yes, because women need to begin looking at how they can best support each other. That's very important right now. People feel so isolated and so alone, and circles can provide much needed support. We need to know that it's not just us, that there's actually a community out there who really cares about us. Just that knowledge in itself provides unbelievable amounts of healing.

Although I like working in circles that are made up of both women and men, I can also see the benefit of having separate circles because there are different issues that come up in the lives of men. Women and men are still raised differently, and there are roles that we're supposed to be taking in life. I have a lot of male friends who are in men's groups where they have the opportunity to just be themselves without the social pressures that come in when you have men and women working together. Men need to learn how to support one another instead of constantly competing, and this in turn will help them become more nurturing in their families.

We in the women's circle movement are not so arrogant as to believe we can survive without men or without their influence, nor would we want to. We appreciate those males who are supportive, and we honor the teachings of males such as Mahatma Gandhi, Martin Luther King Jr., Carl Jung, Henry David Thoreau, Joseph Campbell, Nelson Mandela and Matthew Fox. And yet, we understand that at times women and men need to be separated in order to do their individual emotional and spiritual work. We follow the example of Native Americans and other tribes of indigenous people throughout the world by advocating separate healing circles for women and men. Like native people, we believe that each sex has its own lessons to learn and its own special medicine.

For example, according to Robert Lawlor, author of *Voices of the First Day: Awakening in the Aboriginal Dreamtime,* not only do Australian aboriginal women have separate initiation rites, but the campsite of an aboriginal band is divided into a women's camp and a men's camp, as well as a general camp. During certain ritual occasions and phases in their lives, tribal law requires that the people live in either the men's or the women's camp.

The Women's Circle Movement

The women's liberation movement was about women becoming free from the confines of the limiting roles placed on us by the males in our society—sex goddess, doting wife, primary parent. The women's circle movement is also about becoming free from the limits we place on ourselves.

The women's circle movement is based on women's *strength* and *power,* not on *victimization.* It is based on the belief that we can and will make a difference in our lives, the lives of our children and the lives of every person and creature on the planet by utilizing our feminine wisdom, strength, creativity and compassion.

While those in the women's circle movement actively support and are involved in many organizations working for peace, ecology and other important causes, we recognize that it is even more important to work for peace within our own families and communities, and to clean up our own acts and our own backyards. We recognize that each individual has the power to change the world by her daily actions and spiritual practices, and that a circle of honorable women who respect others and Mother Earth can create an unimaginably powerful energy in the universe.

Most of those in the women's circle movement are more *humanist* than *feminist* and have a decidedly spiritual focus. Although one of the strongest principles guiding the women's circle movement is the support and acceptance of everyone's right to their own beliefs, some of the values that fuel and shape the new movement are:

- respect for the diversity of all humanity and all life
- respect for the Earth and a keen environmental sensitivity
- a belief in the creativity, fruitfulness and inner wisdom inherent in every person
- a strong belief in nonviolence and the need for consensus and mediation
- a strong belief in compassion versus judgment
- a belief in gratitude as a way of life
- a belief in generosity versus the accumulation of wealth
- a belief in simplicity versus consumerism
- a strong belief in freedom—of religion, sexual preference, political ideology

- a belief that patience coupled with tenacity can move mountains
- a respect for our elders, ancestors and spiritual leaders

Ultimately, the women's circle movement emphasizes quiet action, contemplation and prayer versus disruptive and aggressive action. Or as Brooke Medicine Eagle cautions:

We must solve our current problems without creating new ones. We must place more emphasis on being receptive rather than aggressive; on relating to one another rather than on maintaining separation; on power in the flow with the great forces rather than on personal dominion over others; on nurturing rather than fighting; on supporting rather than destroying; on a deep and sacred ecology that deals respectfully with All Our Relations. Gentler forms cannot be held down. They are reemerging like grass growing through concrete.

So far we have discussed the benefits of women meeting in circle in a very general way. In the following section we will discuss the specific benefits that meeting in circle can offer individual women as well as women as a whole.

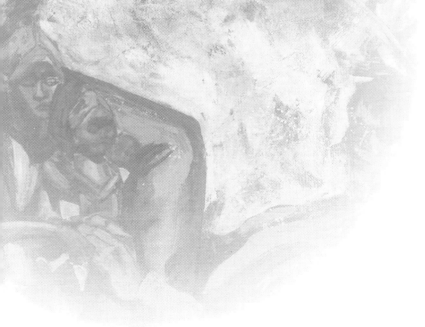

PART TWO

Gifts of the Circle: Community, Healing, Empowerment and Sacredness

THREE

Circle as Community

Community.
Somewhere there are people
to whom we can speak with passion without
having the words catch in our throats.
Somewhere a circle of hands will open to receive us,
eyes will light up as we enter, voices will celebrate
with us whenever we come into our own power.
Community means strength that joins our strength
to do the work that needs to be done.
Arms to hold us when we falter.
A circle of healing. A circle of friends.
Somewhere where we can be free.

STARHAWK
DREAMING THE DARK

Perhaps the most powerful benefit of women meeting in circle is the sense of community that is created. No matter how happy a woman is with the rest of her life—her work, her family—many women experience a deep sense of loneliness and isolation. They miss the friendship and camaraderie of other women.

Our lives are so busy that few of us take the time to establish and maintain friendships the way we once did. Unlike our mothers and grandmothers, women no longer meet together in sewing groups, bridge groups or consciousness-raising groups. This leaves women feeling hungry for the companionship of other women, for the sense of connectedness that can only be achieved when women get together and open up their hearts and souls to one another.

The circle reminds us that we are all connected. In this time of separateness and alienation, meeting in circle is a way to connect with one another in a nonthreatening, uncomplicated way, a way to bring us back to our humanness and our sacredness. No one can survive entirely by themselves for very long, and circle reminds us of our need for one another, reminds us that we are better together and can accomplish much more working together, supporting one another.

As Sandra Ingerman writes in *Soul Retrieval:*

In ancient times, small communities were central to human life. These tribal societies, acting as a single organism, fostered interdependence among all members. Based on my study of shamanism, I believe the health and healing of each member of the community was the responsibility of the entire community. Every individual had tremendous support in the emotional, spiritual and physical healing process.

As humans evolved and developed more sophisticated technology, communities gave way to cities, with their crowding, anonymity and indifference. We moved from tribal societies to a culture in which families took the place of the community. As society became more mobile, family clans broke into smaller and more isolated units, down to the "nuclear family." Even now the nuclear family is dissolving into individual members who live separately.

I bring this up because the disintegration of community into ever more discrete units of human interaction has a dramatic effect on soul loss. Not only do many of us today have no community support to draw on, but also the isolation many of us feel is itself a major cause of soul loss.

A Community of Women

Women have always banded together along what Barbara Walker refers to as "the underside of male-dominated social structures." Aside from the obvious natural bonds among female family members, women have always created all-female groups that served to provide mutual support for one another whenever they could. Old-fashioned sewing circles and quilting bees gave their members more than a chance to learn needlework techniques. They provided women a sense of connection and the satisfaction of working together toward a common goal. Afternoon teas and luncheons provided more rewards than learning the latest gossip or exchanging recipes. They provided an opportunity to share with other women the kinds of feelings that were uncomfortable or unacceptable to share in the company of men. Community services, volunteer groups, neighborhood committees, social clubs, and church and charity organizations all gave women the opportunity to meet and work with one another, to communicate, cooperate and widen their circle of friends.

Women working together on almost any kind of project have inevitably formed mutually supportive relationships out of their common needs and shared life experiences. And whenever a woman has had to face any of life's common crises, be it birth, death, illness, sudden misfortune or troubles with love, there have usually been other women there to help her.

Today women seldom work together to accomplish a task. In fact, they are often pitted against one another, especially in the corporate world as we scramble to break the glass ceiling. Today women tend to see one another as rivals instead of as supporters. Women have grown to see life from a perspective of scarcity—not enough jobs, not enough money, not enough men. Therefore we feel we must fight for the available jobs and men, and we view every woman as a potential threat.

One of the benefits of meeting in circle is that it helps women to stop viewing one another as competitors. As we sit in a circle, facing one another, no one taking a higher or more prominent position, we are encouraged to set aside our own self-interests for the interests of the circle. Instead of envying or competing with one another, women begin to inspire one another. We begin to understand that our lives no longer depend on getting the men we were once in competition for, and that as long as we cripple ourselves with envy—either toward men or other women—we hold ourselves down.

The circle reminds us that we are all whole and complete just as we are. We don't need to be like anyone else; just being ourselves is enough. By looking at one another for support and validation, as opposed to looking at one another as competitors, we find we are stronger than we ever imagined.

We live in a time and a world that cultivate separateness between people. But when women join together in circle, they become keenly aware that such separateness does not really exist on a deeper level. Circles help alleviate the feeling that each woman stands alone against the oppressiveness and harshness of modern society. They remind us we are all one and encourage us to band together as one force against negativity, oppression and envy from the outside.

As the talking stick is passed around the circle, allowing each person to speak on an issue, it becomes evident how much we are all concerned with the same issues. As stated in *The Ceremonial Circle:* "This state of compassion is the building block of community. When the magic of the circle is active, separateness is experienced as the illusion that it is."

Circles don't have to be large numbers of women gathering together, and they don't have to be about lofty goals and ideas. All that is needed is that your intention is to meet for the mutual benefit of all. As long as you have at least four like-minded women who wish to connect with one another and with self in a meaningful way, you can form a circle. Your intention can be as simple as that of exploring a particular issue, connecting on a higher level, or meeting together to establish a closer bond. And, although ritual is certainly an important part of circle, it doesn't have to be elaborate. The ritual can be as simple as lighting a candle and sitting in a circle.

To illustrate this point, I'd like to share with you an incredibly powerful experience I had while writing this book. I decided to get together with three friends to discuss a mutual desire of ours (the reason is unimportant). One of the women asked if a friend, who had similar interests, could join us. All but this last woman knew that I was writing this book, but nothing was said about our meeting being a circle. In fact, we decided to make it a potluck dinner.

As we all sat down at a table, I asked that we light candles and toast to our mutual goal and friendship. This, plus our intention, was enough to set the stage for a remarkable evening. We drank wine and shared in a very general way while eating dinner, but it was immediately apparent that this was not a typical gathering. Each woman began opening up in a very intimate way, and we all became increasingly aware that we had much in common—most especially, that we were what one woman called "motherless children."

All of us had been either emotionally or physically abandoned by our mothers shortly after our birth and throughout our lifetimes. And all of us had reached a point in our lives where we had come to some kind of resolution about our mothers: reaching an understanding about a mother's behavior; coming to a place where we had stopped trying to please a mother who clearly was never going to be pleased; or realizing for the first time that a mother's behavior wasn't personal, that she treated everyone the same way. We talked about forgiveness, and about our mutual realization that we all have a dark side and are capable of evil. We even contemplated whether perhaps in former lifetimes we had been abusive or neglectful ourselves, perhaps to our own mothers.

The conversation was rich with insight, filled with compassion. It was clear not only that we had had similar life experiences, but that we had all managed to overcome and transcend them, albeit by different vehicles. We shared our transition points, those moments of clarity when we finally "got" our lessons. We shared a variety of experiences— from hypnotic regression to rebirthing, from shamanic journeys to healings through essential oils.

As the evening progressed we spoke of women's power, how women are finally coming into their own, even taking over. Throughout the evening there was a keen awareness that we were all women, and once or twice, those women who had male partners remarked about how different the conversation and the evening would be if males were present. Other than these remarks, we didn't talk about men at all, which for one woman in particular was unusual.

The evening was magical, and we were all keenly aware of it. One by one we made some kind of remark concerning the specialness of the evening. We were listening more closely to one another instead of jumping in and interrupting. Each woman was allowed to voice her opinion fully, even though others might disagree after she had finished. When one woman seemed to be going off on a tangent, we all sat patiently listening for a while, and then silently, as a group, brought her back to the circle, back into the positive energy.

Several times I found myself sitting back in awe and observing the experience. Each woman seemed so powerful. No one was trying to one-up the other; no one was dominating the conversation. We were all an integral part of the conversation and the experience. We were all listening carefully to one another and allowing the others' words to sink in slowly before speaking. Each woman seemed to speak from her heart, not trying to impress the others, not running away from the deeper issues, but staying on track.

By the end of the evening we all agreed that we needed to continue meeting with one another. Even though we hadn't talked too much about our initial purpose for getting together, it was apparent that there was a higher purpose to our gathering.

Once you have been in a circle with other women, a bond is created that will continue even if you rarely see one another or meet together only sporadically. If, on the other hand, you circle with the same women on a regular basis, you will begin to feel an even deeper bond, as if you are part of the same tribe. This is the most potent aspect of circling for community. Becoming an integral part of a group of people provides you with an extended family and will enrich your life in many ways. You will no longer feel the isolation that is so much a part of modern living. Instead, you will feel a sense of communion with others in your circle. This sense of communion with others can then be generalized towards the larger world, helping you feel connected with all humankind.

FOUR

Circle as Healer

The sacred circle, thousands of years old,
speaks to the hearts of all people. Step inside the
sacred circle, listen, and you will hear
Earth Mother calling you.

DOLFYN
SHAMANISM AND NATURE SPIRITUALITY

We are all, as individuals, in much need of healing—physically, emotionally and spiritually. Our families and our communities are also in need of healing. And Mother Earth is crying out for healing. Forming and meeting in circle is one of the most powerful tools we have available to facilitate such healing.

One of the primary functions of a circle, and the one that is most widely known, is to facilitate the calling forth of healing energy. Circles collect and focus energy. This healing energy can be used for the purpose of healing an individual, a community or Mother Earth.

Technically, all circles have the potential for healing, so labeling a circle a "healing circle" is not only redundant but may appear to negate the healing properties of other types of circles. Nevertheless, for our purposes I have made a distinction between those circles that meet expressly for healing and those that also meet for other purposes, such as consensus.

Circles Devoted to Individual Healing

In a circle of friends
The circle is singing
The drum is starting
The shaman is journeying
The shaman is raising up

She brought my soul
back from far away,
with energy for me,
knowledge for me.

A soul-thief unmasked.

Circle, I sing to you.
Sun, I dance to you.

*Soul, I laugh and cry
to welcome you Home.*

Ailo Gaup

We are a fragmented people desperately searching for ways to bring meaning, depth and healing into our lives. Whenever people gather in a circle with their intentions aligned it helps them drop their protective armor, and become more vulnerable and open to change.

There are several ways that healing can occur for an individual when she meets in a circle. The easiest explanation is that something is healed inside whenever we are able to talk openly and honestly about our issues in front of those who understand because they share the same concerns. This is what occurs when individuals who have similar issues, concerns or backgrounds meet together in circle. When we find that we are among those who think as we do, who have experienced the same feelings or who share the same values and goals, we experience an overwhelming feeling of relief. We are not alone; we are supported and understood.

A similar healing takes place when we meet in a circle for the purpose of telling our stories about being misunderstood, mistreated, used or abused. The circle provides a tribal experience of acceptance, support and shared experiences, which in turn allows catharsis—not only for the individual, but for all those who surrender to the healing. Those who are listened to without judgment experience a sense of dignity, hope and self-worth they have never felt before.

Kay Pranis, a restorative justice planner for the Minnesota Department of Corrections and an advocate for Peace-making Circles, has observed the following benefits to individuals in a circle:

- What in other places is considered baggage can be a gift in a circle. People who have been there and who share their stories can now offer gifts to others. Their baggage is then transformed into something positive as we "take the hard things in life and draw out the beauty."
- In the circle it is presumed that everyone has gifts to offer, and circles make it possible for everyone to offer their gifts. For example, one individual may feel overwhelmed in trying to assist someone who is very needy. In a circle, however, each person's gifts can benefit this person until it is enough. Individual gifts may not look like much but when collected they can help make profound changes.
- Circles offer us a refuge from the fast pace of our lives. When we sit in place and go quiet we can experience peace, serenity and wisdom.

Kay is involved in a powerful type of healing circle— circles for victims of crime. These circles normally include the support system of the victim and several other community members who are active in the circle process. According to Kay, this type of healing circle is based on several important principles: respect for each individual, confidentiality, commitment to positive outcomes, openness to hearing the pain of others and an understanding that the pain of one affects all.

The purpose of this type of healing circle is for the community to validate that the victim did not deserve what happened, and to demonstrate that the community cares about the victim and is willing to share the pain the victim is experiencing. As Kay explains it, "Through a healing circle the community can reach out and surround the victim with care, and affirm that what happened was wrong and that the victim was not responsible for the crime." In addition, a healing circle can identify the nature of the harm caused by the crime and the steps which might remedy the harm.

There are also many circles that meet for the express purpose of healing individual problems and illnesses. Twelve-Step programs for alcoholism, drug addiction, sex addiction, compulsive overeating and compulsive gambling are based on circle principles, whether the people in them actually form a circle or not. As we tell our stories and feel truly heard, perhaps for the first time, we find that we become stronger and more hopeful for our future. Many of those who have finally felt heard discover they no longer need to retell their stories again. They are done with them and now more able to move on.

The same holds true for circles that meet with a spiritual intent. As we tell our life story over and over again and dig deeper and deeper into it, we learn from the obstacles we've encountered. We begin to truly understand ourselves and the reasons for our actions. Repetition of important stories is often a crucial aspect of learning our life lessons.

When we are listened to empathetically, without judgment, we are able to gain important insights into ourselves, and recognize our journey and the paths we must take. It is within the sacred circle that healing comes, for it is within the circle that we recreate the wholeness and sacredness of life.

For some, the circle provides a sanctuary where they can be free from roles and masks, and become closer to their true selves. A place where they can sink into a deeper level of self-acceptance. A place where they can be and become. A place where they can fed by watching others grow.

This is how Janice described the healing that takes place in her circle:

My circle has encouraged me to look deep inside myself for inspiration and answers instead of relying on outside sources. We assume that a woman knows what is best for her if she listens to her own heart, and that she can speak her truths if she speaks from the heart. So instead of giving her advice, we listen without judgment—really listen—with our hearts open. Do you know how it feels to really be listened to? It can be a transforming experience. I was severely criticized as I was growing up—so I was afraid to say anything. But in the circle no one criticizes me.

Every time I've been in a group in the past I've been afraid to speak. Sometimes I'd sit there all night not saying a word, letting others dominate the group. But in my circle everyone is given the opportunity to speak when the talking stick is passed and this encouraged me to say something. At first I didn't say a whole lot, but when I noticed that no one judged anyone I slowly gained enough confidence to speak. Now I love the opportunity to speak and share my feelings with others.

Healing Through Ancient Traditions

In addition to healing through the experience of shared communication and mutual support, there are also circles that call upon ancient healing traditions to remove obstacles that stand in a person's way of healing. Through the ages women have been healers, midwives, nurses and herbalists. Today women are bringing back ancient healing practices and inventing new ones that respect the power of the life energy. Throughout the world, these healing circles attribute illness not only to the effect of germs but also to the action of spirit ancestors, to the damage done by violating taboos, to spiritual dysfunction and to antisocial behavior.

Women's healing circles and rituals cross the boundaries among goddess, pagan, Christian, Jewish and Buddhist groups. For example, for wiccan women, healing is one of the principal uses of magic and women's circles. Diane Stein considers healing such a critical element of goddess spirituality that she specifies that all rituals must contain elements of healing, change or transformation. Barbara Walker suggests healing rituals of soothing and comforting, such as cradling, rocking, laying on of hands and massage.

Healing Through Shamanic Journeying

One ancient healing tradition is that of shamanic healing. Every Earth-based culture has a tradition of shamanism, including not only most Native American and African cultures, but also the cultures of the Irish Druids, East Indian Shivites, Persian Zoroastrians, Japanese Shintos, Chinese Taoists, English Bards, Siberians and Poles. The shaman's function has traditionally been to serve the community by evoking sacred powers.

A shaman is a woman or man who connects with her or his helping spirits through the use of what is referred to as a "journey" outside of time and space in order to access information. A shaman is able to access information from these travels into what is called "nonordinary" reality and return with knowledge that will assist in healing. In traditional cultures, it is only the shaman who journeys to nonordinary reality. In some circles today, shamans teach circle members to journey for their own answers or healing. Shamans like Sandra Ingerman teach others how to journey in order to take back parts of themselves lost to trauma. From my own personal experience, these types of circles can be very powerful and healing. While it is difficult to explain how journeying actually takes place, the following examples will give you an idea of how it works.

My Journeys

Because my childhood was one of extreme neglect and abuse, I have been in therapy several times in my life. I was fortunate to find two female therapists who helped me a great deal and also to receive a great deal of help through individual and group Reichian training (a form of body work).

I give you this information as a backdrop to what I am about to share with you and because I do not want to hold out false hope to others who experienced neglect or other trauma by creating the impression that shamanic circles or shamanic journeying can provide some miracle "cure." While the experiences I had were indeed miraculous, I do not believe they could have occurred without the healing I had already experienced through my many years of therapy.

The following accounts are taken directly from the journal I kept of my journeying experiences while sitting in circle with the shamanic practitioner LaWanna Durbin. These accounts were written shortly after each experience—sometimes while I was still sitting in circle—and so the writing is often rough.

September 10, 1995

I am in a primitive village. Drums are beating, dancers are circling the fire. I am lying on my back on the ground, near the fire. There is a man lying next to me. The man is Steve, the man who molested me when I was nine years old. The natives dance and chant around us, the drums grow louder.

All the evil, hurtful, sinful acts I ever committed pass before my mind's eye. I feel all the hurt I ever caused anyone. I feel the burden of all the shame and guilt I've carried around with me. I begin to understand on a very deep level that I am no better or worse than Steve. That we are all the same.

White ashes are put on our naked bodies as part of a ceremony. I reach out to hold Steve's hand and, without words, I find myself forgiving him. As I do this he turns into a handsome young brave and I turn into a beautiful Indian princess. (Steve was, in fact, an American Indian.) We both rise to our feet and walk away together, hand in hand.

April 26, 1996—Journey to Revise My Story

LaWanna instructs us to take a journey to the middle world where we will be given assistance in being able to perceive our life story in an entirely different way:

I am part of a tribe and I am being initiated into womanhood and sexuality. The women of the tribe lovingly prepare me. They pierce my ears and nipples, and paint my body with intricate designs.

The chief of the tribe is to be the man to take my virginity. I am to begin by painting designs on his erect penis. I do this without embarrassment or fear, and end up putting a happy face on the head of his penis. He slowly begins inserting his penis into my vagina, so slowly that my desire builds and builds until I want him to begin thrusting. All during this time the chief is totally focused on me, on my feelings, not on his own pleasure. Throughout the ceremony, the women of the tribe continue to touch me and I feel their love and support.

Each of these journeys has proven to be remarkably healing in my life. Each has had a profound impact on my belief system and behavior. While some may argue that these journeys were merely fantasies on my part or nothing more than "guided imagery" or "group hypnosis," I know the difference. In shamanic cultures, a journey is thought of not as an illusion or a dream but as an actual life experience—albeit an experience in another "reality." This is exactly what it felt like to me. A real experience, as real as any I've ever had in this "reality."

There is no doubt in my mind that my journeying would not have been as powerful had I not been sitting in a circle with others who were journeying at the same time. The energy created by our drumming and our group intention was profound.

Circles Devoted to Healing Mother Earth

The wild realm is counting
on humans to come back into meaningful
community with one another and with it,
I believe the circle is teaching us how
to take our place in the
natural order.

ANN LINNEA

Our planet desperately needs the power that circles create in order to heal the neglect and abuse done by humans. We humans have the power to reverse this damage if we put our minds, hearts and souls to the task. Not only can circling with other like-minded people create a healing energy that will benefit Mother Earth, but circling can also motivate us to take action—to band together to protect those lands that are as yet unpopulated and unpolluted, and to clean up those lands that have been damaged.

Just as an individual responds to healing energy, so does Mother Earth. Healing circles are often held in order to heal a part of the Earth that has been ravaged by exploitation or carelessness. Often people choose to gather on a beach that has been damaged by an oil spill, in a forest that has been clear-cut or on a piece of land that has been polluted by garbage. The impact of such healing circles can be subtle yet powerful and is often marked by a sign from Spirit.

Recently in my community a day was set aside to heal a contaminated beach area that had been so severely ravaged by an oil spill that not only was the water deemed polluted, but the town itself had to be demolished. The purpose of "Avila Drum Day" was to balance the energy of Avila Beach and, through the healing energy, restore balance, rhythm and harmony to the community. In addition to performances by top percussionists from around the world, there was a massive drum circle at the end where everyone was encouraged to participate.

Meeting in circles helps us to develop what is currently being called "eco-consciousness"—the ability to extend our sense of self to include the natural world and cultivate a feeling of being one with that world. This kind of consciousness comes naturally to indigenous people who are raised in a tradition of animistic culture—or what Native Americans call "nature spirituality."

The shamanic world view of nature spirituality, or Earth religion, is the oldest known religion, going back to Neolithic times. All the tribal and primal peoples of the Earth (American Indians, Australian aborigines and the Huichols [pronounced "wee-choles"] of Mexico) continue to practice nature spirituality as they have done for thousands of years. The symbols of Earth religion—stone circles, goddess and Earth Mother images—have been found in the caves of the earliest peoples.

In a nature religion, a feeling of oneness with the animals, the trees, the ocean, the sun, the moon and the Earth is sought. It is believed that the forces of nature created us, and that their creative ability and power are within us. Living in cities it is easy to lose our connectedness with nature, to become increasingly desensitized to the degradation of our living planet. We must begin once again to avail ourselves of the forces of nature. We must listen to them and take heed of their messages. Creating circles, especially circles in nature, can help us to once again align ourselves with nature, to follow her laws and to be loving and reverent towards her.

Nature spirituality is based on the belief that the Earth is alive and conscious, that she is our Mother, and that we can pray to her for help and comfort. Furthermore, we can communicate directly with trees, animals and stones—in fact, with all forms of life on Earth. It is believed that these beings of nature have a wisdom that is more ancient than human knowledge, which can be tapped for guidance, healing and love.

If we accept that we are totally part of this living Earth, then we must recognize that isolated healing is an illusion. Healing ourselves and healing the Earth is the same work.

Our hearts long to return to the time when humans were in a harmonic vibration with the Earth. Only by beginning to take the interests of all life forms as *self*-interest can we begin to mend the ecological damage we have done.

Whether we meet in circle to heal individual woundings, to heal the Earth or to transform the world, we are exerting a powerful force in the universe, a force that is most definitely felt.

FIVE

Consensus and Mediation

*The heart pulls, entices, and
sometimes drags us into circle because
we need what is waiting for us there. We need
refuge from isolation, refuge from judgment
and criticism, refuge from competition
and power-mongering.*

CHRISTINA BALDWIN
CALLING THE CIRCLE: THE FIRST AND FUTURE CULTURE

*Perhaps the greatest work the circle
can do in the Western world is to teach us how
to combine and balance the need for respect
and the drive for accomplishment.*

CHRISTINA BALDWIN
CALLING THE CIRCLE: THE FIRST AND FUTURE CULTURE

We have become a culture that no longer knows how to treat one another with respect and consideration. Even in our closest relationships we seem to lack the skills to truly listen to and learn from one another. We have lost the ability to share our point of view without insisting on being right. Instead of agreeing to disagree or looking for a way to compromise, we dig our heels in, argue and blame one another.

We often view others not as individuals with the same needs and rights we have, but as obstacles in the way of achieving our goals. We often need help remembering how to behave in respectful ways with one another. This lack of respect is unconscious and unintentional since it has become the social norm. In Western cultures achieving our goals is more important than how we treat people along the way.

In addition to creating community and providing healing, the circle can also be used for consensus and mediation, and as a tool for teaching us how to treat one another with respect. In fact, the circle was the original forum for working out the rules and taboos of social conduct. By establishing specific ground rules to govern the way our circles are conducted, we create a model from which all our social interactions can evolve.

In *Calling the Circle: The First and Future Culture*, Christina Baldwin outlines many of the ways she envisions circles functioning. One of these ways is as a social practice:

> *The circle as a social practice asks us to be willing to arrive, to pay attention, to speak as clearly as we know how, and to help action and accomplishment arise out of the group. . . . However, it's nearly impossible to show up at a meeting that really never gets called to order; impossible to pay attention within chaos and domination; impossible to speak clearly or tell the truth when nobody's listening; and impossible to remain unattached to outcome if outcome has already been determined by those in power or if the process is diverted away from accomplishment.*

Council Circles

Sitting in council is a term used to describe circles that meet for the purpose of members openly sharing their stories, feelings and thoughts with one another. Often council circles meet to explore a particular issue or to obtain consensus in the group. Council circles are particularly beneficial for groups of people meeting for a specific purpose, such as focusing on racism, sexism or voluntary simplicity. Council circles work equally well for people who share a particular experience—such as breast cancer survivors, AIDS patients and people who work together in an organization. Last but not least, council circles are extremely beneficial as a way for those whose life experiences are very different from one another to learn from one another and begin to recognize similarities as well as differences.

According to *The Ceremonial Circle:*

> *One of the important uses of the circle is to find consensus or, as the Quakers say, the sense of the meeting. To sit in council allows an opening of the heart and mind to new possibilities of understanding. It provides the opportunity to be really heard. All participants agree to speak from their hearts and listen from their hearts in order to come to a deeper understanding of themselves, one another, and whatever is being discussed.*

The circle is the perfect forum for joining divergent groups of people. This is because the circle contains a magical power that defies superficial boundaries. For example, if we want to bring peace between the races it is important to meet in small, interracial circles. To bring understanding between women and men we must meet in mixed gender groups, and talk honestly and openly with one another.

The difference between meeting in a council circle and meeting in a support or therapy group is that advice is kept at a minimum. While there may or may not be a leader of the circle, everyone is considered equal, and therefore no one "lectures" others or tells them what they should do. This is based on the belief that individuals know what is best for them to do at any given time. They only need the space, the opportunity and the encouragement to find their own truth.

In council circles we come to realize that an issue can always be seen from a variety of viewpoints and that each viewpoint has a truth to it. We come to see that there are always many options to resolving any challenge or difficult situation. Through the circle process, these options become apparent.

In a council circle deep truth telling is valued over asserting oneself, competing with others or achieving dominance. There is no right way to feel, no right way to think. Those who meet in circle over a period of time discover that instead of competing with one another for attention or trying to prove that they are right or special, they come to accept one another, and themselves, as they are. They begin to recognize and honor the fact that each person brings something special to the circle, and they begin to see that we are all equal in our contributions.

As we continue to remain open and vulnerable, a true sense of community can develop. We gain the strength and willingness to remove the barriers that separate us and prevent equality.

According to Kay Pranis, an advocate for Peacemaking Circles, the benefits of meeting in council circles include the following:

- Everyone has a voice.
- There is an opening for a multiplicity of perspectives. Kay compares what occurs in circles with chaos theory (and what occurs in the real world) versus traditional linear processes. While not totally random, the outcome of a circle is not predictable. Although what occurs in circles may look chaotic on some level, there are boundaries, and patterns may emerge. Because a circle has the capacity to take in a tremendous number of perspectives and accommodate the turbulence that occurs because of this, higher-order solutions emerge.
- Circles create a space for entirely different types of spirituality to emerge. In circles, people can share what is spiritual for them without being judged and without being viewed as proselytizing. Issues that have been polarizing in the past can be discussed openly.
- Circles allow people to talk about difficult situations without imposing one another's values on others.
- Circles are a *respectful* process. They teach members to respect the interaction around an issue.
- Circles are enormously flexible. They can accommodate everything from the silly to the profound.
- Circles are a way of creating a "we" out of a number of isolated individuals.

Bringing the Circle into Business and Educational Environments

Council circles are also important tools for helping us to shift from a hierarchical system of leadership to one based on shared leadership and consensus. Shared leadership is fast becoming the preferred way of conducting business and managing organizations.

Christina Baldwin and Ann Linnea, the creators of PeerSpirit Circles, have focused a great deal of energy bringing the circle and circle principles into the business environment, from small businesses to large corporations. A great deal of this focus has been in the health care industry, which Christina describes as a very "stratified environment."

In one major hospital setting, for example, Christina and Ann have been meeting with eighteen of the top administration teams for the past four years. Each year they go back to determine where the circle can take them now. This all started when one of the vice presidents read *Calling the Circle*. In order to find a way out of management's "silo type of thinking" (where each management team is self-contained and doesn't know what the other is doing), they brought in Christina and Ann to teach them how to talk to each other and develop quality communication between management teams.

The management teams meet twice a month for two hours, and leadership rotates constantly. When someone has an agenda, that person takes charge, oversees the circle and assumes responsibility for initiating actions.

"Checking-in" and "checking-out" have been particularly effective circle components. Council members check in with where they are at the moment, including discussing both what needs celebrating and what needs healing. At the end of the council, each person checks out with what they are still carrying and what they are leaving behind.

Another example of effective council circling that Christina shared with me involved two female psychologists who had recently bought a practice. They decided to meet in council with their staff to establish a new sense of shared staffing and mutual responsibility for the quality of service they provide. This was in direct contrast to the traditional setup of someone being the "director" and shouldering all the responsibility and power

Council circles are particularly valuable in helping groups set goals, write mission statements and come to group agreements. Councils are also being utilized in various teaching environments since they encourage class participation and demonstrate that there are several ways to perceive an issue or topic.

Mary K. Sandford, the associate dean of the College of Arts and Sciences at the University of North Carolina at Greensboro, has used council circles in her classrooms for several years. One of her colleagues, Dr. Eileen Jackson, is the first person she knows to have worked with circles in a university setting. Sandford uses council circles in a program designed to prepare undergraduates for science careers and to provide them with actual research experiences. This is how she describes the experience:

Students are challenged in ways they haven't been before. Not only are they doing research for the first time but they are beginning to question the role of science in their futures. By using council circles to do check-in we are better able to keep track of where each student is in his or her development.

Also, the circle is particularly valuable for discussing topics where students have lots of different perspectives. Circles are also an excellent teaching technique in some situations since teachers can tell more readily whether students are learning and thinking about the material. Circles encourage class participation and research shows that students often learn more effectively when they are active learners and collaborate with one another versus when they sit passively listening to lectures. Although students often hate group work, when we introduced council circles and asked them to discuss, "What is it about working in groups that you typically don't like," they took to it right away. They were able to generate group agreements as to what they wanted their experience in this class to be like and created a great mission statement.

The idea is to get students involved in the co-creation of the classroom. In co-creation everyone has a sense of ownership and a greater sense of responsibility. This translates into people having a greater investment and more willingness to share responsibility as the group goes forward.

Interview with Mary K. Sandford

The Race and Gender Institute, a professional development opportunity for faculty and staff, has been going on at the campus of the University of North Carolina at Greensboro for several years. This year the College of Arts and Sciences is its sponsor and Mary K. Sandford is the coordinator. Faculty and staff in the program are exploring the use of circle councils in their work with one another and in the classroom.

Beverly: Would you explain more about the Race and Gender Institute?

Mary K.: The Race and Gender Institute focuses on helping to discover ways to raise and explore race and gender issues in the classroom and across the university. We are also attempting to get a better understanding of the status of race and gender across our campus, to determine what measures can be taken to further an awareness of diversity in our university community.

We are working with sixteen faculty and staff who have chosen to work together on the Race and Gender project throughout the year. We attend a variety of special events offered on campus that address race issues as a group and meet regularly once a month.

Beverly: How did you come up with the idea of utilizing circles in this process?

Mary K.: We decided to begin by meeting together at a retreat to start talking about what we want to accomplish this year. I decided to introduce the form of council to the faculty at the retreat. I had previously been introduced to PeerSpirit Circles and had attended a circle practicum. I was very impressed with this format. When I contacted Christina Baldwin and Ann Linnea to tell them of my plans with the Race and Gender Institute, Christina offered to co-facilitate the retreat with me.

Christina asked each person to bring an object to the retreat that they associated with race and gender in a positive way. We then opened the circle by having people put the object in the center of the circle and to tell the story of what the object meant to them.

We also used council in the evening to reflect on race and gender issues and how they pertain to our own life. Included in this was a writing exercise—each person was asked to write about an experience in their life in which they felt supported by their race and gender. Later they were asked to write about an experience where they felt hindered by their race or gender.

On the first day we started developing our group agreements and throughout the retreat Christina introduced different aspects of the form such as the importance of the talking piece and the concept of the guardian.

The next day we broke into dyads to discuss, "What is your vision of the Race and Gender Institute and what do you want us to accomplish by the end of the year?"

In the afternoon, we divided up into different groups to plan various aspects of the project: the mission statement, group agreements, and activities.

The circle was very well received and was extremely productive.

Beverly: What were the specific benefits of using the circle at your retreat?

Mary K.: Because of the introduction and the knowledge already gained about this form, we have already established an excellent working relationship among all the members. These sixteen faculty and staff members are learning together about race and gender issues and are learning how to suppport and encourage one another.

And the amount of work that gets done in this setting is phenomenal. Whenever one hears about circles they may think of it as "touchy-feely," but, in actuality, circles are productive ways to help groups find more effective ways of communicating in a positive manner. Circles provide a way to get a lot of tangible things accomplished in a relatively short amount of time.

I love to work in circles so much that I've taken the PeerSpirit practicum. It is the most exciting, rewarding work. The most *feeling* work I do.

Healing Differences That Arise in a Circle

In addition to meeting in council circles for all the previously mentioned reasons, any type of women's circle may need to use the council circle format in order to resolve disputes within their circle.

For a community of women to remain vital and effective, the energies between members need to be kept clear. Unfortunately, women have a tendency to become envious of one another, and power struggles may occur between them. If we can't learn to overcome petty struggles and support one another unconditionally, how can we hope to have a healthy community? An even more important question might be, "If we can't heal our own communities, how can we heal the world?"

According to Sedonia Cahill and Joshua Halpern in *The Ceremonial Circle*, in order to encourage and facilitate a healing between conflicting parties, a healing council can be held which includes the entire community. Unless this is done, the conflict will fester and spread like a disease throughout the community, causing members to take sides, avoid one another, gossip and backstab.

The ability to resolve conflicts in constructive ways is not something that most of us have been taught. It certainly is not something we have witnessed, either in our families or on a larger scale. It can only be learned in the context of a community that encourages conflict resolution through a healing council.

It takes courage to bring a conflict into a healing council. You must be willing to give up being "right" and be able to move from your position to a place where no one is really right or wrong. Instead, each person is seen as a mirror of one's self and a vehicle for one another's learning and achieving wholeness.

According to Sedonia Cahill and Joshua Halpern, the purpose of this particular type of healing circle is to create a safe environment for aggrieved persons to meet and be heard by those with whom they have an issue. The "issue" is evidence of a dysfunction both between individuals and within the larger community.

Each aggrieved party should select witnesses from the community to aid in the healing process of the council. The function of the witnesses is to support the healing process—rather than taking sides or deciding who's right or wrong—and make certain that the aggrieved parties have really heard one another.

Much more will be discussed about conducting consensus circles in Part Three, "Creating Your Own Circle." For now, suffice it to say that in a world that encourages separateness between people and impatience toward diversity, consensus circles may be our best teachers. They help us open our minds to—and accept—viewpoints that are different from our own. And they encourage us to open our hearts to those who are different from ourselves.

SIX

Our Hunger for the Sacred

The purpose of ritual is to
wake up the old mind, to put it to work.
The old ones inside us, the collective unconscious,
the many lives, the different eternal parts,
the senses and the parts of the brain that have
been ignored. Those parts do not speak English.
They do not care about television. But they
do understand candlelight and colors.
They do understand nature.

Z. BUDAPEST
DRAWING DOWN THE MOON

One of the primary purposes—and benefits—of meeting in circles is to bring sacredness back into daily life. We are living in a time when we have lost our deep and abiding connection with the spiritual, or what is commonly referred to as soul. Unfortunately for many of us, we have come to know soul only in its complaints, only when it stirs and causes us to feel its pain. We feel the symptoms of our disconnection with soul and sacredness on a daily basis: our feelings of emptiness, meaninglessness; a loss of values; disillusionment about marriage, family and relationship; and a vague depression for seemingly unknown reasons. Increasingly we find ourselves yearning for personal fulfillment and hungering for spirituality.

Meeting in circle can help satisfy our hunger for spirituality and for the sacred. It can help us reconnect with what is genuine and true about ourselves, others and the world in general. It can help fill us up with meaning, depth and purpose, and it can assist us in defining values that are meaningful, values that we can believe in and live by.

We need to be reminded that every moment is an expression of Spirit and that all life is sacred—every rock, every tree, every animal, every person. Unfortunately we often lose sight of this in the hustle and bustle of our busy lives. We may designate a certain time of the week or year as sacred time, and certain places, such as churches or temples, as sacred spaces. But we forget that every piece of ground we stand on is sacred ground. The circle, with its ritual and ceremony, helps us remember this.

The Need for Sacred Community

While it is necessary for our spiritual development to experience the sacred on an individual basis, to be alone and complete within ourselves, if we all continue to experience the sacred alone our culture will continue to deteriorate. By gathering together to experience sacredness, by sitting in circle and taking the time to deeply connect with others, we participate in the regeneration of our culture and in the expansion of our own souls.

Sitting around the campfire late at night our ancestors more than likely spent their time creating a mythology about our creation and our reasons for being. They created rituals of gratitude for the spirit beings that protected them from danger. They danced and drummed and sang around the fire. Thus the fire and the circle itself became a sacred symbol.

But we have long since stopped meeting together to experience the sanctuary, sacredness and growth of circle. And many of us haven't engaged in sacred community for years. Such was Melanie's experience:

Before I joined my women's spirituality circle, I hadn't worshipped with others since childhood. As a child I had some very negative experiences with organized religion and vowed to stay clear of it in the future. But I began to miss sharing a spiritual experience with others and realized I had "thrown the baby out with the bathwater," so to speak. And so I decided to try a women's circle.

I liked the fact that women of all spiritual persuasions were part of the circle. Finally I've found a place to connect with my spirituality without being preached to or made to feel "sinful" or bad. What a blessing!

The Need for Women's Spirituality Circles

Ellie Mercer, an ordained clergywoman with the United Church of Christ, served at various churches for many years when she began to discover a need for spiritual or inner work not being addressed by most churches. Along with psychotherapist Meredith Jordan, she developed a body of work that addresses the place where psychology and spirituality must meet to complete each other. Their work is grounded in a variety of faith traditions but not bound by them.

In 1994 we began to offer circles called "Deepening in the Spirit for Women." We could see there was a need for women to explore their own unfolding spiritual development apart from the experiences of men. We wanted women to have the opportunity to hear their own stories, to boldly search for their own words, and to feel supported as they navigated the course of their faith lives, their inner lives and their spiritual journeys.

Historically, institutional churches and religious traditions have been dominated by men. The voices and stories of women have been lost or silenced. The language used in churches and the images used to name the Sacred have, for the most part, been the language and images of men. The consequence of this is that the language and images of faith have been passed down to us in a form which does not fit the spiritual experience of many women. Church hymns, prayers and liturgies are steeped in masculine images.

In our initial women's circles, we found that new words, new forms, new images, emerged naturally and effortlessly as we listened to each other speak without interruption. The circle was a model of cooperation which encouraged us to speak from the heart. With this gentle support, we were able to go deeper. We found we didn't have to censor our words and our thoughts.

Together, we explored the language of dreams, poetry, art and dance—language not readily found in the institutional church. We were able to identify this as language of the spirit and found ourselves sharing this expression with one another, telling our stories in ways that we hadn't told them before.

A particular woman comes immediately to mind, a woman for whom words did not come easily. She found a way to tell her story in an especially poignant way, a way that fit who she really is. She brought an empty glass vase into the center of the circle and began to drop stones into it.

These, she said, represented the many obstacles she faced through the years as she tried to identify her spiritual path within the context of the institutional church. Then she added water, which, she explained, was like the water of baptism, inviting her out of the wilderness into new life. Finally, one by one, she added a variety of flowers, as a way of demonstrating the fullness of life that has the potential of emerging from the blocked, stony places of our lives.

Another woman never spoke a word but danced her story for the women of her circle. Still another spread magnificent and yet horrifying pieces of her artwork all over the room. They told the story of her search for God in the midst of profound abuse. What is so moving about this process is that it opens the channels of the heart—a process that is so often missing in the more cognitive, academic, intellectual exchanges of our religious settings.

These particular circles continued for several years. We met for two hours on Sunday afternoons for ten to twelve weeks. The results were powerful. Our experiences of interconnectedness with each other and with the Sacred were among the most meaningful many of us had ever had. I didn't fully realize the impact of these first circles until recently, when I heard a poem read as a eulogy at a memorial service for Maureen, one of the first circle members. Maureen had written that poem in gratitude for her profound experience of finding sisterhood in the circle. No one at Maureen's memorial service knew the origin of the poem but the women of her circle, and that was enough.

Ritual and Ceremony

Ritual and ceremony help us bring the sacred into everyday life—by satisfying our deep human need to regain our sense of reverence and awe, and by helping us feel connected to something larger than ourselves.

Through ritual and ceremony, two important components of circle, we can connect to the home where our souls reside, midway between understanding and unconsciousness. Ritual and ceremony help us play the instrument of soul, which is neither the mind nor the body, but imagination. They take us back to our roots and connect us with the rites and traditions that helped shape our souls and psyches. They help ground us in the Earth and, at the same time, encourage us to reach for the heavens.

Just as we have the memory of fire and circle deep inside us, we have the memory of ritual and ceremony. Many indigenous cultures believe that there is a deep, pre-verbal part of us which understands only the language of ritual. Because we have lost touch with the rituals and ceremonies in our lives, we hunger for them.

Indigenous cultures, with their natural sense of Earth wisdom and awareness of the sacredness in all things, seem to have always understood that humans are coded for ritual. In an article for *Awareness* magazine, Jenny Lipscomb, the founder of the All One Tribe Foundation, quoted an unnamed writer friend who shared with her

this profound insight: "Dreams are the way the unconscious speaks to the conscious mind. And ritual is the way
the conscious mind speaks back."

What exactly are ritual and ceremony? Technically, if we
are true to the dictionary meanings, the word *ritual* means
an established form for a ceremony, a ceremonial act or
action. The word *ceremony* means a formal act or series of
acts prescribed by ritual, protocol or convention.

Unfortunately, confusion about these terms has arisen
since people tend to use the two words interchangeably in
our culture, including people in the women's circle movement. Depending on who you talk to, ritual can mean a
ceremony, a celebration, a religious service, a rite of passage or the use of ritual magic. The word ritual is used
when talking about a repeated act or acting on a habit. It
can also be said, when someone is doing something in a
formal way, that he or she is ritualizing it.

For our purposes, I will stick to the dictionary meanings as much as possible and first look at ceremony—
with the understanding that since the words are used
interchangeably by so many in the circle movement, there
is bound to be some crossover in meaning.

Ceremonies

Ceremonies are an important aspect of every culture. They are events that bind a culture together, that create a center or heart for a people. By creating a strong group bond, ceremonies help build community, establishing a meeting ground where people can share deep feelings and a place where people can sing, drum, play, howl or maintain a solemn silence.

For example, throughout adulthood a traditional American Indian participates in numerous communal ceremonies. These ceremonies serve to keep the community in balance, to renew attitudes of respect and gratitude, and to fulfill obligations toward the land. A wide variety of ceremonies celebrate events within the year's cycle of unfolding creation. The Iroquois, for instance, offer communal gratitude for the manifestations of maple sap, green corn and strawberries. Other ceremonies, such as the sacred dramas danced throughout the year by the Pueblo peoples, are renewals of nurture, power and union with the sacred whole. The O'odhdam respond to the Sonoran desert as if it were a sacred calendar, celebrating their place in the cycles of change. In all instances, Indian ceremonies are regarded as spiritual responsibilities, human expressions of the reciprocal interdependence that constitutes the cosmic processes.

The process of ceremony, with or without ritual, inserts

a depth of feeling into any setting where it is introduced. One of the main reasons we have ceremonies is to mark what are called rites of passage. These rites of passage honor the various stages of a person's life, the stages we all go through in our lifetimes. We have ceremonies such as christenings to officially welcome a child into the world and to announce his or her name. We have graduation ceremonies when a child completes a certain number of years of school. And finally, to commemorate the final stage of life, we have a funeral ceremony to celebrate a person's life and to mourn our loss.

Ceremonies also bind us to one another. Ceremonies such as baptisms, marriages and baby showers create a sense of belonging. Symbolic actions such as blowing out candles on a birthday cake, smashing a glass or throwing rice at a wedding are often more potent than words in stirring our emotions and opening us to a sense of unity.

Ritual

Ceremony requires a certain amount of respect, and this is often where ritual comes in. Ritual is a necessary component of ceremony, adding meaning, emotional satisfaction and texture to it. As such, ritual is a central tool for women's self-empowerment. The term ritual often refers to any patterned movement of energy created to accomplish a purpose. A ritual must have purpose and a focal point for the energy raising to be effective and have meaning. There must be structure along with content. When we repeat a ritual in a mindful way, over a period of time, it gains even more power.

Ritual is an essential part of all circles and a necessary element in establishing what is called "a sacred time and place." In order to be effective, ritual needs to trigger the subconscious and let it know that something important is happening. Rituals consist of evocative words and symbolic actions that are meant to invoke a sense of sanctuary and sacredness.

For example, an opening ritual of lighting candles may symbolize the inner spark of wisdom we are seeking or the light of our creator. For this reason, an opening ritual, or any other ritual used in the circle, needs to have meaning for everyone present.

A ritual also needs to tell our subconscious that we are ready to change and are in a safe place to change. Ritual sets the stage, provides the structure, gives us an emotional "kick start" to effect change.

An opening ritual also begins the process of connecting members of the group to one another and laying the groundwork for a shift in consciousness from "I" to "We," from the individual to the group. In an intact indigenous community every member is taught essential spiritual rituals upon which the survival of the group depends. Everyone is expected to take responsibility for performing the rituals that maintain the connection to the sacred in their personal and communal lives. If an individual fails to perform his or her ritual role in maintaining the order that holds the life of the tribe together, the whole order suffers.

This sense of responsibility for collective spiritual integrity, while most powerful in tribes of indigenous people, also exists in other cultures and religions. For example, in Judaism the role of ritual is to hallow life (to honor the whole of life). This happens when a Jew sees the world as reflecting the source of all holiness, namely Yahweh. The route to such seeing is piety (spiritual devotion or reverence). The opposite of piety is to accept the good things of life—most of which come to us quite apart from our own efforts—as if they were matters of course, with no relationship to God. In the Talmud, to eat or drink without first making a blessing over the meal is compared to robbing God of this property. Jewish law sanctions the good things of life—eating, marriage, children, nature—but on the condition that they be hallowed.

Jewish belief holds that without attention, the human sense of wonder and the sacred will stir occasionally but will not become a steady flame unless it is tended to. One of the ways to do this is by steeping oneself in tradition—the Sabbath eve with its candles and cup of sanctification, the Passover feast with its many symbols, the austere solemnity of the Day of Atonement, the ram's horn sounding the New Year, the scroll of the Torah adorned with breastplate and crown. The Jew finds nothing less than the meaning of life in these things, a meaning that spans the centuries in affirming God's great goodness to his people. This in turn creates a feeling of centeredness, of being focused on the present, on the here and now.

We all have rituals in our lives, but in most cases we have forgotten their original meaning. These rituals were designed to remind us over and over again of what should be our true relationship to life: that of a grateful, amazed supplicant at the feet of our creator or the universe.

Ritual has many other functions in addition to those just discussed. According to Nancy Brady Cunningham, in her book *I Am Woman by Rite: A Book of Women's Rituals*, ritual can be any and all of the following:

- an acknowledgment of the movement of the seasons and a way to put us in sync with the rhythms of nature
- actions taken when words are insufficient to express the momentousness of an occasion
- a way to give expression to the nonverbal part of us through movement, song, dance and poetry
- meditation made visible
- an attempt to heal the opposites within us through a rite of passage

In my interview with Sandra Ingerman she stressed how important ritual is to her. One of the reasons she gave was that whenever we do a ritual, our body, mind and spirit all become engaged. The body performs the ritual, the mind has to think about how the ritual is going to be done and the spirit is there supporting the ritual. For Sandra, the nature of ritual is that it creates change. She told the story of how she was in Switzerland teaching a workshop and talking about the power of ritual when a woman said to her that the root word for ritual is a German word spelled *rta*, which literally translates to English as "the truth." When one is engaged in ritual, some truth is being brought forth.

Women's Rituals

According to Lesley A. Northup, editor of *Women and Religious Ritual* and author of *Ritualizing Women: Patterns of Spirituality*, although the specific rituals will vary from circle to circle, most women's rituals seem to include the following central elements:

- a concern for preserving women's history
- a reclamation of the connection of women with nature
- respect and gratitude for the bounty of the Earth
- a celebration of women's reproductive and nurturing power
- an emphasis on the stages of women's lives (maiden,

mother, crone), which is particularly important for women

The following interview will further explore the importance of ritual and ceremony, and elaborate on their roles. Julie Steinbach is a ceremonialist living in Southern California. She is also the woman who conducted the ceremony for my fiftieth birthday, the details of which I share with you later.

Interview with Julie Steinbach

Beverly: Before we get started, let's clear up some terms here. Do you make a distinction between the words ritual and ceremony and, if so, what is the difference in your mind?

Julie: I think the words are used interchangeably but generally speaking I use the word ceremony to mean celebratory and the word ritual to mean transformative.

Beverly: What in your opinion is the importance of ritual and ceremony in our culture?

Julie: Ritual helps us to slow down. Slowing down puts us in the framework to pay attention. It provides the space and the opportunity to connect and reconnect with what is important—sense of sacredness, nature, the cycles of life. When I am more regular with my individual rituals I feel more alive, more present, more open.

Ritual also signals life transitions. They are important not only to the person who is being acknowledged but to all those in attendance who use it as a measure or mirror for themselves. It is also through witnessing that people honor each other and themselves.

Beverly: Do you feel ritual is an important aspect of circle?

Julie: I can't imagine a circle without it. Sitting in a circle is itself a ritualistic act. I don't see how a circle can function without some aspect of ritual. In fact, ritual makes a circle a circle.

A circle's rituals fulfill our need for connection and encourage us to slow down and pay attention. Most important, they create a structure and space to articulate and give public voice to the important things we want to say to each other but usually don't say because they feel too charged or too embarrassing.

Beverly: How did you first become interested in conducting ceremonies?

Julie: I've always loved ritual and ceremony. Loved honoring birthdays. I came out of a traditional German-Lutheran background. After Christmas dinner we always sat around in a circle in the living room singing songs and listening to the children recite their Christmas pieces.

My mother kept a diary every day of her life, starting when she was eleven. She sent her friend of fifty years flowers on the anniversary of the day they met. I find I'm the kind of person who remembers anniversaries too. I was the chaplain in my sorority one year and I loved it, loved being responsible for the nightly devotionals.

Right after I began attending the Cambria circle I moved into a new house. I was used to having a big annual Christmas party at my house when I lived in Los Angeles, and so I decided to have one there and to include a house-naming contest. I also decided to have a house-naming ceremony and asked a local ceremonialist named Kristin to conduct it. She led a very beautiful ceremony and as she was doing it I thought to myself, "I could do that." And so I started conducting ceremonies for special occasions and the more ceremonies I did, the more I wanted to do.

In 1992 my sister asked me to do a house blessing for her new home, and so it felt like I'd come full circle.

Beverly: How has becoming a ceremonialist benefited you personally?

Julie: It has helped me with my own deepening, growth and understanding. It continually reminds me to pay attention, stay in the present and stay open.

Beverly: Do you use rituals that you've learned or do you create your own?

Julie: I create each ritual. It's a process that sometimes takes weeks or months. By now I have an idea of a structure that works.

While I've participated in many of Julie's rituals and have been deeply touched by them, I hadn't realized that she created each one. I'd assumed she was using rituals she'd learned from other women or rituals that had been passed down from other circles. The most important thing I learned from talking with Julie, which I want to pass on to you, is that you can create your own rituals to fit your particular circle or any occasion.

I encourage you to create your own rituals, rituals that have special meaning for your circle of women. As mentioned earlier, since there are so many possibilities for opening and closing rituals, in the spirit of the circle it is important to create or find rituals that hold positive meaning and have positive associations for everyone. As your circle meets over time you will no doubt discover favorite rituals that are particularly meaningful and inspiring for everyone.

You will notice while reading this book that many circles have adopted the ceremonies and rituals of the Native Americans and other indigenous peoples around the world. I believe this is because women resonate to tribal living so well. If you decide to form your own circle, you, too, may wish to incorporate some of these rituals, or you may wish to explore and rekindle the traditions of your family, your heritage or your religion. Those in the women's circle movement draw their rituals from a widely divergent array of disciplines and traditions, including Native American, Buddhist, Christian, African, Taoist, shamanic, neopagan, New Age and the occult.

Some of you reading this book may be frightened or nervous about the use of ritual in circles. Rituals may remind you too much of pagan ceremonies, or they may feel antireligious to you. This is what Pamela had to say about her initial fears:

> When a friend invited me to join her circle I was reluctant. I'm Catholic and all that hocus-pocus they do frightened me. It seemed too "New Age," and I was afraid they were involved with satanic rituals or something. But my friend assured me that there were women of all religious backgrounds in the circle, including other Catholic women, and that there was nothing "satanic" about women's circles; in fact, they were very spiritual.
>
> After meeting for a few weeks all my fears subsided. I

recognized that the ceremonies were no different from the lighting of candles we do at our church or the offering of incense that the priests make. And each woman respects the religious beliefs of the others. No one proselytizes and no one judges. In fact, one of the greatest benefits of the circle for me is that I find I am becoming less judgmental.

The women in my circle are very special. They are good women who are really working on becoming better people. That's the most important thing, not what religion they believe in.

If you have fears similar to Pamela's, don't let them get in the way of your experiencing the sanctuary, sacredness and growth possible in a women's circle. Either attend an existing circle for a few weeks to see if it is right for you, or create your own circle with rituals consistent with your beliefs.

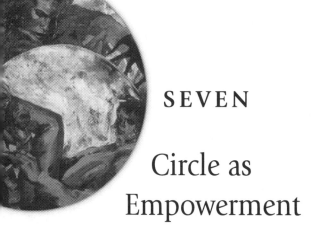

SEVEN

Circle as Empowerment

We don't need someone to show us the ropes.
We are the ones we've been waiting for.
Deep inside us we know the feelings we need to guide us.
Our task is to learn to trust our inner knowing.

SONIA JOHNSON
GOING OUT OF OUR MINDS

I see a finely wrought chain of tempered silver,
delicate yet strong, stretching back through time,
reaching deep into the earth. . . . A chain of women,
each listening to each, being present to her as she waits
for her self to be born, for her feeling values to come to
form and to birth. . . .Woman after woman after
woman, being present, as each finds her voice.

JUDITH DUERK
A CIRCLE OF STONES: WOMAN'S JOURNEY TO HERSELF

E ven though women were oppressed and treated as second-class citizens for many, many years, we are now learning that we are indeed equal to men, although our energies and talents may lie in different directions. The next step is for women to own their power, to stop giving it away and to channel it in positive directions.

Circles are excellent places for women to learn positive lessons about power that can replace the negative ones they learned early on. Since most circles rotate leadership, each woman gets a chance to experience the role of the leader, including those women who wouldn't ordinarily take a leadership position. Conversely, those women to whom the leadership position comes naturally will learn to abdicate responsibility and allow others to share the power of leadership.

The circle teaches us a new model for interacting with others, a new way of relating in which we are neither inferior or superior, where no one person's opinions are more important than another's. This is in sharp contrast to the typical hierarchical model of relating where one person is seen as the authority and all others as subordinates.

When we are in a subordinate position, we tend to distrust our own judgment. We then begin to look to authority figures for the answers instead of trusting our own instincts and our own wisdom. Because we have "disowned" our own power, we also may begin to sabotage those with more power. Conversely, when we are in a superior position, we tend to become arrogant. We stop listening and learning, and we begin to close ourselves off from new information. We tend to become defensive and hostile if anyone questions us.

Circles advocate equality over domination or submission, and power from within versus power over. As Starhawk noted, power from within can be likened to the power we sense in a seed, in the growth of a child, or the power we feel when creating. In fact, the root meaning of the word "power" is from the Latin *podere* or "to be able."

Women's Power

Many believe that women tend to address the issue of power differently from men and generally exercise power differently. This belief is echoed by many women writers such as Susan Starr Sered, the author of *Priestess, Mother, Sacred Sister: Religions Dominated by Women:* "It [women's power] is more often personal than positional, it tends to be situationally oriented, and is frequently exercised outside of the traditional authority structure of society."

Starhawk also argues that women exercise power differently. She has outlined three levels of power: dominative, charismatic and "coactive." The first she equates with patriarchy, the second and third with "good" uses of power by women.

Many female psychologists have also observed that power among women is practiced more as "power with" others than as "power over" them. Nowhere is this proven to be more true than in women's circles where leadership is generally shared or rotated, and where strength through consensus is valued over strength through dominance.

In my interview with Christina Baldwin she notes that:

There is an incredible sense of empowerment that occurs when someone sits in circle and is acknowledged. People come away from the experience thinking, "I have a voice" and, in turn, begin to act as if they have a voice. A good example of this is what happened when we were working with a Catholic organization in deep crisis. Recently the organization had become ruled by a secular administration and there were only four religious sisters left. One of the sisters came to a circle training. For days she wept about the changes in the organization and held that point on the rim. But she came out of the training with a tremendous feeling of empowerment. She went to the CEO and spoke her truth. She spoke her truth to those in the hallway. Within a period of six months she was elected to an administrative position. All because she had experienced a sense of empowerment in the training from being heard, and now felt that empowerment enough to speak up and be heard by the people she worked with.

Another important benefit of sitting in circle is that of entitlement—learning to act as though you have the right to speak up. This is an important shift, especially for women. I've often said that it is easier for women to make amends than to get permission. This sense of entitlement, of seeing themselves as equal members of the community, is important for women to bring into any organization, whether it be their job, their church or their marriage.

The Spiritual Aspects of Power

Circles are also excellent places in which to experience spiritual power. When we make a sacred circle we are creating a very powerful space—a space where we can share in the mysteries of body and spirit. Those in sacred circles experience how the circle allows them to raise and project energy and manifest it in the world. The circle teaches us to contain, intensify and direct the energy we raise.

As Christina Baldwin states in *Calling the Circle:*

To call in the potency of the circle challenges everything we have been taught about power. To move self-assuredly within the circle, we need to have a way of personally turning to spiritual guidance. We need to be able to hold our own authority and to acknowledge that our authority springs from a spiritual, rather than egotistical source.

Over time, calling on a spiritual source changes how we perceive events and how we react to them. As soon as we stop to ask what Spirit wants in any situation, we create a receptivity for spiritual guidance. Agreeing to maintain silence until we feel spiritually directed to speak helps us connect with our inner source of power.

For over twenty years I conducted support groups for survivors of childhood sexual abuse. In these groups women sat in a circle and told their deepest, most shameful stories to one another. They supported one another as they experienced their pain and anger together and as they became empowered together. These support groups were circles in almost all respects except that they lacked a spiritual focus.

A few years ago I began conducting Empowerment Circles for women who had histories of abuse of any kind, as children or as adults. Although the problems discussed were the same, meeting in the circle format with circle principles and guidelines has produced very different results. The main difference is each woman in the circle has become far more empowered. Instead of looking to me, the therapist, for all the answers, participants learn to value the wisdom of other women in the circle. This, in turn, encourages them to value their own wisdom.

Recently, I asked the participants of one of my Empowerment Circles how our circle is different from regular support groups and what they have gained from the circle. Here are a few of their responses:

"At first the fact that you could only talk when you had

the talking stick was difficult, but it wasn't too long before I saw the benefit of it. Each woman had a chance to say what she needed to say instead of being interrupted."

"When I first came into the circle I was afraid to tell my story—it was so horrible. I was afraid the other women would get turned off or judge me. But I found that the talking stick empowered me to speak. It was a physical thing—holding onto it gave me the courage to talk."

"Not allowing any cross talk was a good thing for me. I was so sensitive when I first came that I might have been offended if someone had given me advice or said anything to me in response to what I'd shared."

"I felt relieved by the rule that there was to be no advice giving. This told me it was not my place to give advice and this freed me up to focus on my own problems instead of always trying to solve the problems of others."

"The circle provided us with strong, focused energy. Other groups are too chaotic and diffuse for me."

"I was shy about talking, and holding the stick gave me more courage."

"The use of the talking stick and the no advice-giving rule kept the horses from charging in. It helped me contain myself, and I needed the discipline. And since I couldn't say what I wanted to say right away I usually forgot it. This kept me focused on myself more. I finally came to realize that if I kept thinking about what I wanted to say I missed all the treasures others had to say."

Many of the women in my Empowerment Circles have strong spiritual beliefs. In the past I believed that spirituality needed to be kept out of the therapy arena and I therefore discouraged women from sharing their spiritual beliefs in group. But since I didn't consider our Empowerment Circles to be therapy, I didn't discourage discussions about spirituality. Again, I was surprised at the results.

It seems I had underestimated the women's ability to be discriminating—to take what fit and disregard what didn't. When a woman shared her spiritual wisdom or beliefs with the others, no one seemed to feel they were being preached to. And the person who shared her wisdom was empowered from having been listened to.

I had also previously believed that at times spirituality and personal growth were mutually exclusive. For years I had seen people stay in denial about atrocious acts of violence because of their belief in God. I had witnessed women staying in abusive relationships with men partly because they believed that they should obey their husbands. And I had experiences with hundreds of women who could not become angry with even the most abusive or neglectful parent because of their belief that they should "honor their parents."

But in our Empowerment Circles we found a way to blend spirituality with personal growth, to rely on Spirit but not give up self-responsibility. We could express our anger and, at the same time, work toward understanding, compassion and forgiveness.

Just as all circles have the potential for healing, all circles can be empowering. Nevertheless, some circles are specifically focused on empowerment for women.

Goddess-centered spirituality circles teach that when women focus on themselves as divine beings and as co-creators, they become uplifted and begin to feel better about themselves and become more assertive—exercising their own authority in their lives.

Other circles, such as the Empowerment Circles I have created, encourage women to overcome victimization and to stop giving their power away to others. They empower women to have the courage to overcome an obstacle, stop losing themselves in their relationships with men, or complete a particular goal.

Reconnecting with Our Power

Just as many women no longer identify themselves as being part of the women's liberation movement, many women don't identify themselves as victims or even as survivors. Today women simply identify themselves as women—women seekers, women visionaries and women warriors. Women who are striving to discover, reconnect with and nurture their power.

Throughout history, women have depended on men to protect and provide for them. In more primitive times, women depended on men to do the hunting and to protect them against enemies—whether man or beast. Even as recently as thirty to forty years ago, women were seen as helpless victims in need of protection from the world and financial support from men in order to survive. But all that is changing. Today it is becoming abundantly clear that women do not need men for survival. Women not only take care of themselves but their children. In some cases, women are even carrying the full emotional and financial burden of their entire family, including taking care of unemployed, ailing or irresponsible men.

Today more and more women are single, either by choice or by chance. Many are becoming single parents and, as women get older, more and more are remaining unmarried. For all these reasons, women are discovering that they need each other more than ever.

It is my belief that if there is any hope for this planet it is through women coming back together in circle as they once did—to support one another, to view one another as sisters instead of enemies. Meeting in circle is the most viable way of accomplishing this.

This belief is shared by Sandra Ingerman, who wrote in her book *Soul Retrieval:*

> *The problems we have in society today—social injustice, crime, environmental problems—require that we move out of our lives of isolation and band together, acting communally to find solutions that extend beyond the scope of the problems. Without discarding the concept of self-healing, we must recognize the need for a healing process of power and love that involves the support of others.*

Once women have come back together and received the support they so desperately need, once they are nurtured and nourished by one another, they will feel rejuvenated and empowered. This empowerment will in turn encourage them to stand up for what they believe in, stand up to social injustice and male domination, and work toward saving the children, the poor and the planet.

Women have an unlimited amount of energy—creative and otherwise that, if channeled in the right directions, can be used to change the world. Some call what women have to offer our "female intuition," but this is often said in a very disparaging way. What exactly is "intuition"? Intuition means feeling, inspiration, instinct—traits that women have in abundance, traits that are needed if we are to turn this world around.

By joining hands and hearts we find we can overcome

even the greatest of obstacles. Women banding together can become a force strong enough to someday wipe out poverty, racism, child abuse and pollution. We can counter and eventually overpower the war-driven, dog-eat-dog mentality that permeates our planet. Women banding together have already changed the world in significant ways and we can do even more.

This is our time in history. Our planet needs our power—the power of the feminine. We need to stop giving our power away. We need to stand up and say no to the masculine drive to obtain more things, to possess, to have power over.

If we have any hope in saving the world, women must heal one another and stop feeling threatened and envious of one another. We must stop giving our power away to men and stop waiting for men to take care of our needs. We must stand up and stand together. The circle can help us do so.

PART THREE

Creating Your Own Circle

EIGHT

Choosing a Women's Circle to Create— An Overview

*This is our challenge: to rediscover
this innate knowing of circle and to fit that
knowing into the realities of
the modern world.*

CHRISTINA BALDWIN
CALLING THE CIRCLE: THE FIRST AND FUTURE CULTURE

*The energy of a circle can create a space that
can allow for the unorthodox to enter
and the unexpected to happen.*

SEDONIA CAHILL AND JOSHUA HALPERN
THE CEREMONIAL CIRCLE

O ne of my intentions in writing this book is to help
you become empowered to start a circle of your

own or to integrate circling into an already functioning group. In this section I present an overview of the various types of circles available as well as information on how to go about creating and structuring your own circle.

For purposes of simplicity and clarity I have divided circles into two broad categories—council circles and sacred circles. Council circles include all circles that meet for the purpose of reaching consensus, and discovering and nurturing the wisdom that lies within. While these circles usually have a spiritual element, they tend to be more *verbal* than *nonverbal*. Sacred, healing or ceremonial circles tend to rely far more heavily on rituals and ceremonies and to focus more on communication with spirit guides than on verbal communication between circle participants. This does not mean that council circles are not healing since all circles provide healing and encourage wholeness. Nor does it mean that sacred circles don't also sometimes meet for the purpose of achieving consensus and mediation.

Some of the circles I describe may sound either too "far out" or too complicated for some of you. For this reason, keep in mind that you can form a circle of women that can be equally powerful just by inviting at least four like-minded women together and by observing the six elements of circle: intention, sacredness, commitment, equality, heart consciousness and gratitude.

In order to present you with the full range of ways that

circling is being utilized, I have tried to include a wide variety of circles. Some of you may be uncomfortable with or even offended by some of the circles I have included. If this is the case, please be reminded that the philosophy of the circle is based on inclusion, nonjudgment and the idea that everyone has a right to their beliefs. As the Twelve-Step saying goes, "Please take what fits and leave the rest."

The first thing you will need to do before creating your circle is decide which type of circle you wish to create. This decision is best made by carefully considering your *intent.* Do this by asking yourself, "What is my main reason for wanting to form a circle?" Some of you will undoubtedly wish to gather for the purpose of healing, worship or ceremony. Some may wish to meet in circle in order to resolve individual problems. Others will wish to meet in circle in order to tackle community problems, while still others want to meet in order to focus on resolving world problems such as hunger or the environment.

In this chapter I introduce you to several types of women's circles. Each of these circles has certain underlying principles and rules of organization based on a philosophical system. Whenever possible I will attempt to explain these to you. In the next chapter, "The Structure of Circle, the Circle as Structure," I focus on how each circle applies these principles and rules within the circle's structure.

Council Circles

PeerSpirit Circles

We need a revolution in the West: not violent over-throw, but a willingness to take responsibility for the course of history being set forth in our names. We need a revolution determined to activate broad, inclusive social change. We need to insist that our homes, schools, neighborhoods, places of work, cities, states and nations dialogue with us about the values set in place for this next millennium.

CHRISTINA BALDWIN
CALLING THE CIRCLE: THE FIRST AND FUTURE CULTURE

Christina Baldwin and Ann Linnea, the cofounders of PeerSpirit circles, envision the circle as a vehicle for social change and world transformation starting at the level of dialogue and community building. They were among the first people to devise a specific structure for modern-day circles, incorporating all the elements of circle I've mentioned earlier. As their *Guide to PeerSpirit Circling** states: "PeerSpirit is a movement dedicated to bringing the circle

---

This booklet, available through PeerSpirit (see Appendix II), condenses the struc-ture of the circle for easy introduction.

into culture. We form a circle around the belief that by rotating leadership, sharing responsibility and attending to Spirit, people may align their lives with their own dreams, social awareness, spiritual values and respond to the pressing needs of the earth, its peoples and creatures."

In her book *Calling the Circle*, Christina further explains:

> *As Ann and I and our circle colleagues have clarified our vision of the piece of this work we feel called to carry, we have evolved a structure for the circle that is peer-led and spirit-centered. We call this structure the PeerSpirit circle.*
>
> *The basic experiment in PeerSpirit circling is to invite groups of people to become self-facilitating. PeerSpirit is an all-leader circle that counts on all members to assume increments of leadership, according to their skills and the needs of the moment. PeerSpirit is a form of collective accountability that trusts all members to share responsibility for the functioning of the group on every level, from interpersonal respect to accomplishing the work that binds the group together. PeerSpirit encourages people to relinquish part of our commonly held autonomy to the center, so that all members may rely on spiritual energy—collective group synergy— to act as a force of cohesion and guidance.*

Christina and Ann, and a growing number of circle colleagues, are reintroducing circle to women, men and mixed groups, in settings as varied as wilderness retreats to corporate boardrooms. In her book, Christina reaches back to the dawn of human society and identifies the circle as the common First Culture that grew out of the campfire to the tribe, the village and eventually became lost in the modern world.

Now she believes the circle is calling us again to a common experience of renewed community that she names "Third Culture." Christina uses the term "Third Culture" to suggest a context for bringing the circle back into the world as more than a ceremonial experience. As she explains, her intention is to make the wisdom of thirty thousand years of council available to us in order to help us choose how to reframe society in the twenty-first century:

> *This Third Culture is not a country we visit, or a formula already devised. You and I will choose what Third Culture is. We will set the context. One circle at a time, we will decide what Third Culture looks like and how it acts toward its citizens.*
>
> *Third Culture is an interpersonal practice. It is the practice of learning how to behave with respect toward each other, toward our earthly resources and toward Spirit. When we change how we interpret and interact with the circumstances and people right around us, we create Third Culture. . . . Who knows what risks we will take if we are asked, if the task is explained clearly, if our contribution is valued, if we can count on each other. Even the smallest child responds to the challenge of contribution when s/he is*

relied upon. Even the most outcast member of society has something of value to offer the whole.

The PeerSpirit methodology for circling has been used extensively in community organizations and work environments. It is often introduced when an existing group is ready to shift from a designated-leader model to an all-leader model or when a new group seeks to become self-governing. In *Calling the Circle,* the circle model is applied to parents and teachers negotiating conflict in a school system, to a project team, to women's groups and to many other anecdotal situations.

As Christina states in her book: "I hope a person introduced to PeerSpirit in the workplace can understand this structure and apply it to call a circle at home or in his/her neighborhood. I hope a person who practices PeerSpirit within his/her family can adapt the structure to work, or church or conflict resolution. . . ."

PeerSpirit circles often meet in order to accomplish a specific task in the form of a shared, verbalized intention so that everyone knows why they are gathered. The circle self-governs and corrects its course through the adoption of commonsense agreements of behavior.

Examples of such agreements include:

1. What is said in circle belongs in circle.
2. The circle is a practice of discernment, not judgment.

3. Each person takes responsibility for asking the circle for the support they want and need.

4. Each person takes responsibility for agreeing or not agreeing to participate in specific requests.

5. When troubled, someone in the circle may call for silence, song, time-out or ritual to reestablish the focus on center and remind participants of the need for spiritual guidance.

When confusion arises, or the way is momentarily lost, everyone agrees to fall into reflective silence, refocus on the group's highest purpose, and follow protocols for problem solving that reestablish trust and cohesion.

One of the most exciting dynamics about this form of circle is that the agreements empower everyone equally and release a group to practice "democracy." It is the redistribution of power and the rise of collaboration that most deeply inform Baldwin's perspective on the circle.

Wisdom Circles

There is nothing so wise as a circle.

Rainer Maria Rilke

Founded by Cindy Spring, Sedonia Cahill and Charles Garfield, Wisdom Circles offer people a unique opportunity for self-disclosure and a way to engage one another in increasingly deeper levels of wisdom and compassion.

The basic philosophy of the Wisdom Circle is that within all of us lies the elemental wisdom to inform us of what it means to be human, what it means to love one another, to do our best work and to be our best selves. But sometimes it takes a special setting to help us remember this wisdom and to draw it out of ourselves. Wisdom Circles provide such a setting.

Wisdom, as the creators of Wisdom Circles use the word, is an "emergent quality" that surfaces when people agree to form a circle with a loving heart and open mind for the purpose of mutual discovery. Circle members work in partnership to reveal the essence and wisdom of one another's stories.

According to the Wisdom Circles' founders:

> The wisdom circles process provides a way to deepen the values that sustain our lives. Inside the safe space of a wisdom circle it feels natural to be authentic, trusting, caring and open to change. As we come to realize how many of us there are who share these life-affirming values, and are committed to them as a basis for action in the world, we develop greater self-awareness as well as the strength of mutual support.

A Wisdom Circle serves many purposes. It is a place to practice heart-to-heart communication skills, to heal the wounds of loss, illness and abuse, to find the courage to act upon that "still small voice within." It is a place to share a vision, discover a mission. It is a place within which to create a feeling of community, where individuals can learn to be more fully themselves, while simultaneously becoming an integral part of the group.

Wisdom Circles have been used in a variety of settings— at conferences, in organizations, at the Institute of Noetic Sciences and in Unitarian-Universalist and United Church of Christ groups. They have been used by hospice nurses, diversity trainers, social activists, corporate work teams, a medical school staff and a single fathers' group. Cindy helped integrate the Wisdom Circle format into the viewer's guide for a PBS series called *Reaching Out,* which focuses on the role of community service in relation to racism and the assault on the environment. Charles Garfield, Cindy's husband, introduced Wisdom Circles into the AIDS caregiving community throughout the country.

The Wisdom Circle format has the potential to facilitate communication among people who see themselves as very different.

By listening and speaking from the heart—the primary conditions for Wisdom Circles—real communion can take place, which in turn can help us begin to resolve our differences based on race, gender, ethnicity, religion, class, political ideology or sexual orientation.

Wisdom Circles also serve those who have been following a solitary spiritual path but who now feel the need to connect with kindred spirits. Such circles help them to sustain an honest self-inquiry and to counteract tendencies toward cynicism, despair and self-doubt.

Interview with Cindy Spring

Cindy Spring is one of the cofounders of Wisdom Circles and coauthor of *Wisdom Circles: A Guide to Self-Discovery and Community Building in Small Groups.*

Beverly: How did Wisdom Circles begin?

Cindy: My initial motivation for starting Wisdom Circles came during a vision quest in the Nevada desert led by Sedonia [Cahill]. For years I had been looking for a way to make my work more meaningful, for a way to make a difference and to regain my faith in humankind—values I had held as a social activist in the 1960s. During that week in the desert, I came to understand the power that circles have to create community and to plumb the depths of our experience. The circles formed during that vision quest supported and challenged me more than the consciousness-raising groups I was used to and I discovered new levels of honesty in myself. I came away with a new mission: to encourage people to meet in circles and then find a way to network those circles. I asked my husband, Charlie, and Sedonia to join me, and in 1994 we founded the organization called Wisdom Circles.

Beverly: What are the most important aspects of your Wisdom Circles?

Cindy: There are two aspects of Wisdom Circles that I feel are the most important. The first, and the thing I want to be known for the most is: We have so much to learn from each other. This is the essence of Wisdom Circles. We can tap into our own divinity to deal with the problems we all share.

Of particular interest to me is bringing people who may not see each other as kindred spirits into circle together. Listening from the heart and speaking from the heart is the place to start. This is the way to resolve problems like environmental destruction and racism, two issues I am particularly interested in.

The second idea is that the Wisdom Circle is a *dojo*—the martial arts word for "training area." It is the place to learn the skills of life, like how to express gratitude. As in a martial arts dojo, a Wisdom Circle is a place where we practice the ways we want to be in our daily lives.

Beverly: Do you feel ritual is an important element of circles?

Cindy: I feel it is very important, but it need not be elaborate. It may be holding a moment of silence or lighting a candle. Anything that marks the beginning of the circle.

Beverly: Many forms of circles utilize traditions of indigenous peoples such as Native Americans. Do Wisdom Circles utilize such traditions and practices?

Cindy: Aside from the talking stick, Wisdom Circles do not utilize other practices from indigenous people. I drew as much or more from support groups and from Quaker circles.

Beverly: What changes have you witnessed in others because of their participation in circles?

Cindy: I'll speak for myself. I was in circles back in the '60s—women's consciousness circles. Then I went on a vision quest in 1993 and 1994 with Sedona Cahill and was given this form of circle. Wisdom circles have helped me to open my heart. I tend to be very heady, to focus on intellectual pursuits. Wisdom Circles taught me to listen and speak from the heart. I also tended to be very judgmental. I didn't like it, but it was a knee-jerk reaction. I didn't know how to stop, how to change it. Now I am far less judgmental.

I also used to prefer working alone, living a more solitary life. Now I hunger for community and what I learn from others. I used to feel that the only people I could learn from were the so-called "experts." For several years I read stacks of spiritual, metaphysical books. Another sign of my maturity is that now I learn from the people around me. That is where the wisdom I need comes from.

Beverly: I know that your circles include both women and men. But do you feel that circles have a particular significance for women?

Cindy: Eighty to eighty-five percent of the people who have responded to our Wisdom Circles are women. Women take to circle like ducks to water. Circles are not only for women; women just have the courage to use them. We understand that the source of spirit is community. This doesn't denigrate solitary work at all. It is just that we are moving into a time where the major form of spirituality will be the circle.

Beverly: Is there a particular message you would like to convey to my readers?

Cindy: My highest vision is for people to think of circle the way they do meditation. We don't think about where meditation comes from or who "invented" it. It has just become a part of our culture. I'd like people to think of circle in the same way. As an important tool to be used for certain reasons.

Empowerment Circles

*Everything the Power of the World
does is done in a circle.*

BLACK ELK
BLACK ELK SPEAKS

I created Empowerment Circles as an offshoot of my many years of working with victims of childhood abuse and my dedication to helping those women who tend to continually give their power to others. In addition, there are literally thousands of women who have been suffering alone with their problem of losing themselves in relationships. I wanted these women to discover, through circle, that they are not alone and to feel the empowerment that can come from connecting with and being supported by other women.

Empowerment Circles help women in many other ways as well:

- By being able to talk openly about their issues, women begin to feel they are really being heard, seen and respected, perhaps for the first time in their life.
- By learning to ask for the kind of feedback and support they want, women not only become more assertive, but more clear about what their real needs are.
- By receiving feedback from other women about what they have said in the past and what they have stated they wanted, women begin to know themselves better and take more responsibility for their words and actions.
- By learning to give feedback that is without judgment, women learn to remain more objective (and therefore tend not to lose themselves in relationships), to respect

others' rights and needs to be separate; and begin to judge themselves less harshly.

The Core Belief of Empowerment Circles

Our deepest fear is not our fear of being inadequate, but our fear of our own power. It is much easier to let others control our lives than to take charge ourselves. It is much easier to pretend to be meek than to take responsibility for our power. It is much easier to allow others to abuse us than it is to own our own tendency to abuse ourselves.

Empowerment Circles keep women honest—about their power, about their feelings and about their intentions. If a woman states an intention or makes a proclamation about what is really important to her in front of a circle of women she deeply respects, it is far more difficult to take actions outside the circle that go against her stated intention or beliefs.

The guidelines for Empowerment Circles are as follows:

- We share leadership of the group and meet in a circle to remind us that we are all equal. Since we are all still learning about ourselves, no one can afford to take on the role of leader as a way of distracting herself from her own work.
- We use the talking stick to remind us that each person has something important to say, that we each deserve

a turn at speaking, and that it is important that only one person speak at a time.

- We will endeavor to focus our entire attention on the person who is speaking, not allowing our minds to wander or our hearts to close. We know how painful it is to go unheard, unseen and misunderstood, and so we give our attention and our understanding as a gift whenever possible.

- We refrain from giving advice to one another because we believe that deep inside every woman knows what is best for her. We want to encourage each woman to come to her own decisions.

- We refrain from criticism and judgment of one another because we understand how it robs us all of our self-confidence, our trust in ourselves and our ability to be strong and independent.

- We offer our own experiences, not to take the focus off someone else, not to show that we know best, but to let others know they are not alone, to help others feel connected with one another, and to remind ourselves of our own issues.

- We expect each woman in the group to be responsible for asking for what she needs from the group.

- We hold each woman accountable for what she has stated she wants from the group and for her life. Therefore, if a woman is doing something counter to her stated objectives we will point this out. While we all have a right to change our minds, we need to be aware that we are doing so.

- Even though we have, in fact, been victimized by our families, our partners, and by the way women are treated in our culture, we do not see ourselves as victims today, nor do we wish to continue to behave like victims. This means that whenever possible, we take responsibility for our actions, particularly when it comes to our relationship with men.

Simplicity Circles

Most of the luxuries, and many of
the so-called comforts of life, are not only not
indispensable, but positive hindrances to the
elevation of mankind. With respect to luxuries and
comforts, the wisest have ever lived a more
simple and meager life than the poor.

HENRY DAVID THOREAU

The Earth has enough for every man's need,
but not for every man's greed.

MAHATMA GANDHI

In her book, *The Circle of Simplicity,* Cecile Andrews defined one of the goals of voluntary simplicity as the following:

We want to create a society in which the quality of life both for people and for the planet are more important than the attainment of wealth. . . . [This includes] moving from an egocentric ethic in which people are motivated by greed to an egocentric ethic that values people and the planet. We need to create a belief system that makes the welfare of people and the planet a higher priority than the belief in the right of a few people to get rich. . . .

Simplicity study circles or voluntary simplicity circles, as some people call them, follow the basic circle format discussed throughout this book. Most have a spiritual focus, most share leadership and most encourage self-reflection and nonjudgmental listening. Some operate more like "study circles," using books such as *Voluntary Simplicity* by Duane Elgin or *The Circle of Simplicity* by Cecile Andrews as their context or guide.

Crone Circles

*At fifty-one we become an adult.
It takes that much time to begin to understand
the mysteries within us. At fifty-one, understanding
cause and effect, one voice arises clearly.
At fifty-one we may look to the Western gate and
decide what negative thoughts and attitudes can be
cast out so that we may resonate a song of peace*

and harmony for all people, so that they live without
fear. At fifty-one we decide, "Shall I continue for the
benefit of the family, the clan, the nation and
the planet?" At fifty-one we commit ourselves
to bringing forth beauty for all people, and one may
begin to become a grandparent at that time.
At fifty-one, in the Tsalagi tradition,
we become an adult.

DHYANI YWAHOO
VOICES OF OUR ANCESTORS

In some tribes of indigenous peoples once a woman passes her "thirteenth moon-time," which means that she hasn't bled for one lunar year, she is considered a wise elder. She is expected to provide a voice of wisdom to the children of the tribe, and all tribal decisions have to pass her close scrutiny.

Unfortunately, many in contemporary society fear the wise woman's wisdom and as a result we have made elder women virtually invisible. Because they are left alone to deal with the negative and misunderstood aspects of menopause, the power released in women at this significant time is often turned inward, resulting in depression, mood swings and a general feeling of being lost, useless and impotent.

Because we no longer honor our elder women they are

often unable to find a new and vital identity. And we as a society flail about without their direction and wisdom. According to *The Ceremonial Circle:* "The result is that we are on the brink of extinction and find ourselves living in a morass of dysfunction."

In order to save ourselves we must recover the voice of the grandmother. We must understand that people will listen to elder women when we are ready to claim our wisdom and our right to speak it. We as women must reclaim the power and vitality of this stage of life and make our voices heard.

Crone circles are a way for women to honor the wisdom and strength that comes with aging. By sharing and grieving together, and by creating meaningful ceremonies of initiation, women can become more aware of the possibilities of this powerful transition, and more connected to the power and beauty of the wise woman or grandmother. By sharing their fears around growing old and being alone and unloved, women's fears can be transformed into power.

Creative Circles

*All sorrows can be borne if
you put them into a story and tell
a story about them.*

ISAK DINESEN

If you want to write the
truth, you must write about yourself.
I am the only truth I know.

JEAN RHYS

There are many forms of art or creative circles. Many are conducted as leaderless groups, obtaining their structure from books such as *The Artist's Way* by Julia Cameron. Others are led by art therapists but are conducted with circle principles.

Patricia Waters is a registered art therapist and registered expressive arts therapist who conducts creative circles and teaches private classes using the format of the circle. Here is what she has to share about creative circles:

My groups are focused on creative arts processes for healing and personal and spiritual growth. We always start in a circle, usually sitting in chairs, and until recently I had been putting a bowl of rocks with a candle in it in the center of the circle to invite Spirit to be with us. I left the candle lit for the length of the group. More recently I've been putting a circular tray of sand in the center on a small table. Each person lights a candle and places it in the tray to invite in the quality of spirit they wish to invoke.

We do a check-in where each woman talks about what is calling her attention, or sometimes we start with a check-in drawing and speak through the art. Then we continue doing art around either a theme I bring in or something that needs to be looked at in the person's life. When I bring in a theme, I always make it clear that people can follow it or not. I work in a person-centered way, i.e., trusting that the individual has her answers and emphasizing empathy, honesty and respect for the individual. I almost always work along with the others and share with them.

In working with and through art, participants not only learn how to express themselves creatively, they learn to come into relationship with their art in nonjudgmental, insightful ways. By going through the challenge of confronting their blocks to the creative process, they confront some of the same blocks they face in their daily life. Creative circles offer a safe venue to practice new ways of working through these blocks. In working in circle without interpretation or judgment, but with respectful listening, owning our own responses and using "I" statements, safety and trust are created. The work is transformational.

Participants are empowered through their work in circle and through the sharing with and support of the other circle members. And they bring this into their daily life. Community is built through this deep sharing. The woman who is not enlivened and empowered by this work is a rarity.

Dream Circles

Circles are an excellent format for processing dreams. Ellie Mercer and Meredith Jordan conduct dream circles based on Jeremy Taylor's model and his book *Where People Fly and Water Runs Uphill*. As Ellie shared with me, "Jeremy said that 'Dreams are the language of the divine' and I agree."

As their Web site states: "When we gather with others to explore the meaning of our dreams, we are giving and are offering insights that go unnoticed in solitary dream work. The creative ideas that emerge for others in the circle help us to move beyond our personal blind spots into greater appreciation of how dreams teach, guide and serve us."

The following are ideas for structuring your own dream circle:

1. Create a sacred space using incense, candles, music, etc. Invite people to come into the space quietly. Start with reading or music.
2. Do a brief check-in. This is the time for people to follow-up with feedback about dreams discussed in previous circles, etc.
3. Ask who has a pressing dream to talk about.
4. Ellie Mercer asks that each circle member preface her comments with "If it were my dream . . ."

Peacemaking Circles

Peacemaking Circles began in the United States as part of the criminal justice process known as restorative justice and through the work of Kay Pranis. Now they are being used in a variety of other settings. Peacemaking Circles may be used for decision making, problem solving, support, conflict resolution, sharing, mutual education and brainstorming. The following are examples of how Peacemaking Circles have been utilized in a variety of settings:

- *Child abuse and neglect cases* to develop a support system and a plan for the family
- *Staff renewal* to help refocus on underlying values, share challenges, support one another
- *Team building* in a unit or agency
- *Workplace conflict and discrimination complaints*
- *Neighborhood issues*
- *Ceremonies of closure at conferences*
- *School discipline procedures*
- *Workshops and trainings*
- *Healing for a group working together* and experiencing conflict
- *Resolution to a criminal incident* to promote healing for all parties and to determine sentence or obligations for offender

- *Community reintegration* of an individual after place-
  ment in a residential facility or prison.

According to Kay Pranis, Peacemaking Circles provide
a structure for bringing people together as equals to talk
about very difficult issues and painful experiences in an
atmosphere of respect and concern. The underlying
philosophy acknowledges that those who give help also
receive a benefit in the process. The collective wisdom
of the circle is understood to be drawn from the wisdom of everyone in the circle.

While Peacemaking Circles are most prominent in
Minnesota and Canada, the principles of negotiation,
mediation, consensus building and peacemaking that
shape the Peacemaking Circle process have been part of
dispute resolution processes in many communities for
centuries. The process as it has evolved today, most
recently within Yukon, Canada, draws heavily on the traditions of Canada's aboriginal communities. After being
used for several years in Yukon, Peacemaking Circles
began spreading across Canada. In 1996 the Mille Lacs
band of Chippewa Indians, the Mille Lacs County District
Court, the Minnesota Department of Corrections and
Midstate Probation initiated the first criminal justice
Peacemaking Circle in Minnesota. In rapid succession,
Peacemaking Circles were developed to meet local needs
in rural, suburban and inner-city communities.

Sacred Circles

Shamanic and Sacred Circles or Medicine Wheels

The soul should always stand ajar,
ready to welcome the ecstatic experience.

EMILY DICKINSON

Arising from altered states of
consciousness, from trances, from merging
with Spirits, and from a knowing unity of one's
kinship with all beings, shamans have always
provided visions and images that evoke the
remembering of our Wholeness.

CAROL PROUDFOOT-EDGAR

She say, My first step from the
old white man was trees. Then air. Then birds.
Then other people. But one day when I was
sitting quiet and feeling like a motherless child,
which I was, it came to me: that feeling of being
part of everything, not separate at all. I knew that if
I cut a tree, my arm would bleed. And I laughed

and I cried and I run all around the house.
I just know what it was. In fact, when
it happen, you can't miss it.

ALICE WALKER
THE COLOR PURPLE

Envision a circle. There is a blazing fire or a single candle burning. There is the smell of sage burning as an abalone shell is passed around the circle allowing each person to cleanse herself. The drums begin. The people respond with their bodies, their voices: singing, chanting or allowing strange indescribable sounds to emanate from their throats—voices of their spirit guides, their ancestors, their power animals. At first the drumming sounds are uneven, chaotic. But soon the drum sounds are rhythmical, as all melt into one synchronized beat. The sounds and the power that arise from within the circle unite the people in a common bond, relinking them with one another, with their ancestors who have also chanted, drummed and sang in circle, with the land that supports the people and the spirit that enters into them.

Those who walk a shamanic path worship in a sacred circle or what some indigenous people of this continent refer to as medicine wheels. Ritual is an important element of sacred circles since they touch us at deep subconscious levels, allowing us to fully experience the powers, forces and laws of nature. Once we achieve this connection with nature, the sacred circle helps us draw that powerful positive force into us in order to transform ourselves and our world for the good.

Those who walk a shamanic path also believe that when we connect and communicate with nature in a positive way, we have all life on our side—all the force and power of life is working for us. With this force available to us, we can easily raise and project powerful energy and manifest it in the world. The energy we raise helps transform us into complete and whole beings, and get in touch with the forces of nature and our own higher selves.

Many believe the sacred circle or medicine wheel is an entranceway to the spirit realm, to other dimensions and times—a sacred place "between the worlds" where power is raised for healing and transformation.

Many also believe that the current revival of the shamanic arts and the circle is a response to the deep longing within us all to return to a state of harmony with the Earth. Members of sacred circles and medicine wheels believe that healing comes when we become attuned to the primal energies of the Earth. Moreover, the time has come for each of us to call forth the shaman within, to break down the boundaries between us and to bring people together.

The shaman's function has traditionally been to serve the community by evoking sacred powers. Shamanic practice involves looking deeply into what is called tonal or worldly reality, no matter how disturbing. The shaman accesses information by traveling into nonordinary states of reality and returning with knowledge that will assist him or her in healing individuals in the tribe or the tribe itself.

Circles become entities which hold a shamanic force and take on a presence of their own. The value of learning how to circle in a ceremonial way, utilizing ancient shamanic tools—such as prayer, invoking, the talking stick and the drum—has the potency to bring people together so that the self is connected on a deeper level with the whole of humanity.

Interview with
Carol Proudfoot-Edgar

Carol Proudfoot-Edgar offers retreats that focus primarily on shamanism within community. She is also a faculty member for the Foundation for Shamanic Studies for which she teaches advanced courses in Southern California. She is a founding member of the nonprofit organization, Tending Sacred Circles whose purpose is to support and link shamanic circles globally.

Beverly: What is the significance of the circle for you, both personally and in your work?

Carol: The symbol of the circle represents both metaphor and the reality of the laws of nature. Our human task is to live according to the larger pattern in which we unfold, evolve and contribute to the future health of this earth home.

Somewhere in our evolution as humans we lost our way, became disconnected from ourselves and the larger pattern of the universe. Every culture has its own myth as to how we became lost, and many ancient cultures—whose mythologies and ceremonies are still known to us—offer guidance as to how we can return home to our true relationship to ourselves and to the whole.

Finding our way home is the essence of my work in circling. By returning to our essential selves within the whole, we rediscover our own selves as holy. Knowing our holiness, we know the holiness, the sacred nature of all that is. This knowing inspires us to find ways of manifesting, through our actions, our sacred relationship with all beings. Such manifestations ensure the prospering both of those now living and future generations.

If you look at many ancient symbols of the circle, the circle is usually not completely closed: Sometimes there is an actual spiral shape or sometimes the ends of the circle curve in and out, not quite connected. I think this has to do with the spiritual or shamanic understanding that the circle as a form and as reality is part of this larger pattern.

For me, circles are forms within the great spiral of becoming. Circles are spirals forming, never ending or beginning, simply returning; and in certain places or seasons, forming one round shape like a hogan, a kiva, mountain, cave, creature. When we come together in circle, we give shape to the essential nature of ourselves as women and women in community. I think one comes home when one has the opportunity to grow and learn within a circle.

When I lead circles now, I always leave one space, one chair, empty to indicate the circle is part of the infinite spiral. The empty chair is there for the Spirit, ancestor, descendant or some other being of this greater spiral, an invitation to come and be with us, to remind us that our circle is part of this greater spiral and other circles.

When we hold hands as we include this empty space in our circles, we touch ourselves as one with all beings. In touching and knowing ourselves as one, a deep healing occurs. Healing is remembering and remembering we are one.

So when I teach I always try to symbolize this aspect of circle in order for us to know on some deep physical and soul level that we are being held. We are participating in a way of being together that is consonant with the very essence of all life, of infinity.

The empty space also signifies that we have resources available to us—spiritually and among the other beings of the world—who can assist us in learning how to return home and become home to ourselves. We are pilgrims walking together as we answer the call to be ourselves and manifest our gifts, our knowings, our uniqueness as women.

Finally, I draw upon the richness of circles from the world surrounding us: winds circling the globe, nesting, caving, birthing, living, dying, rebirthing, seasonal patterns, the daily cycles of light and dark, circling sun, circling moon, Earth herself turning. Every analogy from nature teaches us how to become more our circular selves. The variety offered is an incredible feast for the imagination, the heart and the soul—both for the individual and the group as an entity.

Beverly: Could you describe the special energy a circle creates?

Carol: Once we have the experience of listening, speaking, movement and roundness together, a profound power begins to build in a circle. This power can be further experienced by holding hands after activities that build or amplify one's personal spiritual power. For example, after a period of drumming, chanting or dancing together, when you hold hands there is a current that can be felt passing around the circle. This current is as keenly felt as if you had turned on the light in a darkened room.

The power of circle creates a vessel, a huge container within which we can call and attend to what I call spirit beings, winds and other inexplicable but felt entities who join the circle, often working with various individuals upon behalf of healing some other person, creature or the land. This powerful vessel is also experienced as the nature of the circle itself. A circle thus empowered provides a place of safety, love and strength so that each person is able to do the work they are called to do in the midst of supporting witnesses.

I often think a major benefit of the power of the circle is being seen by others without judgment—simply seen. My experience is that our need to be seen is as great as our need to be truly heard. When individuals join to create circle, the major part of the early work is the development of just this kind of power.

Beverly: What role does ritual play in your circles?

Carol: Throughout our time together, in every circle, I use ceremony and ritual. Those two words may be interchangeable for most people, but some hear the word "ritual" and connect it with a fixed and unchanging way of doing a sacred activity. Some people also have a negative response to the word ritual. The word "ceremony" seems to elicit less negative associations and so I prefer to use the word ceremony.

For me, ceremonies are those activities which bring the experience of the eternal into the temporal now. Since we are both of time and eternity, I consider ceremony essential in all my work and in my personal life.

The structure of my workshops is actually created around ceremonial activities from our opening ceremony to our closing ceremony. For example, each day we greet the rising sun, welcome the dark as the sun sets and do some activity associated with the moon's specific phase at the time.

Each session begins with drumming, singing, chanting and calling the spirits to work with us. Other ceremonial activities evolve from the themes upon which we are focused.

From my experience, for ceremony to be sacred and authentic

it needs to arise and be shaped around the events in a circle's life . . . whether that be the needs of some particular individual or the circle as a collective.

I find it difficult to put "ceremony" into a fixed definition of some activity because I think the whole object of our work is to learn how to live ceremonially, and then have particular ceremonies that mark special understandings or special occasions. In that respect, I think of myself as a "ceremonialist." Given that description, I would then say that we also do certain rituals in which we are indeed following an agreed upon way of honoring or blessing some primary event, initiation or understanding of how there are these eternal rhythms in our lives of passage, special holy days, special seasonal shifts.

Beverly: What do you see as the role of the shaman?

Carol: The primary calling of the shaman is to work with spirits in bringing equilibrium to one's people, other inhabitants and Earth herself. Embedded within this calling is the understanding that the "woundings" of the shaman need healing. This is why the shaman or anyone walking this path is referred to as "the wounded healer." These wounds are often a personal manifestation of a collective problem. By being healed, the shaman is thus able to partner with spirits in tending other people or other beings.

Beverly: How do you feel your work benefits those who participate?

Carol: I think the type of work I do benefits individuals in many ways. Some of these benefits are experienced during our time together, some in changes that occur much later as a result of integrating experiences in the workshop.

Often people initially discover how thirsty they are, how large a hunger they have developed, or how estranged they feel from knowing this planet as home. They discover their outer lives may seem meaningful but they themselves feel a loss of spirit, an emptiness of heart.

They are often surprised by how much they have yearned for a sense of authentic, uncensored relationship with other people. Then comes the deeper recognition of the hunger for community. Many people return to my retreats as they seek to further find themselves and learn how to be in community. Eventually they can then begin the process of creating community where they live.

Thus, from these workshops have emerged shamanic circles all around this country and abroad. I keep myself available to consult with these circles as they form. We have lived fragmented from each other so long that I think those of us teaching in this area need to assist others as they begin forming their own circles. It is not easy to form a shamanic, nonhierarchical, ever-renewing circle in a world where competition, hierarchy and linear thinking predominate. If I can have some small influence on the lives of others, it is my hope that this would be in assisting others in knowing how to create such circles, to become such circles—people joining together to tend the sacred circle fires of their peoples and homelands wherever they live.

Beverly: What changes have you seen in participants and how have these changes affected the community?

Carol: I have been delighted to see that as individuals come home to themselves, as they gather and practice shamanism, their lives have become increasingly more meaningful and creative. I think that shamanic circles tap into this rich creative potential and then there is an outpouring of art, music, dance, theater, story. We move from the focus of "impressing" others to "expressing" our deepest selves. I have seen this result in changes that may be difficult, such as leaving jobs, facing marital dissatisfaction, recognizing one's deep woundedness. Yet I see changes primarily in experiencing one's creative powers and the development of compassion for others. I also frequently receive feedback that people are delighted to discover they are living more attentively and respectfully within the natural world.

Beverly: Who benefits the most from your work?

Carol: The individuals who seem to benefit the most from my retreats are those who know they are hungering for "something more" than psychological, political or material benefits. Perhaps they have already been in years of therapy and are looking now for that "something more." Perhaps they have been quite successful in their work but no longer wish for their occupation to be their preoccupation. Generally, they know there is some wider window in their soul that needs opening. The fact that most of my retreats are in semiwilderness or nonurban environments is the first clue for many that they are starved for being in more than just human company. They want to be with others in wilderness sanctuary because they know they've lost touch with nature both within and without. Some ancient memory is calling them to return to touching Mother Earth and taking delight in all creation.

I think eventually each individual who participates in my circle gatherings comes to realize that the natural world offers us something that is not in our human capacity alone to give each other. Simultaneously we begin to discover what we in our humanness have to offer each other. And each person leaves with some knowledge of the need to attend to what I call our "spiritually embodied selves."

Goddess-Centered Spirituality and Wiccan Circles

Mother Goddess is rewakening, and we can begin to recover our primal birthright, the sheer, intoxicating joy of being alive.

Starhawk
The Spiral Dance

In 1985, writer Barbara Walker wrote about a new phenomenon taking shape:

> *Women, the traditional pillars of Judeo-Christian religion, are turning against this faith. Many women prefer to gather in small grassroots groups in each other's homes, where they discuss recent studies of prepatriarchal Goddess worship and engage in rituals aimed at recreating some feeling for those ancient faiths. Because of its private nature, the phenomenon is almost invisible to the public eye.*

The phenomenon she was referring to was the blossoming women's spirituality movement or goddess-centered spirituality movement. One cannot but recognize the similarities between this movement and the women's circle movement in the passage below:

> *The women's spirituality movement has given many women better feelings about themselves, in consequence of joining together with other women in groups, gatherings, circles, covens or conferences. Women touch, embrace, communicate. They share food, feelings, thoughts and ideas. They praise each other's accomplishments. They support each other in trouble. They provide sympathy for hurts, advice for problems, many kinds of mutual education. They laugh or cry together, love or quarrel, lend things, give gifts, do favors. Some find in women's groups the closest relationships of*

their lives, closer than their bonds with husbands, children or parents. Others drop out after a time, but with changed attitudes.

According to Robin Deen Carnes and Sally Craig in their book *Sacred Circles: A Guide to Creating Your Own Women's Spirituality Group*, the women's spirituality movement is one of celebration, not recovery. They are engaged in reclaiming and celebrating female energy. In addition, most goddess-centered circles don't dwell on personalities but instead explore the archetypal, heroic patterns and journeys of people's lives. They explore each woman's connection to the divine, and draw strength and power from female ancestors, from the goddesses, from the archetypal feminine and from honoring their own sacred path in this lifetime.

The goddess is a symbol of the archetypal divine feminine and as such most women involved in the women's spirituality movement find meaning in the goddess, whether they actually worship the goddesses or not.

As Starhawk stated in *The Spiral Dance*, "the image of the goddess inspires women to see themselves as divine, their bodies as sacred, the changing phases of their lives as holy. . . ."

Others find inspiration and comfort in female figures such as Mary, the mother of Jesus, women saints or other women found in religious writings.

Many goddess-centered and wiccan spirituality circles share an interest in the cycles of the moon and the moon's effect on women's lives.

Drumming Circles

In many circles we will sit
drumming around our council fires, and
as we greet the day with strongheart songs, we
will become one body . . . one heart beating . . .
each a little river coming together to make a great
stream. And perhaps from some high place we
will see that all our rivers run to the one great
body of water that embraces our homeland.
Around our fires and in our teaching lodges
we will set upon a journey to find
our old planet again. . . .

SCOUT CLOUD LEE
THE CIRCLE IS SACRED

Drumming is tribal music, and the fact that drumming has become so popular, in and out of circles, is a testament to our need to reclaim our original tribal essence. The growing drumming movement suggests that people are beginning to reclaim their rituals and to reconnect with themselves as they drum. In fact, some would say that the drum is emerging as the transformational tool of our time.

The purpose of the drum in circles is to find the common tone among the group. Because the drumbeat is a universal, vibrational language which communes with the Earth and all her creatures, the drum has come to symbolize our unity as Earth-family citizens. In addition, the drum has the potential to resonate the body into a state of deep feeling and to heal the wounds of the psyche.

Drumming is a spirit-opening act, helping us to be receptive to spirit, to healing and to important insight.

In an article in *Awareness* magazine, Feeny Lipscomb, a drummer and founder of All One Tribe Foundation, wrote of how the most accessible tool for reconnecting with our deeper selves may be the drum. She states that recent research in biofeedback indicates that drumming along with our own heartbeats can alter brain-wave patterns and "meditate" us, dramatically reducing stress. We now know that stress either causes or exacerbates most diseases, and so drumming also helps prevent and treat illness.

Sedonia Cahill includes hand drums in all her circles. As she shared with me:

When we get the same beat it unites us. We relax—I'm sure we all end up in a light trance—and we put down whatever we might be carrying. Drumming makes it easy to be there fully and deeply.

We had a lot of drumming circles several years ago here in Sonoma County. The purpose was to encourage women to start circles. Our drumming circles got very big. When the United States invaded Iraq we held a circle called "Women Drumming and Scheming for Peace," and over three hundred people came. We drummed for a while and then broke up into smaller circles where people could voice their feelings and ideas for peace. We made a sacred container where people could express all their anger and fear.

We also had a large drum circle every solstice. Large circles like that can be exciting.

Dance Circles

. . . Pageants of mystery, enraptured we unfold
Dancers spin in ecstasy while new stories are told
Bodies dissolve, and return as webs of light
Radiant by day and luminous by night.

JOSIE RAVENWING
TRAIL OF POWER AUDIOTAPE

Ancient ceremonial dances had their genesis in birthing and planting, and observing the cyclic flow of the seasons. Dancing is an expression of prayer, gratitude and ecstasy, and is a way of singing to the earth. Just as the Earth sends its healing resonance up through our feet, dancing allows our energy to resonate through our body down into the Earth. It helps keep the Earth in alignment.

In circle dancing the purpose is to get into communion with one another and Mother Earth. The dance can go on for hours or days, depending on the needs and intentions of the group.

Unlike most other kinds of circles, dance circles often require a leader, at least in terms of leading the dance steps. In Mary Elizabeth Thunder's circles, the women make all the decisions, choose the dates, organize everything and then bring it all to her for a final okay.

Interview with Mary Elizabeth Thunder

Mary Elizabeth is a well-known speaker, human rights advocate, sun dancer and peace elder. She is also the author of *Thunder's Grace: Walking the Road of Visions with My Lakota Grandmother*. She travels globally to share the message about the peace and healing of the Earth Mother by healing oneself. She and her husband, Jeffrey "Horse" Hubbell, maintain a ranch which is a spiritual university in West Point, Texas. Here she shares her experiences with sun dancing:

> *My husband, sons and I are traditional sun dancers. This year I have completed my twenty-fifth Sun Dance. Our family's commitment was to and at Crow Dog's Paradise. I*

will also complete a commitment that I have served for the Chipps family in Wamblee, South Dakota, as a female sun dance helper. Eight years ago Charles Chipps asked me to help him as Mother of their sun dance.

Sun dancers dance for four days in the sun, making prayers for the people, so that the people might live. They dance to renew the Earth Mother. When I first saw the sun dance it was still illegal. Native Americans were not given back their rights to religious freedom until 1978.

I am a woman who danced under the sun to thank the Creator and Mother Earth for giving me back my life after my near-death experience on an operating table. My uncle, Leonard Crow Dog, had foretold of this death experience one week to the day before it happened. There were not a lot of women dancing in the early years, but I see many women dance now. Most of the dances I have been to are traditional and have been closed to noncultural society—dances where many old grandmothers and grandfathers dance and pray for their people, families and our Earth. Now, I have lived to see dances like the Ellis Chipps Memorial Sun Dance happen, where people of the four colors dance to the sun together. It is an honor to dance.

Four years ago, over sixty women came together to dance and see and heal and be and enjoy. Dancing in that circle of life, we learned much about ourselves, our own souls and about others. As the leader of the White Buffalo Calf Woman's Dance in the spring, I feel overwhelming pride, connection and friendship with women as I have never felt before. It has taken me out of separation into the wholeness of being female. I am a sun dancer—a more masculine form of a traditional initiationary dance—and I found I could be with men easier than I could women. I put off and put off starting a gathering for women because I believed that women don't get along with each other and I would have nothing but heartache. Wow, was I wrong! It has been nothing but gentle, flowing and nurturing—good food, surroundings, friendship. I now see that I was holding back, yet one more time, to being fully into my feminine.

Women are often in a shell when they first come into our dance circle, but then they begin to open up like a lotus and begin to interact with the other women. People dancing together in a circle can always see each other fully and that's the magic of the circle. I also believe that our woman's dance creates nurturing and healing towards our Mother Earth.

In this chapter I have presented a broad overview of the major types of circles. Although there are undoubtedly some forms of circle I have left out, this will serve to give you a general idea of the intent of each circle and will help you decide which type of circle best suits your needs.

In the following chapter I explain in detail the basic elements that are required for a circle to reach its full potential, no matter what type of circle it is.

Chapters 10 and 11 provide more specific information about how some types of circles are structured, and how you can initiate and conduct your first circle.

NINE

The Structure
of Circle, the Circle
as Structure

Making sacred space is an
intricate process which requires that each
participant get clear about their motivations.
That a space is made sacred does not mean that
the human struggle involved in having an ego
will disappear, merely that it is a safe space
in which to work on one's self.

SEDONIA CAHILL AND JOSHUA HALPERN
THE CEREMONIAL CIRCLE

In the previous chapter I provided an overview of the most common types of circles. Most of you will probably choose to create a circle based on one of these models. Some may choose to create a circle that is a mixture of one or more of the circle forms I've outlined. While you should feel free to pick and choose which aspects you will include in your circle, certain basic elements need to be part of *every* circle in order for it to achieve its full potential. And while circles may take many forms, most people will naturally include these same basic elements when structuring their circles. This is particularly amazing when you realize that there is no central organizing body prescribing the structure of circle, and many circles function autonomously, with no contact with any other circle.

This can be explained to some extent by the universal influence of the traditions of indigenous peoples, such as the American Indian, aboriginal Canadian and New Zealand Maori, combined with the rules and agreements normally set for women's consciousness-raising groups, and therapy and support groups. But I also believe we must be open to the possibility of synchronicity— meaningful coincidence.

The Elements of Circle

The elements of circle listed below are a synthesis of all the information I have gleaned from my research on circling, as well as from my personal experience with circles. You will find that each type of circle tends to advocate their own version of this general list:

- Intention
- Sacredness

- Commitment
- Equality
- Heart Consciousness
- Gratitude

Intention

A circle is held together by clear and strong intentions on the part of all its participants. Therefore, it is best when the intentions of a group have been spelled out and agreed upon by all members. If you have a specific intention in mind, it is up to you to communicate your intention and inquire whether other circle members agree with your vision. This can be done prior to calling the circle and can therefore become a way of screening which women you will actually ask to join your circle. Or you may wish to state your reason for wanting to create a circle at the beginning of the first meeting and then ask each person present their reasons for wanting to create a circle. From this you can arrive at a consensus of what the purpose of the circle will be.

There are also times when the convener of a circle calls a circle and allows a spontaneous and improvised happening to occur. This works particularly well when you don't have a preconceived idea as to what type of circle you want, when you don't have a specific issue to discuss and when the purpose of the circle is purely celebratory.

Whatever your reason for calling a circle, make certain that your intentions are positive ones. Because the circle is so powerful, whatever you do within it will ultimately come back to you, magnified many times. It is important, then, that all you wish and pray for within the circle be both positive and life-affirming.

Sacredness

As mentioned earlier, sitting in circle and deeply connecting with others in the circle can bring us back to an awareness of the sacred. This is achieved primarily by creating sacred time and space. As Sedonia Cahill and Joshua Halpern state in *The Ceremonial Circle:*

> *The internal experience of being in sacred time and space is a feeling of timelessness, in which only the here and now exists, a focus on what is happening both inside and outside of yourself. It also involves an absolute knowing that you are related to all living creatures, a feeling of awe for the beauty of life.*

Creating sacred time and space includes the act of *mindfulness.* When we are mindful we are keenly aware and acutely conscious of what we are doing. We are intently focused on the task at hand, whether it is lighting a candle, praying or listening to another circle member. In turn, mindfulness can be closely attuned to *reverence,* which is the act of honoring or worshipping. When we practice mindfulness we are in a sacred state of mind; we are reverent.

Ceremony and ritual help create sacred space. They help participants let go of their expectations that the circle is just another support group, committee meeting or task force. An opening ritual helps you step out of "ordinary time" into sacred time, opening a door to a sense of deep communion with self and others. An opening ritual helps you focus on the present and let go of everyday concerns and distractions.

When we open and close a circle with a ritual, we are reminded to be mindful as we establish a sense of reverence and awe. Smudging (burning aromatic grasses or wood to create a "protective" smoke) at the beginning of a circle is one way to create sacred space. When the sweet smoke of cedar, sage, sweetgrass or piñon drifts into the ceremonial space it calls for sacred attention. The person or object that is smudged is called to service. The broadcasting (scattering) of cornmeal or tobacco is a way to create a specific boundary for ceremony.

Ceremony and ritual remind us that we are not alone in our struggles and triumphs. They help us regain our sense of connectedness to something larger than ourselves. They remind us that we are a part of a vast circle in which all expressions of life are our sisters and brothers.

Commitment

In order for a circle to successfully come together and remain ongoing there must be a strong commitment on the part of all members. The authors of *The Ceremonial Circle* recommend that your overall commitment be to create a community with a shared intention, a community in which every member has a profound relationship with one another and every member is encouraged to grow.

The act of commitment in itself can produce growth, especially for those who have had difficulty making commitments in the past. Some circles design a commitment ceremony in which each person declares her commitment to the circle and circle members, and makes a ritual gesture of that commitment. The same holds true when individual members decide that it is time to end their circle commitment.

Commitment creates a bond among participants and instills trust. In order to be willing to share the most vulnerable parts of oneself with the group you must have a sense of cohesiveness, stability and continuity. When each member of a circle has expressed and shown her commitment to the circle, to the process and to one another, the entire circle becomes stronger, safer and more powerful.

This commitment also includes having a strong intention to attend each and every circle gathering, and to make the circle a priority on the times when it meets. The only way for you to be really known by other members is for you to be present each time the circle meets. By the same token, other members need your presence each time they reveal something important about themselves.

When members become lax in their commitment and allow excuses to keep them away it causes a rupture in the circle which affects everyone. Some circles require their members to call a designated person if they must miss a circle meeting. Other circles also ask the person who is going to miss a meeting to send energy to the circle during the meeting time. It is believed that this will help the circle remain strong and whole.

Each potential member of a circle needs to determine her level of personal commitment by asking herself certain questions, including:

- Am I willing to attend every meeting unless something unavoidable occurs?
- Will I be on time for every meeting and stay for the full time?
- Am I willing to bring my entire being—my mind, heart and soul to the circle?
- Am I willing to stay alert and present during the circle?
- Will I honor the guidelines of the circle?
- Am I committed enough to self-exploration that I am willing to endure some discomfort or even pain to achieve it?

- Am I willing to be completely present when others speak?
- Am I willing to speak the truth in the circle, even when it is difficult or painful?

In addition to a commitment to attend each circle meeting, each participant needs to make a commitment to each person in the circle and to the group as a whole. This involves being willing to commit to being present to one another emotionally as well as physically—being willing to put aside one's own problems and issues while the other person is speaking and commit to being in a state of total receptivity.

Equality

One of the reasons most circles are so powerful is that the structure itself dictates a lack of hierarchy. By sitting in a circle we are reminded that we are all human beings and we are all equal; no one is "above" the others, no one is "better than" the others.

While the circle structure itself reminds us of this, it does not guarantee it. One of the ways to guarantee a sense of equality is to make sure that each and every person in the circle gets a chance to speak her mind. This is best done with the use of a "talking stick" or "talking bowl."

The talking stick has been a way of life among indigenous

groups since people first sat in circle. They would first pass the pipe and smoke in silence until their hearts beat as one. Then they would pass the talking stick.

There existed a time when each person's word was respected, when people would listen to one another openly and carefully. But today we are raised with the feeling that we are never really heard. Often as children our words were experienced as a nuisance to adults, meaningless prattle. Today we are all so hungry to be heard that we cut one another off in an attempt to get our words out. Instead of listening carefully to what another person has to say we are busy thinking of what we are going to say next. Instead of listening openly without judgment, we are quick to question and contradict. Instead of recognizing that the people speaking need to be heard above all else, we don't take in what they say but instead offer advice.

When you use the talking stick and proceed around the circle, allowing each person to have a chance to share her feelings, her opinions or her stories, there is no competition for air time. Everyone can relax because they know they will have a chance to speak.

By inviting people to share their ideas and by listening to their ideas without judgment, we begin to let go of hierarchical structure. By letting go of our preconceived ideas of what is the right or wrong way to do something we open ourselves up for equality.

Another way to guarantee equality is to make certain that no one "takes over" the circle or "overpowers" the circle. This generally is done by rotating leadership, which allows everyone in the group to take the circle in her own direction when her turn comes. This may include having different women host the circle each time it meets.

If the same people are always out front, if the same people do all the work most of the time, it is natural that they will feel more ownership of the circle and believe they should have more to say about how it runs. Therefore, sharing leadership also means sharing the investment in and ownership of the group.

Heart Consciousness

We all want to be heard. We all want to be accepted. And ultimately, we all want to be loved. Remembering this helps us to become more open-hearted. This space of open-heartedness or heart consciousness is an essential element for circling.

Heart consciousness includes listening from the heart, speaking from the heart and discovering the innate wisdom we hold within our own hearts.

Listening from the Heart

When we listen from the heart, we listen openly and without judgment to what others in the circle are saying. We recognize that each person has a right to his or her own truth, opinions or beliefs, and we do not try to impose our truths, opinions or beliefs onto anyone. Listening from the heart asks us to find what the authors of *Wisdom Circles* call, "that centerpoint of pure receiving," where we relax our assumptions and opinions to make room for new ideas, and where we can "show a greater degree of lovingkindness."

The phrase "listening from the heart" also refers to the fact that members of a circle are encouraged to listen with empathy and compassion. This means that we experience as much as we can of the emotional life of the person speaking. Through our body posture, direct eye contact, attentiveness and respectful silence we convey to the speaker that we are listening empathetically—seeing life through her eyes. We share in her hopes and joy, we feel her fears and sorrow.

As we grow in our capacity to listen and empathize, we find we are able to hear the deeper meanings of what is being said. We are able to understand the more subtle levels of communication that we may have previously missed and are better at discerning nuggets of wisdom normally hidden in everyday speech.

Most importantly, we learn to appreciate the commonalities between ourselves and all people, and in turn feel less separate and more at one with all humanity. By listening from our heart we expand our capacity for unconditional love. Empathetic, compassionate listening helps rid us of stereotypes, long-held prejudices and biases. We are able to look past those obstacles that have kept us from accepting someone in the past. We can listen past those assumptions and expectations that prevented us from truly understanding someone. As we see through the eyes of another our awareness expands tremendously and we become far more than we once were.

Speaking from the Heart

When we speak from the heart, we say what is most true for us without censoring ourself or trying to impress others. Speaking from the heart means that we don't rehearse what we are going to say before saying it, but instead allow what is in our hearts and souls to come forth.

The circle is a place to improve our ability to give voice to our truths and find a way to communicate them in a way that can be truly heard by others. The act of telling our stories and our truths works deeply within us. As we increase our capacity to speak from the heart we will become more and more aware of unconscious aspects of ourselves and begin to hear an even deeper, more meaningful story that we are attempting to tell.

Discovering Your Innate Wisdom

In order to access what is in our heart, to discover our deepest, truest feelings, we must be willing to experience silence. While uncomfortable at first, sitting in silence prior to speaking will allow us to connect with our inner wisdom and our intuitive voice, thus allowing more intuitive responses to surface. Sitting in silence after we have spoken but before passing the talking stick will allow us to discover an even deeper message from the experience we have shared, to make important connections and to know whether we have finished speaking.

Gratitude

The ability to feel and express gratitude is an important aspect of every circle. Gratitude evokes a sense of reverence. It humbles us and connects us to all of life. It is an honoring of all life and of the multitude of gifts we are endowed with every day.

Gratitude can be expressed in many ways. Some offer prayers at the beginning and end of each circle. Prayers can be whispered, spoken, chanted or sung. They can be accompanied by rituals, done in special places with altars or spoken alone in the woods without anything but a momentary silence. It is the force of the individual's will and words that make a prayer powerful.

For example, shamans from every continent believe that they must begin each ceremony with prayers of gratitude in order to connect with the great spirits and call upon their powers for healing. They would no more begin a ceremony without prayers of gratitude than they would consider starting on a long journey without food and water.

Gratitude within the circle can be expressed in a round, with each member of the circle offering gratitude to anyone or anything she chooses. The caller of the circle may suggest the group offer gratitude toward a specific spirit helper or offer a more general prayer such as being in the company of kindred spirits. This can be done by one person speaking for the entire circle, by each person taking turns speaking out loud or in silence.

Each person in a circle may have a different way of identifying her creator or the source of life. Therefore, some circles use general terms such as "Creator," "Higher Power" or "Great Mystery." Circles based on Native American wisdom usually use the term "Great Spirit," and circles based on goddess spirituality use the term "Great Goddesses."

The word "prayer" may have negative associations for some people for whom prayer means asking God publicly or privately for some favor or intervention in the course of events, or thanking God for favors granted. But gratitude is more than prayer. It is an attitude. This attitude of gratitude needs to be in the hearts of each member during the entire circle process.

Having an attitude of gratitude is more akin to contemplative prayer, which in turn resembles the approach of Eastern meditation, in which the meditator does not consider the immediate rewards of prayer. Spoken prayers have their place in circle ritual and in private devotions, but contemplative prayer is essentially a "prayer of the heart."

In addition to expressing gratitude to our creator, we also need to practice gratitude with one another in circle. Acknowledging to others how their words have inspired us, how we have learned from their example, or how much their caring has healed us, is not only a wonderful gift but a way of deepening our connection with one another.

One of the many benefits of expressing gratitude toward one another in a circle is that it engenders a sense of belonging. In their beautiful book *Earth Prayers*, Elizabeth Roberts and Elias Amidon state that, "at the heart of gratefulness, we also find an expression of belonging. When we say 'Thank you' we're really saying 'We belong together.'"

When we show gratitude toward someone or something we are acknowledging our interdependence. Saying "thank you" to someone is, in effect, saying, "I am part of you and you are part of me."

Before closing a circle it is important to express our gratitude for all that was expressed and all that was learned. Those involved in sacred circles always thank their creator, spirit guides or helpers.

Circling increases our awareness, which in turn increases our gratitude. The more we express our gratitude the more we become deeply aware of it. This can be likened to a spiraling ascent, a process of growth in ever-expanding circles around a steady center, a movement leading ever more deeply into gratefulness.

The Question of Leadership

The issue of leadership is an important factor in deciding which type of circle to create. Circles that tend to need a leader include those based on a new or complicated model of circling and those that require an "overseer," "guide" or "guardian" in order to maintain the structure and safety of the circle. Christina Baldwin's PeerSpirit Circles are a good example of circles that require a "leader."

PeerSpirit Circles have what is called the "Guardian of the Circle," a person who volunteers to watch and safeguard group energy. The person serving as guardian does her best to be what Christina calls "extraordinarily aware" of how the group process is functioning. Using a small bell, chime or rattle, the guardian has the group's permission to interrupt and intercede in the group process for the purpose of either "calling the circle back to center," to task, to respectful practice or to suggest a moment of silence or a needed break. She also keeps track of time and of the need for breaks.

Even though there is a guardian in PeerSpirit Circles, everyone shares responsibility for initiating a call for recentering and for helping the guardian fulfill her functions. For example, if discussion has become too heated and no one is listening to each other, if someone has been rambling on and lost the attention of the group, or if someone has shared something that the group needs to sit with for a few minutes, someone may say, "Where is our guardian?" or "Ring the bell."

If silence is needed the guardian holds the silence for anywhere from fifteen seconds to several minutes and then releases the silence by once again resignaling. She then makes a statement as to the intent of the pause: "I called the silence to remind us to listen openly, without judgment." It is customary that the role of guardian rotates session by session so leadership is shared.

Peacemaking Circles are another type of circle that require what Kay Pranis calls a "keeper." According to Kay, the role of the keeper is as follows:

- To create an atmosphere of respect and safety for all
- To create a tone of hope and optimism for constructive solutions
- To guide the process in order to remain true to underlying values
- To articulate the progress and accomplishments of the circle as it proceeds

- To clarify unresolved issues to focus the circle's energy
- To participate as a community member

The Option of Having an Overseer

While many circles advocate shared or rotating leadership in the interest of equality, there are also many circles, such as shamanic circles, that have more permanent leaders. Many women strongly object to the concept of a circle needing a permanent leader. If this is your belief, then by all means honor that. On the other hand, you may also want to make an attempt to break away from rigid beliefs and "open up" so to speak, as the circle encourages us to do.

Consider, for example, the concept of "overseer" or "guide." These words feel best to me when describing those situations when women can gain a great deal from having a person who is a little more objective, and whose primary investment and focus remains on the structure of the circle itself, as opposed to meeting her own needs.

Just because a circle has a leader does not necessarily mean you have to sacrifice the element of equality. A spiritually and emotionally evolved "overseer" or "guide" has worked enough on her issues with ego and power to lead with honor, compassion and equality. Her intention is to encourage each and every woman in the circle to become empowered. She views her role of leadership as the responsibility and honor that it is, as a privilege instead of a right, and she does not abuse this privilege. She knows she acts as a role model for the other women in her circle and she conducts her life accordingly, eliciting respect and love from the other women. Instead of engendering envy she projects these messages: "I represent an achievable goal to which you can aspire. I am just like you. I have the same feelings. I've dealt with and continue to deal with the same issues."

An honorable overseer or guide understands that while she may know more about a particular subject or area of knowledge than some of her peers, this does not mean that she is "better than" anyone. And while she may have reached a place in life where she experiences more balance and harmony than some of her peers, she remembers vividly from where she came. She never gets so far away from her pain or struggles that she forgets what it was like to grapple with them; or becomes impatient with those who are still struggling; or feels superior to those who seem to have a more difficult time with an issue than she may have had.

An honorable overseer or guide never gets to a place where she feels she has resolved all her issues or has become "evolved" and can now rest on her laurels. She is continuously working to become a more compassionate, nonjudgmental, forgiving, nondefensive, objective, caring human being. The more she learns the more she realizes how much she has left to learn and she experiences over-whelming compassion and empathy for both those who struggle and those who triumph.

Neither does an honorable overseer or guide abuse her power. She realizes her position of leadership is a great honor but also a great responsibility, and she takes this responsibility very seriously. She understands she is a role model and because of this, she has a great deal of influence on others even as she consciously works on remaining humble. Certainly she does not take advantage of this position of power by manipulating, coercing or gaining favors from those who hold her in esteem.

Nor does she abuse her power by playing favorites. She continually reminds herself that just as we are all the same, we are also all different, and that differentness does not mean "less than." She knows she can learn as much or more from those she does not gravitate toward, those she dislikes or those who repulse her.

An honorable overseer or guide does not get into power struggles with other circle members. She realizes she can learn a great deal from those who challenge or disagree with her. She doesn't take it personally when others strive to overpower her but recognizes the reasons for their attempts. She does not zealously hold onto her position because she knows it is one that has been given as a gift and can be taken away just as quickly and easily if it is coveted or misused.

If you are interested in joining a circle that has a

permanent leader, and you have some trepidation about doing so, check with the leader and/or past and present members of her circles as to the type of leader she is.

The Circle as Structure

In order to create a safe and supportive environment you must create a circle with a well-defined and purposeful structure. This structure, instead of feeling limiting, will actually put people at ease. We are all afraid of the unknown, and your circle structure forms the foundation from which participants can enter the unknown with some degree of comfort.

In circles with little or no structure the energy tends to dissipate or become too chaotic. While room must be left for the unknown to enter, well-structured circles have tools to bring the energy back into focus. The balance between structure and nonstructure can be very delicate. Too much direction can stifle and inhibit the flow of energy, while too little can scatter it.

In addition, a good circle should have space for all members to create the conditions they need in order to achieve a feeling of safety. For example, an agreement needs to be made among members that everything that is shared in the circle will be held sacred and not revealed to anyone outside the circle. As stated in *The Ceremonial Circle:* "When a circle becomes a well-woven basket, with no place for energy to leak, it becomes a truly safe container where each member can do unsafe things; that is, go through deep revealing and transformation, with the circle as witness."

In my interview with Sandra Ingerman she talked extensively about the importance of establishing safety in a circle:

I spend a lot of time in the beginning of every workshop creating the circle. People come from all over and most aren't comfortable working in group experiences. We all come cold into a circle. We all have our issues and all kinds of judgments come up. So I like to acknowledge these issues in the group. I find that sometimes giving voice to what might be coming up for people allows them to settle into the circle easier.

The first thing I do is welcome people and ask that we hold hands. I ask everyone to try to open up their hearts as much as they can at the present time to let each person in the circle know that they are welcome. I don't ask that people be in a false space of unconditional love or in an artificial space. I just ask that people try to open up their hearts as much as they can at this point in time to silently welcome each person in the room. Basically we all come into the circle for the same reason. We all want to heal, we want to grow. We all come because we need help in our own evolution. And we all come to learn how to heal other people in our communities and in our lives. But it's easy to forget this.

We look around the room and see a lot of strangers. Some people connect right away because they're desperate for that relationship. Some become frightened by the numbers in the groups and tend to isolate themselves a bit. So it's important to make them feel comfortable by saying, "Hey, we're all on this planet and we all want love and we're all here for the same reason. Can we just simply acknowledge and welcome each person in the group?"

By taking the time to do this and letting people know that the circle is a safe place to be and that we honor each person for who they are, not who they think they're supposed to be, I find that people can drop into a deeper level of work. A certain kind of container has been formed for that work to happen. There's a depth in the container, there's a safety in the circle. There's a safety in knowing that everyone's there for the same reasons.

Each circle will have its own norms and limits and, over time, it will become more and more clear what these limits are, what is or is not appropriate in terms of content and focus for the group. For example, in the beginning of a council circle it may not feel safe to explore personal feelings and experiences with racism, religion, homophobia or other potentially divisive subjects. But as the circle continues to meet, and more trust and solidarity are established among members, these tough issues can be more easily explored. My recommendation is that if even one person in a circle objects to a topic it should be shelved. Over time, as circle members come to know one another better, someone may suggest the topic again.

Sitting in a circle provides part of the structure needed to contain the energy generated in the circle. This is one of the reasons it is very important that your group literally form a circle with your bodies. You can choose to sit on the floor or in chairs, but make sure you form a complete circle. When we rearrange our seating it causes us to rearrange our expectations as well.

By each person sitting on what Christina Baldwin calls the "rim" or the edge of the circle, we are also symbolically removing ourselves and our self-interests from the middle of the group. As she explains it, this moving of our bodies from rows to circles and our self-interests from the center to the edge, enables us to reclaim our innate knowledge of circle.

Most people find it useful to mark the physical center of their circle with a cloth placed on the floor or a low table upon which they place objects that remind them that they are gathered in a sacred place for a sacred purpose. Often objects are placed on the altar that are sacred to group members or that signify something meaningful to them. The center can also be formed by each member placing something on the altar that is personally meaningful to her.

Agreements

Working together as a group, you will either need to establish the specific agreements that will help provide the needed structure of your circle or take on the agreements suggested by a specific type of circle (PeerSpirit, Wisdom, etc.).

In order to create a truly democratic circle, each member should have a say in establishing the structure and agreements of the circle. Each suggestion needs to be heard, honored, examined and discussed. This may include a process of adaptation as well. The process of establishing the agreements for your circle can be an exciting one which will begin the bonding experience.

Even if you decide to create your own agreements and structure, there is no sense in reinventing the wheel. Review chapter 8 for the generic circle agreements Christina Baldwin offers in *Calling the Circle.*

Your agreements or rules empower each circle member to take full responsibility for how she interacts, behaves and contributes in circle. It is especially helpful both to write down rules and make them available to all members and new members, and to bring rules or agreements up for review from time to time.

Creating Your Circle Structure

The following questions are offered in the hope that they will provide you further help in determining the type of circle you wish to have and the basic structure of your circle:

1. Why am I (we) calling a circle? What is its purpose? What are my (our) intentions?

2. Who do I (we) wish to invite to the circle? People who share a common lifestyle or vision? Or just women? Or will the circle be open to anyone who wants to participate?

   My opinion, and the focus of this book, is that circles are far more productive when men and women meet with their own gender in order to do certain kinds of work. But there are certainly benefits to having both women and men in the same circle, especially when it comes to airing differences.

3. How will members be selected? Unfortunately, it is sometimes necessary to say "no" to someone who may want to join your circle, either because the person doesn't seem like she "fits" with other circle members, or because she appears to be too fragile or distressed to be a member. This is particularly true if your circle is specifically oriented toward healing or shamanic work. Although it can be difficult to do, saying "no" to

someone who doesn't fit, for whatever reason, generally benefits everyone in the group and the circle itself, especially when a circle is originally being formed.

4. Where will the circle meet? Determining where the circle will meet will play an important part in determining its structure. If it meets at the home or office of the convener, more responsibility will naturally fall on that person. This responsibility can be interpreted as leadership. If a circle meets outside, the boundaries will probably not be as well-defined (unless you create a permanent circle and altar).

This brings up an important issue. When a circle meets in the same location over a period of time a vortex of energy is created that energizes and supports all future circles. This vortex can help the work done in the circle to become deeper and more clear. Anyone who is considering volunteering to use her home as the permanent location for a circle should have this information as part of the decision-making process.

5. How often will the circle meet? Weekly? Bimonthly? Monthly? Obviously, a circle that meets once a week, at least in the beginning, has a stronger chance of becoming a viable circle. When a circle meets regularly it engenders a certain level of intimacy and trust allowing for inner work that often does not occur otherwise. But because we all have such busy schedules, meeting weekly may be prohibitive for some people.

A circle can also be called to celebrate or acknowledge a special occasion. Many women's circles meet
each month on the new and full moon.

6. Will there be a leader or will the circle be leaderless?
If there is a facilitator, will leadership rotate among
members? What will the duties and responsibilities
of the facilitator be? If it is a leaderless circle, how
will the group make decisions?

In order to form a circle, someone has to be
responsible for initiating it. Since this person has
such a commitment to the circle, it is often assumed
she will be the leader. But this does not necessarily
have to transpire. Several of the types of circles I have
described advocate leaderless circles, shared leadership or rotating leadership.

Whether there is to be a leader or not depends
largely on the purpose of the circle. For example,
circles that meet for teaching or therapy usually have
a leader, while circles with well-defined guidelines,
such as Wisdom Circles, can function very well with
rotating leadership.

Entering and Leaving a Circle

Many people struggle with feelings of fear or shyness in
the beginning of a new circle. It is best to be honest about
this rather than to pretend you are feeling otherwise.

Entering an already functioning circle can be even more anxiety-provoking. Give yourself permission to just sit quietly and be in the space of not knowing until you become familiar with the circle structure.

It is best to prepare yourself for being in circle by taking a few deep breaths into your belly for several minutes. This will allow your actions and words to come from a more grounded or centered place. In time you will begin to feel part of the circle and will want to share from your heart when it is important to do so.

Meeting in circle can bring you to a place of connectedness with others you have never known, but it takes time and patience to grow past our feelings of isolation and alienation. It is often tempting when things become difficult or challenging in a circle for people to retreat back into protective isolation, and some are tempted to leave a circle at such times. If this should happen to you, it is important to remind yourself that becoming a part of a circle requires taking risks. While you certainly need to give yourself time to decide whether a particular circle provides a safe place for you to take such risks, you may want to contain your natural tendency to flee whenever you come up against a particularly threatening experience.

People find all sorts of reasons for leaving a circle when things get too real or frightening. For example, it is sometimes easier at these times to decide that everyone in the circle is wrong—rather than admitting our fear—or to blow out of proportion one small aspect of the circle that we do not like. When someone leaves a circle without some resolution or closure, it can be very disruptive to the group. It leaves a huge energy leak that will have to be mended or healed.

One way to avoid this is to have everyone make an agreement to participate in a closure ceremony before leaving the circle. Unfortunately, if someone is really upset she may refuse to keep this agreement and then the circle will have to find a way to mend itself. One way of doing this is to symbolically place the missing person in the center of the circle and have everyone speak to her, sharing their anger and pain, as well as feelings of goodwill. This process should continue until everyone in the circle feels closure and is able to release the person with blessings.

When any member leaves the circle for any reason she should assure the remaining members that she will honor her original agreement not to reveal other members' secrets to those outside the circle.

There is no right way to form a circle. Generally speaking, one learns to create and participate in circles by being a part of them. You will undoubtedly learn new ways of circling as you go along. As stated in *The Ceremonial Circle,* "every time and place in which a circle is formed is a new experience and adds to the body of knowledge of all circles."

In the next two chapters I give strategies for setting up specific types of circles. Although it should be understood that there is great overlap in circle setups. I have once again divided circles into two broad categories: council, or consensus, circles and sacred, or ceremonial, circles.

Council circles tend to focus more on verbal interaction, while ceremonial circles tend to be more centered around nonverbal ways of communicating, including ritual and ceremony. While ritual and ceremony may sometimes include verbalizations, in ceremonial circles, a great deal of emphasis is put on silence, meditation, dancing and drumming, as well as on chanting and singing.

TEN

Creating Council Circles

To sit in council in a circle
allows an opening of heart and mind to
new possibilities of understanding. It provides the
opportunity to be really heard. All the participants
agree to speak from their hearts and listen
with their hearts in order to come to a deeper
understanding of themselves, one another
and whatever is being discussed.

SEDONIA CAHILL AND JOSHUA HALPERN
THE CEREMONIAL CIRCLE

A n excellent way to start a council circle and to help
the group clarify its direction and purpose is to ask
each member to state her intention concerning the circle.
Another way to start a new circle is to present a question

and then ask all participants to respond.

In later meetings someone can initiate a question concerning an issue that is important to her, asking the group for their input. Questions can be large and abstract or small and personal. Other council circles use the check-in approach in order to facilitate the surfacing of topics.

Many council circles use questions to center and help focus the group. A well-formulated question encourages deep truth-telling which in turn bonds the group together. These questions are often presented by the person who is facilitating the circle for the evening.

At times there may be no agenda or agreed-upon topic of discussion. Instead, the time is used to share whatever is most important to each group member at the moment.

In order to facilitate communication, the talking stick or talking piece is usually used when meeting in council. The talking piece can be a specially carved stick, a medicine pipe, a feather, a crystal—or anything the group decides upon. Some circles prefer to use a stick found in nature as a reminder of the simplicity of speaking and sharing from the heart. Some prefer to find a stick or other object while focusing on an upcoming meeting or special occasion. Still others prefer a talking bowl which they believe better represents the feminine.

Only the person holding the talking piece is allowed to talk, and no one is allowed to interrupt the person holding it. Whoever holds the stick should have the total attention of the group and each member needs to make a commitment to listen from the heart. This means listening with a neutral, compassionate, nonintervening attitude, allowing the speaker the freedom to be really heard.

The talking piece can be passed from one speaker to the next in a clockwise direction, or it can be placed in the center of the circle and picked up when the next person is ready to speak. Some circles pass the talking stick around only once while others pass it many times.

Since speaking from the heart can be difficult, it is important not to rush the talking stick. The talking stick allows everyone in the circle to have a chance to speak, whereas in most groups, those who are most verbally adept tend to dominate the meeting.

The talking piece reminds us that speaking is a privilege and that words are sacred. As stated in *The Ceremonial Circle:*

> *To select one's words with care and thoughtfulness is to speak in a sacred manner. The talking staff helps us awaken from the stupor of too many words and of good words that have been used in evil ways. It is one of the most important tools of the circler.*
>
> *The point is to allow Spirit to speak through you when the staff reaches your hands. This usually takes time and experience, so be easy on yourself. If you find your mind rehearsing, just take some deep breaths and focus on the speaker. The speaker, like you, deserves to be heard. In this way you*

*honor yourself, the speaker, the circle and Spirit. It is impor-
tant to understand that when a member of the group speaks
in a sacred and heartfelt way, your careful listening may
reveal some previously ignored part of your own heart.*

Kay Pranis shares the following list of advantages of the
talking piece:

- The talking piece helps to manage the discussion of
  very emotional issues. Emotions can be expressed
  without the emotions taking over the dialogue.
  Because participants must wait for the talking piece to
  speak, they cannot respond without thinking. Because
  the talking piece must go around the full circle, it pre-
  vents two individuals from getting into a back-and-
  forth emotional exchange. If the words of one
  participant anger another, multiple members of the
  circle may address the issues raised before the talking
  piece reaches the angry participant, thus relieving the
  angry participant from a sense of needing to defend
  him/herself alone.
- The talking piece creates space for the contributions
  of quiet people who might otherwise not assert themselves to claim room in the dialogue. These people
  often have valuable insights which are lost in an open
  dialogue process.
- The talking piece spreads responsibility for peacemaking

to all participants. In traditional mediation, participants expect the mediator to control the dialogue. In
the circle process the keeper does not interrupt the
flow of the talking piece, thus every participant carries
responsibility to address conflict which may be arising
between some participants of the circle.

- The talking piece promotes better listening.
  Participants listen when they know that they will not
  have an opportunity to speak until the talking piece
  reaches them. In open dialogue we often stop listening and begin formulating our response before a
  speaker is finished because we need to rush into an
  opening in the dialogue.
- The talking piece encourages the use of silence in the
  process.
- The talking piece reinforces the principle of equality
  in the circle because it provides equal opportunity for
  all to participate and presumes equal capacity for
  contributions from all participants.

Described by Brooke Medicine Eagle, one method for
finding consensus in a circle is for everyone to look into
the center instead of at the speaker. In days gone by,
indigenous tribes would always have a fire in the center of
the circle which served to connect everyone to a deep,
centered place. (You may choose to have an altar or
candles.) Fire represents the great Spirit which lies at the

heart of everything, and this metaphor brings recognition that there is a place where consensus and harmony rest, and that the discussion will draw the circle closer and closer until all are finally in agreement.

PeerSpirit Circles

A PeerSpirit Circle is usually started when someone has an idea or desire and wants to find a group of fairly compatible—like-minded and like-hearted—people to fulfill that idea or need. This person, the caller of the circle, sets out the basic intention, invites participants and models the circle's basic structure at the first meeting while others become accustomed to the form.

PeerSpirit, like most models presented here, is not a rigid methodology, but has a definitive structure that gives it a distinctive place in the circle movement. Christina Baldwin, author of *Calling the Circle: The First and Future Culture*, is cofounder of this form with Ann Linnea. The two women work out of their homes on Whidbey Island, north of Seattle. They also travel extensively, spreading the word of the circle throughout the world.

One distinction between PeerSpirit Circles and some other types of circles may be that PeerSpirit encourages groups to become self-facilitating and self-governing. The structure for doing this is presented through three principles, three practices and four basic agreements.

The three PeerSpirit principles of council are:

- Leadership rotates
- Responsibility is shared
- Ultimate reliance is on Spirit

The three practices are:

- To listen attentively
- To speak intentionally
- To consciously self-monitor

The four basic agreements are:

- What is said in the circle remains in the circle
- People listen with discernment, not judgment
- People ask for what they need and offer what they can
- When in doubt or need, the group will pause and ask for guidance

It's amazing to see these laid out, as Baldwin has done, condensing her 200-page book to a business card. She did this, she professes, so that the structure of the circle would be accessible and not intimidating.

When I asked Christina to share a suggestion for coming into circle she offered the following:

It helps to ask people to bring some object that is special to them, put it in the middle of the circle and to share a little anecdote about themselves. This varies according to where the circle is called and for what purpose, but the stories are always interesting, and they help all of us to pay attention to each other more closely. By the end of a few minutes, every voice has been heard, and the center of the space has a new quality to it because part of everybody is symbolically represented.

During our interview Christina Baldwin also shared the following exercise she uses in PeerSpirit Circles for women:

When I do a women's circle I like to play "20 Questions." We have each woman write down a statement about what is up for herself, what issues she is dealing with. Then we have her make a list of questions pertaining to this statement. We time it so she has seven minutes to do this. When the time is over we have each woman rise up and go to the person sitting on her left and say, "Here's my statement. Please ask me five more questions." We have the women keep on doing this process over and over until each has a long list of questions about their issue. This helps them to get a totally different perspective about the issue. It's like saying, "Here, you'll see the issue differently if you just look through this lens."

If you want to know more about PeerSpirit Circles, you will want to read Christina Baldwin's book, *Calling the Circle* (Bantam Books, 1998). Since she also offers workshops you may want to look up PeerSpirit in Appendix II for more information.

Wisdom Circles

Wisdom circles are opened and closed with some kind of simple ritual. A topic that has been chosen by the members is sometimes posed in the form of a question, and all members then take turns responding to it. The basic orienting question, "What can we learn from our own and each other's experiences?" has wide application in support groups, study groups and organizations of all kinds.

As stated in the book *Wisdom Circles*, the wisdom circle inquiry is ideally an opportunity to uncover a basic insight about ourselves that reminds us of who we truly are and what we truly value. An example given in the book of such a question is: "Tell us something you did that you feel proud of."

Coming up with incisive, truth-eliciting questions can be a challenge. The authors of *Wisdom Circles* suggest these two generic questions:

- What unique talents or qualities do I bring to this circle?
- Tell us about a watershed event that changed the course of your life.

The authors also offer these helpful guidelines for determining which questions to ask:

- Choose questions or topics that require thinking, and

even more important, to feeling one's way into an answer.

- Choose questions that require reflection on personal experience as opposed to those that elicit answers based on a belief system.
- Choose questions or topics that motivate group members to bring their full emotional, intellectual and intuitive energies to the question at hand and to the group.
- Choose a topic that carries within it a universal concern such as learning about ourselves, healing past wounds or creating a vision for the future.
- Choose a topic that will help people discover the wisdom in their own experiences.

For further help with the types of questions to ask and more suggestions for topics, please read *Wisdom Circles: A Guide to Self-Discovery and Community Building in Small Groups* by Charles Garfield, Cindy Spring and Sedonia Cahill.

After a question or topic is chosen and stated, each speaker holds a talking stick or other symbolic object and speaks without interruption. Those not speaking are asked to listen openly, without judgment. No advice giving or cross talk is allowed. Silence is valued as much as words.

Although no two Wisdom Circles are alike, there are elements that all share. The Wisdom Circle is shaped by a set of guidelines called the Ten Constants. These constants have been inspired by councils of indigenous peoples, informed by support and dialogue groups, and drawn from the founding circle's own experience. They create a safe "container" in which participants can tap their innate capacity to relate to each other in a context of wisdom and compassion.

The Wisdom Circle constants are explained below:

1. *Honor the circle as sacred time and space* by doing simple rituals to mark the beginning and end of a circle gathering. A ritual creates a shared sensory experience and a demarcation from ordinary life. Light a candle, for example, or take a moment to breathe deeply. Share a brief period of silence, or burn some incense or sage. Listen to a selection of music or to a guided meditation. You can be as creative as you want.

2. *Create a collective center* by mutually agreeing upon a topic or intention. This might be visioning the future, healing wounds, going within to learn more about ourselves, making decisions or planning actions that sustain and enrich life for yourself and others. A group may choose a focus specific to its needs, or it can allow for topics to surface determined by individual needs.

3. *Ask to be informed* by your highest values, such as

compassion and truth, the wisdom of those who have gone before you, and by the needs of those yet to be born. One person can speak for the group or each person can take a turn.

4. *Express gratitude* for the blessings and teachings of life. In silence, or by taking turns, give thanks for those things great and small whose gifts and life energy enrich your life.

5. *Create a container for full participation and deep truth telling.* Allow each person to speak without interruption or cross talking. Use a talking object (a stick, rock, flower or any other thing that has symbolic significance). The object may be passed around the circle or taken from and returned to the center. Respect a member's right to silence. Keep everything confidential.

6. *Listen from the heart* and serve as a compassionate witness to the other people in the circle. To be an effective witness requires paying attention to what's being said without interpretation, judgment or trying to "fix" or rescue the person speaking. It also means a willingness to discover something about yourself in the stories of other people. Offer feedback only when solicited by the speaker.

7. *Speak from the heart* and from direct experience. When you are moved to speak, do so thoughtfully and with care. Avoid abstract, conceptual language, and stay in

touch as deeply as possible with your feelings. As this capacity develops, a person may be moved to share those feelings and to say difficult things without self-judgment and without blaming others.

8. *Make room for silence to enter* to allow for reflection, for meditation, for feelings to surface and for a sense of the sacred to emerge as the circle proceeds.

9. *Empower each member to be a co-facilitator of the process.* Designate a different person to be the circle maker each time. This person readies the physical setting, initiates the opening and closing ritual, and facilitates consensus on a topic. Encourage each other to give voice to feelings of satisfaction or discomfort with the group's process.

10. *Commit to an ongoing relationship* with each person in the circle so as to engender trust and caring among members. Extend that caring to other people, to the Earth and all her creatures by practicing the capacities developed within the Wisdom Circle in daily life.

Simplicity Circles

In *The Circle of Simplicity,* Cecile Andrews provides the following suggestions for conducting a simplicity study circle:

• Except for the first meeting, begin each session with a

brief check-in. This involves going around the circle with people reporting on the concrete actions they took that week to simplify their lives.

- Each person is encouraged to conduct personal research on issues. Learning to draw your own conclusions from your own experience is valued as much as learning from books or television.
- Everyone is encouraged to keep a journal or notebook to write down thoughts and notes during study circle meetings, and to record thoughts and observations during the week.
- At the end of each session each person commits to an action she or he will take the following week.

Cecile advocates breaking the larger circle up into smaller groups of two or three to discuss a particular question, and then returning to the larger circle and answering the question again, this time more succinctly, by taking turns going around the circle.

She makes the following suggestions for questions to ask at the first meeting:

- Why are you here? What is going on in your life that attracts you to the subject of voluntary simplicity?
- How do you define voluntary simplicity?
- What are you already doing to simplify your life?

For more information on how to conduct Simplicity

Study Groups, read either *The Circle of Simplicity* by Cecile Andrews or *Voluntary Simplicity* by Duane Elgin.

Crone Circles

Crone circles usually include only those who are approaching or are in the midst of menopause. Some women meet for the purpose of exploring this important rite of passage; others meet in order to honor and encourage the wisdom of the crone; and still others meet in order to share information about health issues such as which herbs are helpful, natural sources of estrogen, and which exercise and diet programs are most effective.

Those who meet to explore menopause as a rite of passage conduct circles with some or all of the following rituals and exercises:

- A storytelling circle in which each woman tells the story of her first moontime (the time she began menstruating). In some circles everyone brings a photo of herself at puberty to place on the altar. This sharing of beautiful, sad and funny stories brings women together and reminds them of the passage of time.

- A circle in which women share their grief about no longer celebrating the moon's tides with their blood and about their fears of growing old. Most women feel relieved to realize that other women have the same fears, and there is healing in sharing these fears and having them witnessed and understood.

- A powerful ceremony into cronehood that honors what has been and what is being sacrificed, and that celebrates the power that is just beginning for each woman. For example, each woman may come to the circle dressed in an old garment representing her old self. She removes and burns the old garment which symbolizes her passage from the past into the present. The old garment is then replaced with a beautiful new one symbolizing a powerful new phase in her life. Some women choose to take a new ceremonial name which expresses her commitment to this exciting time.

Those who wish to focus on exploring their fear of aging or fear of death may wish to try the following:

- Make masks of yourselves as old women, wear them in the circle and allow yourself to really experience being very old. Then talk about how you would like your old age to be, including where you would like to live, whether you would like to be single or involved with someone, and what you would like to do with your time.
- Have a circle in which you explore death issues, sharing with one another how you would like death to come, how you want your burial service to be, and what you believe happens after death.

A Circle for My Fiftieth Birthday

Even though I had heard that turning fifty can be a tremendously positive event for women, marking a transition into what they describe as the best years of their life, turning fifty can also be a very difficult time for many women and I was one of them. No matter how many books I read on the subject or how many pep talks I received, nothing lifted my spirits. The thought of turning fifty sent me into a depression that lasted several months. I knew I needed the powerful healing of a women's circle. I knew I needed to transform the painful ordeal of turning fifty into a ritual of renewal.

I called fourteen women from my community to join with me on the eve of my birthday for a women's circle. Instead of bringing presents, I asked the women to bring something to share—a poem, a journal entry, a personal story—that might help me make my transition a positive experience.

It was raining hard on the night of the circle, but every woman I invited, with the exception of one, weathered the storm to attend. This in itself made me feel loved and supported. As we joined hands in a circle we could hear the wind howling outside. But with dozens of candles lit around the room, a fire burning in the fireplace and the energy we were creating in our circle, we felt comforted and protected.

I asked each woman to share with me and the other women both her pain and her joy about turning fifty. Since most of the women had already made this transition, they all had plenty to say. Their words of wisdom were very healing for me.

In addition to sharing their stories, some of the women shared a poem or ceremony with me. One of the women had each of us hold a lit candle while we went around the circle, each woman saying the following words to me: "As a woman I wish you . . ."

One by one my dear friends filled in the sentence with such powerful words and phrases as "authenticity," "recognition," "good health," and "the ability to receive and give love." I felt overwhelmed by my friends' love and good wishes, and had to struggle to take them all in.

This circle was truly one of the most meaningful experiences of my life. By the time the circle was closed I was filled up with love and hope, no longer feeling alone with my fears, but feeling a part of the great community of women.

Peacemaking Circles

Peacemaking Circles use traditional circle ritual and structure to create a respectful space in which all can speak from the heart in a shared search for understanding of a specific event. According to Kay Pranis, the peacemaking process usually follows this format:

1. A welcoming
2. An opening ritual (often this is a smudging, but each circle is encouraged to create their own ritual that will clear the heads, hearts and spirits of each member)
3. Making a contract with one another as to how circle members will interact with one another. This usually includes:
   - passing the talking piece
   - observing confidentiality
   - agreeing to stay with the circle, i.e., not dumping a problem and then walking away; or leaving a problem in circle and not giving the circle a chance to resolve it
   - talking and listening with respect
4. Working toward making the circle a safe place. Passing the talking piece and asking the question: "What else can we do to make the circle safe?"
5. Reminding the group of the guidelines, which have been agreed to by the entire circle
6. Beginning with a round of introductions and encouraging each person to give more than her name (to share something significant about herself)
7. Introducing an issue or topic
8. Passing the talking piece for one or more rounds to get perspectives and concerns of all participants on the issue

9. Passing the talking piece to explore possible actions to be taken regarding the issue

10. Checking with participants on possible areas of consensus. Clarifying commitments made and plans for next steps

11. Passing the talking piece for final comments

12. Ending with a ritual. Our endings often include the sharing of food

Peacemaking Circles were originally developed in partnership with the criminal justice system. The goal was to involve all those affected by an offense in deciding an appropriate sentencing plan which addressed the concerns of all participants.

When used in this way, these "Sentencing Circles" include: the victim, victim supporters, the offender, offender supporters, the judge, the prosecutor, defense counsel, police, court workers and all interested community members. There are several steps leading up to the actual sentencing:

- an application by the offender to the circle process
- the creation of a support system for the offender
- the creation of a support system for the victim
- a healing circle for the victim
- a healing circle and preparation circles for the offender
- the Sentencing Circle

After the Sentencing Circle, there may be follow-up circles at appropriate intervals to review progress on the sentencing agreement.

The following excerpt from an article written by Kay Pranis for *Corrections Today* describes how the Sentencing Circle works:

A young man in his early twenties sits, his head hanging down, in a circle of chairs. Around the circle sit community members, elders, the young man's sister, a judge and a probation officer. Notably missing are his mother and friends, many of whom had agreed to attend this Sentencing Circle. The Keeper, a respected community member skilled in peacemaking and consensus building, opens the session with a prayer and a reminder that the circle has been convened to address the behavior of this young man, who killed his sister's cat in a drunken outburst. An eagle feather is passed, each member of the circle expresses his or her feelings about the crime and raises questions or concerns. The young man expresses regret about his actions and a desire to change his harmful behavior. His sister, the victim of this crime, talks about her anger and sadness, but also about her love for her brother. An elder mentions that the young man owes something to the animal kingdom and suggests building a bird feeder and feeding the birds. Another community member comments on the inability of the young man to cry and suggests grief and anger counseling. Attendance at Alcoholics

Anonymous and community service also are suggested. One community member volunteers to help the young man with the bird feeder and several others offer to accompany him on his first visit to the counselor when he acknowledges that it may be difficult for him to go alone.

Community members also speak about the young man's strengths and potential. As the evening progresses, the young man holds his head higher and higher. Toward the end of the discussion, he tells the group that he had no idea he had so much support in the community. The suggestions of the group are incorporated into a sentencing agreement. The circle ends with a prayer honoring participants for their wisdom and support. The group then adjourns for a potluck supper and chatter.

The Sentencing Circle provided an opportunity for all those impacted by the crime to talk about their feelings and concerns. But this circle did more than determine a sentence for the perpetrator. The young man later joined the Community Justice Committee and today participates in healing and Sentencing Circles for others.

In this chapter I provided some suggestions on how to structure some of the most common types of council circles. In the next chapter you'll learn how to structure ceremonial and sacred circles.

ELEVEN

Creating Ceremonial and Sacred Circles

Ritual is a component of ceremony.
The ceremony is like a canvas and the ritual
the color to be added. Ritual can be done
unconsciously; there is no magic technique for
waking up and being present, but when
ritual is done consciously it adds a
beautiful texture to a ceremony.

THE CEREMONIAL CIRCLE

Ceremonial Circles

As you've already learned, ritual is a central component of most circles, but ceremonial circles rely especially heavily on ritual. Some ceremonial circles come together for the express purpose of enacting a ritual rite of passage. Birth, puberty, menopause, death, marriage, divorce, jobs beginning or ending, and moving are just some of the reasons for creating a special ritual. These rituals acknowledge and support the changes that are occurring and enrich all those who are part of the circle.

Many women recognize the potential for great power in ritual—the type of power many women are only beginning to discover but are afraid to experience. Because of this fear, many women who are just beginning to do rituals follow ritual forms suggested in books, or those based on Native American traditions or other indigenous tribe traditions or those based in goddess spirituality. No matter how innovative a group may be, creating new rituals can be difficult, especially when you are just beginning. In her book, *Ritualizing Women*, Leslie A. Northup lists the following inspirational sources for rituals:

- **The Western Liturgical Tradition**

    In spite of the oppressive patriarchy of Western religions, many women continue to find meaning in Christian and Jewish rituals such as sharing a loaf of blessed bread or blessing parts of the body with ritual water.

- **Eastern Religions**

    Since the 1960s American women have been exposed

to Asian religious teachings and practices, including such ritual elements as extended meditation, posture and breathing exercises, chakra concentration and making mandalas. They have also found ritual material in New Age spirituality, which often adapts Eastern spiritual techniques to help people focus on personal well-being.

- **Ancient Ritual Traditions**

    Many women's circles draw on the ritualistic traditions of goddess-worship, midwives, herbal healers, witches, Santerias and visionaries—traditions that have been passed down through the centuries as oral narratives and history "read between the lines."

- **The Rituals of Other Cultures**

    The practices of Native Americans, Africans and other tribal cultures, especially those that show a respect for women and nature, have inspired many women's rituals.

- **Nature Patterns, Symbols and Objects**

    It is not surprising that the use of natural objects and symbols is a common source of ritual since female identities have commonly been ascribed to the Earth, the sea and the moon. In spite of the stereotyping such identification can imply, women are particularly attuned to Gaia theology, creation theology, the ecological movement and their own natural fertility rhythms.

- **Personal Experience**

  One of the most significant sources for creating women's rituals is the personal experience of women themselves. Female rituals are often rooted in the lives and activities of women who do housework, prepare meals, produce handicrafts, overcome abuse, give birth and raise children, succeed against all odds in business and professional roles, and survive in community.

- **The Women's Movement and Feminist Consciousness**

  Feminist writings, theory and insights often inform women's rituals, provide their thematic content and inspire women to work for change.

- **Women's Creativity**

  Many elements in women's rituals are created by women using their imagination, artistry, interests and talents. These rituals may come out of a response to current events, the particulars of members' lives, or shared backgrounds and concerns. Successful attempts may be repeated or revised; failures are seldom repeated.

Some women, like Sedonia Cahill, believe that by relying on books or by writing and memorizing elaborate scripts you lose the meaning and spontaneity of ritual making. She believes that by following the rituals of others you are prevented both from discovering the variety of ways there are to do ritual, and from experiencing the freedom of action and movement that comes from developing your own rituals.

My purpose in discussing the ways to create and perform rituals is to provide new choices to women in circles, thus making room for creativity and spontaneity to enter in.

According to *The Ceremonial Circle* every ceremony is divided into three distinct parts. These parts need to be honored and harmonized in order for the circle to touch us deeply:

1. *Severance* is the act of moving from the world of our habits into sacred ceremonial time and space.
2. *Threshold/Liminality* is the phase that is the heart of the circle: We go beyond ourselves, leaving behind our limited identities.
3. *Reincorporation* is a process of returning to the "everyday world" with new self-knowledge and a way to integrate and use that knowledge in daily life.

Some of the rituals that go into creating a meaningful ceremony include:

Praying

Making invocations

Building and lighting fires

Creating an altar

Lighting candles

Burning sage

Using incense

Using smoke

Purifying

Making offerings

Using power objects

Fasting

Feasting

Playing music

Singing/Chanting

Drumming

Dancing

Performing mimetic acts

Practicing silence

Wearing masks

Wearing symbolic clothing

Using special gestures

Hand-holding/Embracing

Exchanging special gifts

Making taboos

Keeping vigils

Inducing stress

Facing ordeals

Knocking down/Breaking objects

Burning objects

Burying objects

Untying and tying objects

Washing

Moving within and outside circle

Crossing thresholds

Using a special power name

Performing symbolic deaths and rebirths

Cahill and Halpern divided these rituals into ten general categories:

Speaking to Spirit (prayer, invocation, dance, singing, special gestures)

The purpose of ceremony is to connect with higher powers. In order to do this many believe one must declare one's intention to speak with Spirit. There are various ways of doing this, including those listed above. In addition, many people begin by casting or calling their circle in a specific direction (eastward, clockwise, counterclockwise) in order to create a wholeness to the circle and a protective energy around it. (See "Creating a Medicine Wheel" later in the chapter.)

Sacrifice (fasting, ordeals, sleeplessness, stress induction, vigils, making taboos, silence)

The word sacrifice means "to make sacred." It is often necessary to give up something—such as food, sleep, sex, speech, physical comfort or even safety—in order to make oneself more open to Spirit. These sacrifices sensitize the body and help people connect with what is happening inside. Some spiritual teachers also believe these practices make us transparent, thus inviting the entrance of Spirit.

Worship (altars, power objects, offerings)

At some ceremonies it is appropriate to build an altar which expresses the intention and diversity of the circle members. An animal skin or a handmade rug or cloth can be placed on the ground and each circle member may carefully place an object that has special and symbolic meaning on it. Some people choose to clarify the object's meaning to the group while others do not. Objects such as crystals, rocks, pieces of jewelry, animal totems and rattles can offer protection, healing or other special energy for the circle. And since they get energetically "charged" from the ceremony, they can be used for healing purposes at a later time.

Some circle groups choose to create a permanent altar. If you wish to do this make certain that your altar is blessed and purified on a regular basis since it is a way of honoring Spirit.

Exorcising (breaking, unifying, burying, burning, making offerings, knocking down objects, cutting hair)

An important part of ceremony is a breaking away from the old and making way for a new consciousness or behavior. Two of the most common types of exorcising rituals are:

1. Making a list of your faults, shortcomings or addictions, placing them in a "burning bowl" and lighting them
2. Building a pile of rocks—each representing a part of the past that you are ready to leave behind—and knocking down the pile to show your commitment to moving on to the new

Purification (washing, immersion in water, smudging, prayer lodge)

Purification is a process of cleansing away the mundane and preparing to enter the sacred. Therefore, most circles begin with some kind of purification process. The Native American sweat lodge utilizes both fire and water to cleanse the body and mind of accumulated waste and to free the spirit, but any of the above methods can be used effectively to prepare yourself for ceremony.

Communing (music, singing, dancing, mimetic arts, ritual silence, incense)

Opening up the body and bringing forth sounds and movements that express the inner world is the most ancient way of communing with Spirit. As long as the sound you make is true it will be heard and accepted by Spirit. Dances often involve gestures that imitate an animal that you wish to commune with and be empowered by. Another ritual commonly used to commune with Spirit is to send one's prayers on the ceremonial smoke of burning incense, tobacco or other herbs.

Symbolic Deaths (moving in and out of circle, crossing thresholds, symbols, death and rebirth, burying)

Crossing a symbolic threshold or doorway symbolizes the death of the old you. Moving back out through the threshold is a symbol of rebirth. One effective severance ritual is for the group to moan as the quester moves outside of the circle.

Calling the Light (lighting candles, building fires)

Fire is one of our most powerful tools when used in a ceremonial way. In winter solstice ceremonies each participant lights a candle to honor the returning light. Vision-questers often have small fires in their circles during their solo times and will slowly feed the fire with twigs and sticks that represent the various parts of their bodies or psyches to be burned in the transforming fire.

Rebirth (masks, wearing symbolic clothing, power names)

Painting your face, wearing a mask or donning symbolic clothing can bring forth an archetypal part of yourself that you want other circle members to witness. This might be an animal totem, a deity or a member of your inner family. Sharing a name that you have chosen to represent your commitment to a spiritual path is to make a declaration of powerful intention that you are a new person. Many people use their power names only in ceremonial context while others make them their everyday names.

Community (giving gifts, feasting, hand-holding/embracing)

One of the greatest joys of circling is sharing what you have been able to create together as a tribe. Sharing food, gifts or touch is a way of honoring the sacred space that has been created.

As Cahill and Halpern explain, these ritual tools can be used in many combinations. The important thing is that they be used with total mindfulness and an awareness of their symbolic meanings for the individual and the group.

Sacred Circles

Healing Circles

There are many ways to structure a healing circle. Such circles are often conducted outdoors beneath the clear expanse of sky and near a forest, meadow, the ocean or a running stream. This allows nature to endow the circle with its powers, and helps participants connect with the power and healing nature of Mother Earth. Since the circle itself contains the force of nature, a healing circle can also be held indoors and still be effective. One of the most effective healing ceremonies is to have the person in need of healing stand or sit in the center of the circle and have all members of the circle sing the name of the one in the center. The healing that can occur when the person in the center allows this powerful positive energy and focus to seep into her every cell can be incredibly potent. The person in the center may ask that the positive energy be directed at a certain part of her body or that everyone visualize her body in perfect health and balance.

An even more potent ritual for healing is a laying-on of hands. Some kind of purification ritual, such as smudging, needs to be conducted before beginning. Again, the person in need of healing goes to the center of the circle. All the members of the circle then position themselves around the one in the center. Those who know the person better may choose to position themselves nearest her head and feet. Before the laying-on of hands the group can sing a healing song, say "Om" or sing the person's name. At the same time, they all visualize the person in perfect health, balance and harmony. Each member of the circle may then place her hands gently on the body of the one in the center, making sure her hands remain quiet and steady, and her thoughts remain positive and loving.

Creating a Medicine Wheel

It is actually very easy and natural to create a medicine wheel. Unfortunately, it is made complex by some authors, teachers and hierarchical spiritual authorities. They would have you believe that every sacred circle must be created in a very specific way, and they insist that the smallest ceremonial details must be followed exactly or negative energy will result.

But no teacher or group of people own the power or shape of the circle. Circling is the most common event in the universe, the primary motif of creation. The sacred circle belongs to all beings born on Mother Earth.

Therefore, you can take the ancient symbol of the circle, combine it with various ceremonial elements that are common to all primal peoples, and create your own sacred circle or medicine wheel. You can combine these various elements differently for each circle using your spontaneity and imagination. Or you may find one way to do a circle that is right for you and continue to do it that way.

A sacred circle can be as simple or elaborate as you choose to make it. The only limit is that your intention should be to work for the benefit of all beings. You can create a sacred circle for anything positive. As stated earlier in the book, any medicine power or energy you raise or shape in a medicine wheel is magnified and focused by the circle itself. Any energy you send will return to you magnified many times. If you send out healing energy, you get healing energy back.

People often use the medicine power that is raised in a sacred circle for self-transformation. They create a medicine wheel, raise power and direct it towards that which they need to change in themselves.

While some people ask for very specific things for themselves—such as love, prosperity and good health—some part of your circle should be devoted to your spirit. After all, this is what matters most. And it is good to devote part of every circle to healing and protecting nature in some way.

For beginners it is best to concentrate on self-transformative circles and to work with this focus until you are confident and at ease with channeling medicine power positively. When you see how powerfully it works, you will become very careful about using it.

When we create a medicine wheel or sacred circle we are setting aside a place that is holy, powerful and mysterious. Sacred space can be anywhere. You may have discovered your own sacred space in a natural setting where you feel particularly exhilarated or peaceful. By creating a medicine wheel we can also create sacred space and time anywhere.

Your sacred circle can be indoors or outdoors, but it should be a quiet place where you will not be disturbed. You can sit or stand during any part of the medicine wheel. If you are moved to dance or lie down, feel free to do so.

The only requirement, aside from a positive intent, is to create your medicine with a grateful heart and a reverence for all life. With this in mind, establish an atmosphere of reverence by lighting candles, burning incense or starting a fire in the center of the circle. Some people place sacred objects, such as a medicine pouch or a crystal, in the circle area. Symbolic representations of the four elements are frequently placed in or around the medicine wheel. For instance, a feather can be placed in or around the eastern quadrant of the circle to represent the element air; a candle in the southern section can represent fire; a bowl of water or a seashell in the western section can represent the element water; a container of earth or a stone in the northern quadrant of the medicine wheel can represent earth.

Creating or Casting the Circle

The circle acts as a focal point, a concentrator of energy. It will call to the spirits of the universe asking that you wish to be heard. To cast your circle, start at a place that is significant to you and cast a complete circle from that point around. The east is a good starting point because it is where the sun rises each day. For this reason many people begin casting the circle in the east and go clockwise until they end again in the east.

But you can begin at any point that has personal meaning for your ritual. For example, you can cast the circle clockwise, or sunwise, which is the direction the sun travels. This is associated with invoking, increasing or raising energy. Or, you could cast your circle counterclockwise, which is associated with banishing, releasing or cleansing energy.

You may wish to cast your medicine wheel or sacred circle following the traditions of the indigenous people of the world. Some sprinkle cornmeal around the circle as they walk sunwise around the perimeter. Others draw the circle in the soil, using a variety of ritual objects, such as a staff. Others place stones or crystals around the perimeter.

Some simply sit or stand in a circle as each participant sings a sacred song, chants or prays out loud, one at a time, around the circle in a clockwise direction. Others dance as a group, so that the dance creates the circle. Still others combine two or more of these methods. The important thing is that you perform the casting in some way that clearly marks off your medicine wheel from the mundane world.

Following is a summary of the actions involved (in their recommended order) to create a typical sacred circle or medicine wheel:

- **Cleansing**

    Cleanse yourself with water or smoke from a sacred fire, or brush off unwanted energies with a large feather. As you symbolically cleanse your thoughts, feelings and spirit, you might choose to speak aloud to the spirits of the element you are cleansing with and ask for purification.

- **Shielding**

    Use a shield to remind yourself of what you are trying to accomplish and to protect yourself from unwanted energies. A simple way to shield is to visualize yourself surrounded by white light. Some people visualize themselves or the entire circle surrounded by a favorite being of nature (a plant, a tree, an animal).

- **Grounding**

    "Ground" yourself in order to feel more calm, centered and rooted. You can do this by breathing deeply, holding hands with others around the circle, feeling your feet or your body on the earth, or visualizing becoming a tree that grows roots in the earth.

- **Casting (Closing)**

  Casting (or closing) a circle symbolizes marking off or separating yourself from the mundane world. You can do this by drawing a circle on the ground with a sacred object or with cornmeal, going around the circle and having each person call out something in nature, or passing a candle around a circle as each member states her intent.

- **Calling in the Directions**

  One person walks around the circle, stops at the east, south, west and north sections of the circle, and asks each direction to join the circle. Or, four different people stand at the four directions, facing outward from the circle and inviting the directions in. An invitational chant may also be spoken or sung by the group.

- **Invoking Mother Earth and Other Positive Spirits**

  Humans cannot and should not work alone with the powerful medicine of a circle. Therefore, we call in, invite or invoke positive spirits and deities into the medicine wheel. Any positive deity or spirit can be invited into the circle to help raise the medicine power. One or more persons can pray, chant, invoke or dance these positive energies into the circle.

- **Raising and Projecting the Energy**

    The nature spirits understand symbols, pictures, song, rhyme, dance and emotion better than words alone. Let as much of yourself as possible get involved with such activities and energies—the ideas for raising and projecting energy are limitless.

- **Opening (Undoing) the Circle**

    Thank the directions and the deities invoked. Some people also like to walk three times in the opposite direction that the circle was cast in to open or undo the circle.

A Simple Way to Cast a Sacred Circle

Prepare the ground by cleaning the area. Build a sacred circle by sprinkling cornmeal, starting from the east and moving clockwise. Make the circle big enough for you and your tools to enter.

Before entering the circle, do a smudging ceremony. Light sweet grass and sage and move the smoke around your body. Take the smoke into your heart through your breath. Feel the earth and the presence of the four-legged, winged, finned and crawling ones—all our relations.

Periodically cleanse your circle by smudging, moving the smoke from the sweet grass and sage mixture around the grounds and blessing the grounds through prayer.

Feed the sacred circle grounds by "giving away" to all creatures and relations, using tobacco, cornmeal and seeds. Give away to your wheel, so that all who come to the wheel will give away to you. This is the sacred circle.

Goddess-Centered Spirituality/Wiccan Circles

According to Barbara Ardinger, in her book *A Woman's Book of Rituals and Celebrations*, each goddess-centered or wiccan tradition, coven, circle or school—witchy, wiccan, crafty and neo-pagan—has its own structure. Based on her research, however, there are seven basic procedural steps that seem to be common among all such circles, and they are very similar to those used in opening a sacred circle or medicine wheel:

- **Purification**

  Incense, salt water or visualization is used to purify circle members and tools. Sometimes the space is purified as well.

- **Casting the Circle**

  The circle is cast, or closed, by calling in the powers of the four (or six or seven) directions, the four elements, the goddess and sometimes the god. This may be done by the priestess and her assistant or by group members. When the circle has been cast, it usually means that no one is permitted to come in or go out, though sometimes special provisions are made for some people to enter and leave at will.

- **Stating the Intention**

    This is the purpose of the gathering—its will to be done—and can be a sabbat celebration, healing, a working for world or personal peace, a prosperity ritual or any other special occasion.

- **Raising the Power**

    The group chants, sings or makes music by drumming or clapping, does a prescribed dance or visualizes the rising power. The raised power is often referred to as a "cone of power."

- **Trance Work**

    The priestess leads a guided meditation that uses the power just raised for a specific purpose. The power is then grounded. Sometimes the cone of power is aimed and sent out to a specific target.

- **Grounding Energy**

    The energy must be returned to the earth.

- **Opening the Circle**

    All invisible powers are thanked and sent back to where they came from. The people adjourn for refreshment and a social hour.

At the start of a goddess-centered or wiccan circle, women may "check in" with each other first, bringing everyone up-to-date on how their lives have been going and how they're presently feeling. Checking in can include self-introductions if guests are present. Sometimes the intention is stated before the circle is cast. People working with the Gardnerian traditions read the Charge of the Goddess and draw down the full moon—or at least its power—into the high priestess and then into the circle. Not every ritual includes trance work, and many groups celebrate the sabbats by staging dramatic rituals and acting out the appropriate mythological story.

Ceremonial Objects and Tools for Circling

The Talking Stick or Talking Piece

The talking piece of a sacred circle is often a special object that has been created by one or more circle members from objects found in the environment or objects that represent sacredness to the circle members.

There may be one talking piece for each circle, or each person may have her own personal talking piece made to represent what is sacred to that person. It is important to devote prayer and attention to the making of a talking piece that will carry one's voice to the circle or represent all the voices of those in a circle.

When one holds the talking piece, everyone is supposed to listen. The person with the piece speaks into the center of the circle with no thought of influencing others. She simply speaks the truth. Since she sits at one point on the circle, she represents one viewpoint. Each person in the circle represents another. Those who listen should look into the center with open hearts and minds, knowing that whatever is meant for their spirits will come to them and what is not meant for them will pass away.

A powerful way for the person who is holding the talking stick to begin speaking is to say: "I am (name) and I will speak." There is something empowering about saying one's name and making this announcement.

When the speaker has finished, some circle advocates suggest that she say, "I am (name) and I have spoken."

The talking piece teaches about options and choices. It teaches that each person has a unique voice and a right to her opinion.

The talking stick is also an important tool for creating sacred time. In order for the talking piece to work, both the speaker and the listeners need to be in present time. The talking piece encourages this.

A feeling of compassion is generated as the talking piece passes from hand to hand, and this state of compassion is the building block of community. Soon it becomes evident how much we are all concerned with the same issues and connected to the same great Spirit.

Drums and Rattles

For centuries, almost all healing ceremonies used rattles and drums to syncopate bodily rhythms and energies and to drive away unwanted spirits. The wisdom of the rattle encourages us to "Wake up! Wake up!" The soul of the drum urges us to "Listen to the heartbeat of the Earth. It is the heartbeat of all things." Drums are used to bring us into harmony with Mother Earth.

While the human voice (chanting, singing, sounding) is powerful alone, the power is increased geometrically if someone is beating a drum or shaking a rattle.

Drums

The real power of drumming is the feeling you get, the energy you circulate. Drumming echoes the beat of your pulse and magnifies it. It resonates in every cell of your body. It alters your consciousness.

Circles based on shamanic or American Indian traditions use the drum to call in spirits and to help them in their journeying.

You'll find several kinds of drums in pagan rituals, including toy drums, hollowed out tree trunks and conga drums. Three other types of drums are commonly used: frame drums, tom-toms and doumbeks.

Frame drums may be the oldest of the drums. A frame

drum's diameter is greater than its height. On one-headed frame drums there are often leather fastenings gathered into a ring on the back. You can hold the drum by the ring or by a thong in the rim, or you can rest it on your thigh while you strike it with a leather-tipped mallet or your fingertips. On Native American two-headed frame drums, one head (which has a slightly higher pitch) is named for Father Sky, and the other (which has a slightly lower pitch) is named for Mother Earth. Drumming patterns use one or both sides, and sometimes set up dialogues between masculine and feminine energies. Traditionally, men have tended to use mallets and women their hands, but many women use mallets because you can't make enough noise with bare hands.

Tom-toms are taller than they are round and vary in size from a few inches to the yards-wide drums that four men play together at Native American powwows. You can decorate tom-toms and frame drums with ribbons, beads, feathers, shells and totems which are tied to the frame, or you can paint designs on the heads.

Doumbeks are especially popular with pagans and harmonize beautifully with other percussion instruments. They are the womb-shaped drums you find in Middle Eastern belly-dancing orchestras. They are made of clay, hammered copper, brass or nickel-plated tin, and they have skin or artificial membrane (mylar) heads.

Rattles

You can purchase rattles from instrument and import stores in all shapes, sizes and materials, representing all cultures of the world. You can buy elaborate gourd rattles at Native American stores or at powwows, or you can make a rattle out of an empty water bottle (six-pack size). Be sure the bottle is completely dry inside, then pour in about one-fourth cup (total) of a combination of popcorn, rice, dried beans, beads and tiny shells. Shake the rattle, adjusting the amount and proportion of ingredients until the sound pleases you, then glue the cap on. Decorate the neck of the bottle with ribbons, feathers— whatever you please.

Sticks, Tambourines and Rainsticks

In addition to drums and rattles, other percussion instruments are also used in circle, including sticks, tambourines and rainsticks.

You can buy beautiful hardwood sticks from instrument or music stores, or purchase two pieces of broomstick from a lumberyard. The best sticks are Mexican *claves*, which have a musical tone because they're made of rosewood, ebony or similar tropical woods. Broomsticks are much less melodic, but they do make the rhythm. The sticks—beaten together—should be six inches to one foot in length.

Tambourines—which are both shaken and tapped—come in many sizes and prices. Some women paint the rims of their tambourines or put ribbons through the finger holes.

Rainsticks, which are usually made of bamboo, can be very expensive, but you need only a small one (two- to three-feet long) to use as a musical instrument. Tipped up and down or shaken, rainsticks are filled with beans and shells that fall against baffles inside the length of the stick.

Even with all the information I've provided, the work of starting a circle can be difficult and lonely. You may not succeed with your first attempt. If this happens, know that you aren't alone. Many successful circles started out the same way. It is important to continue trying because every attempt to create a circle sets in motion a healing energy. Even if this healing energy is not realized in the way you envisioned, it does not mean there has been no positive effect. And I guarantee that if you persevere, you will find a community of women with which to circle.

In Appendix II you will find a listing of active circles and other resources to help you connect with others who are circling. While the optimal situation is to have a circle community where you live, you may have to travel in order to participate in an existing circle. You will find that even traveling long distances is worth the time and energy in terms of enhancing your life. Circling has such a strong bonding effect that a feeling of community and communion can be established even if the members live hundreds of miles apart. Many women plan their year so that their vacations and holidays are spent in a circling community.

We are, indeed, a global community. Whether that community begins in our own neighborhood or extends across the miles, it is vital that each of us feel a part of it and of the larger circle of women.

PART FOUR

Women Circling
the Earth

TWELVE

The Women Who Are Circling the Earth

*If we are going to live on this planet
and truly celebrate life, then it is time to come
home. . . . Let's take the energy we have created in
this book to create a circle. Imagine being a part of
a great planetary circle committed to life and
wholeness. Imagine joining hands with others like
you who are seeking wholeness and healing for their
own selves and others. Feel the power that comes
from joining hands with like-minded people.
If you can't feel it, imagine it. Know that, step by
step, we are working on a wonderful healing
journey for all life. You are now part of an unseen
circle, a circle of love held together by people and
helping spirits. Know the circle is supporting you on
your own soul's journey. Please take from the power*

*of the circle when you need to, and give back to it
when you have some extra to give. Know that
circles don't end—they continue. . . .*

SANDRA INGERMAN
SOUL RETRIEVAL

I n this final section we focus on how women are symbolically and literally circling the Earth in order to connect with others and pass on circle principles. First you
will meet some of the leaders of the women's circle movement. Each will share with you her concerns, her triumphs
and her visions. Then you will learn how you, too, can join
the circle and become a "woman circling the earth."

As you have seen throughout this book, there are many
people actively working with the healing potential of
circles, and more and more people are being called to this
work every day. In this chapter you will be introduced to
more of the leaders in the circle movement, and you will
further get to know some of the leaders you met earlier in
the book.

All of these women have dedicated their life to circle
and made circle their way of life. As Christina Baldwin
says, "Circle is a spiritual practice, a social practice and a
social movement." All are doing work that is important
for women in particular, but also crucial for every being
on the planet—as well as for the planet itself.

Christina Baldwin

Christina travels throughout North America facilitating circles and training people to start their own PeerSpirit Circles. Her book, *Calling the Circle: The First and Future Culture,* has been published in the United States and the United Kingdom, and there are plans for other translation editions.

When I called her home, which overlooks Puget Sound in Washington state, and asked to interview her by phone, there was a pause on the other end of the line. After a few seconds she said, "I'm lighting a candle here at my desk so we can have this conversation in council space." This is a woman who really walks her talk.

Christina wrote the first edition of *Calling the Circle* in 1993 and 1994, and it was published by a small press. In 1998 she extensively revised the book and it was republished by Bantam.

Beverly: Isn't it unusual to rewrite a book so quickly?

Christina: I think it's indicative of how fast our concept of the circle is evolving. The circle never completely disappeared, but for a long time it was seen as child's play, or a form of meeting that remained outside the mainstream, not something that a person could take to the office or bring home from the office.

Beverly: What do you think is changing? Why are our perceptions shifting?

Christina: The Twelve-Step program reintroduced the circle over fifty years ago, employing a model very similar to the three principles of PeerSpirit. In any Twelve-Step program, anywhere in the world, you will find chairs in a circle, leadership that is rotating, responsibility shared and the group relying on Spirit for guidance. Even those who have never been in a Twelve-Step program have been affected since this movement set a strong imprint of the circle back into our culture. Then the civil rights and peace movements experimented with council and consensus based on Gandhi's work. Then came the women's movement and the early consciousness-raising circles, which have been followed by other movements for recognition and community cohesion—the men's movement, the gay and lesbian movement, the empowerment of elders and so on. And, well, books help change things. Starhawk began writing about the circle in the early 1980s, and now, at the end of the 1990s, there are half a dozen new books on the circle. I think we are looking carefully at the circle, asking how it can be adapted and honored, rather than how to keep it marginalized.

Beverly: How do you describe the special energy the circle can create?

Christina: The circle creates containment. The way meetings are usually held, attention is haphazard. Pagers buzz; people answer or place phone calls when someone right in front of them is in the middle of a sentence. People come and go from the table or room. We get caught up moving at a fast, mechanized pace and have forgotten the basic practices of communication and respect, and the components of clear decision making.

Calling a circle creates an energetic container and a distinction between getting to the meeting and being in the meeting. Something has to stop and something else needs to begin. The pace needs to slow. When a circle is called it gives people a chance to look up and look around. Beepers are turned off, papers are moved over. People get ready to attend to each other and attend to the business at hand. Women in circle do this—they light a candle, have a moment of silence, read a poem. There's a starting point and what happens after that is held differently.

When the circle is in place our words are received by attentive listeners—like pouring water into a chalice. The circle allows everyone's voice to be heard, everyone's contribution to be appreciated by others, even if the wisdom is coming from an unexpected source. In indigenous cultures people traditionally listen for the voice of wisdom, no matter who it comes from. When we invite wisdom to come forth it is amazing what happens.

Beverly: Would you say there is a type of person who benefits the most from your work? If so, how would you describe this type of person?

Christina: I think a better way of putting this is, "What are the attributes of the contributor?" The people I see who are most deeply sustained by circle and most able to contribute have a sense of maturity. They are usually graduates of some kind of personal growth work, whether recovery or therapy. They have an ability to assess their behavior and its impact on the group. For example, if a woman comes into her circle on a particular night and says, "I need time to share what I'm going through," it allows the circle to respond with a sense of volunteerism. A mood of willingness and cooperation develops because each person has been honored by being asked. This is different than when someone commandeers group time and energy by having needs for attention that are not negotiated.

Beverly: But doesn't this constant negotiating make the circle feel stilted?

Christina: Occasionally, but it also has dividends. When the moment is smooth, the exchange is barely noticed. A woman asks, her circle responds, their hearts remain open to each other and what happens has a deep component of healing. And then, when the moment is not smooth, their practice with each other allows them to enter into truthful dialogues that are contained within the circle, that are held by the history of compassion they have with each other.

I do run into people who are highly resistant to structure, afraid that structure will interfere with the heart's longing. But over and over again in the circle, I find structure helps fulfill the heart's longing. For example, if I'm going to share a vulnerable piece of my story, I want certain structures in place: confidentiality, no judgment, the assurance that you are also taking care of yourself while you are listening or interacting with me, and that someone will have the sense to help us pause and call for guidance. That's when the circle's full magic occurs.

Beverly: Most of us tend to focus on what the group can do for us.

Christina: I think this is because most groups are fundamentally competitive. Competition is culturally ingrained in all of us. As well as asking "How can the circle benefit me?", being in circle gives us a chance to ask, "What serves? How can I benefit the situation?" In circle we are always on two tracks at the same time: what the self wants and what the group wants.

Beverly: I understand that your work is not confined to women only, but do you agree that women's circles play a significant role in helping to heal the Earth and bringing needed change to our consciousness?

Christina: Yes. Especially when we practice our ability to hold both the personal and the collective in creative tension. People make decisions which appear reasonable or life-affirming individually, but which have unreasonable and life-negating impact on the wider community or natural world. This is not usually intentional; we need retraining to see our interconnectedness. Because the circle is a container, energetically the impact of everything we say and do is mirrored back to us. This is not always comfortable, but it sure is a teaching tool!

And for women, using the circle itself as a teacher has changed the end of the twentieth century. We are telling our stories, discovering our similarities and differences, and creating community. This gives us the courage to confront the larger culture and stand up for the kinds of change that align with deeply feminine values.

Beverly: So do you think women are in the forefront here? That women come to circle naturally, while men often have difficulty with it?

Christina: I don't know, because I think the most intimate circles of men often occur without women present, just as the most intimate circles of women often occur without men present. I think this may be too bad, but it's where Western culture has taken us. I see the circle as a deeply feminine form, but not because it belongs to women. It calls for attributes of open-heartedness that have been labeled as feminine. I believe our only hope as a species is to find ways to reintegrate the split between defined masculine and feminine energies—to become more fully human and more fully one of the planet's creatures, not the planet's rapists.

Beverly: If someone is interested in calling a PeerSpirit Circle, what is the best way to go about it? Do they need to attend your workshops or can they learn enough from reading your book, *Calling the Circle?*

Christina: People have done both. Those with experience facilitating groups often feel comfortable starting a circle after reading the book. Others feel they need the workshops. We encourage people to read the book and if they feel they resonate with it to go ahead and call the circle in an arena where they are comfortable. A mother who suggests to her family that people take turns speaking and listening to each other at supper and passes the salt shaker as a talking piece can have a marvelous experience of circle. If someone runs into difficulties, there are many resources becoming available.

Beverly: Do you really feel it is possible to achieve world peace through meeting in circles?

Christina: Yes. The circle is the primary unit of society. When people come into circle it triggers genetic memory because the circle is a globally indigenous form. We begin to remember, "This used to work, didn't it?" Sometimes the heart softens so suddenly, I've seen people quietly begin to cry with relief at coming home to space that is held with respect. This recognition of the circle as our birthright gives me great hope for the future. The pathway to the heart is still there, encoded within us, and as times change and the destructive aspects of western culture crumble, the circle will be with us: the light in the window, the hearth in the living room . . . the campfire. We will gather and tell our stories, and listen to each other, and ask for what we need, and offer what we can, and pray for help and guidance.

Sedonia Cahill

Sedonia Cahill is a pioneer in the women's circle movement. Her book *The Ceremonial Circle* was one of the first books on circling. She is also coauthor of *Wisdom Circles: A Guide to Self-Discovery and Community Building in Small Groups.* During her lifetime she was committed to introducing women around the world to circling and traveled all over the United States and Canada, to Ukraine, Asia and Australia, helping people start circles. She also lead vision quests, and circles are the heart of this work. She had a master's degree in psychology.

Sedonia died on February 1, 2000, just weeks before this book was going to press. She was killed instantly in a car accident while vacationing in Morocco. She would have been sixty-four years old on February 12.

At the time of her death she was working on another book entitled, *Living from the Inside Out.* I don't know if her coauthor has plans to finish the book or not.

Myself and many others have been deeply saddened by her death. Sedonia and I weren't friends; we'd only connected during the time of the writing of this book. Yet during this time I was impressed with her warmth, generosity, graciousness and her dedication to her work.

LaWanna Durbin, one of my spiritual teachers, explained to me that we are living in a time of great intensity and that many people are choosing to check out now, not to avoid these times, but to assist in another way. This intuitively felt like the truth to me for Sedonia who has recently been looking to Spirit for "a new engagement." Her affairs were perfectly and tidily in order, and she seemed to leave no loose ends, only the thousands of people whose lives she had touched and who mourn her passing.

Since the interviews in this book may be the last words we hear from this warm, wise and wonderful woman, I am especially honored and pleased to offer them to you.

Beverly: How did you first come to the practice of circling?

Sedonia: In 1955, when I was a sophomore in college, I attended a weekend retreat led by a very charismatic campus pastor. I was a very unhappy person and usually avoided the activities held by my prestigious social sorority because I felt so out of place. But we were all required to attend this retreat and so I tried to endure it. As a closure to the weekend the minister spoke a few words and then asked that all of us—about fifty young women—stand and hold hands in a circle. I responded with little enthusiasm, taking the hands of the two young women nearest me, closed my eyes and half listened to the words of the prayer.

What happened during the next few minutes was of such power and magnitude that it literally shaped the direction of my life. In those brief moments I no longer felt like a lonely, lost, directionless child. I suddenly felt like a member of a strong group—a tribe. I felt my mind becoming one with those of the others; we were, in fact, one. It was no longer necessary to compare myself with the others and find myself lacking. In that moment, in that circle, we were all equal.

I wish I could say that those wonderful feelings of unity and belonging stayed with me, but instead I was left with a spiritual hunger which became a prime motivator in my life.

Beverly: How did you first come to women's circles?

Sedonia: Even though I participated in numerous circles over the next several years—circles for peace, circles of dancing, circles of shared sacraments, circles surrounding newly emerging holy men and sages, prophets and gurus—and even though I found some of the freedom I sought for myself and my family, something was missing. I began to meditate, do yoga and T'ai Chi, study the tarot and I Ching, cabala and magic, macrobiotics, the Tao and Sufi dancing. But I found that I wasn't really connecting with any of it. As soon as the novelty of each new experience wore off I was ready to move on.

Throughout all of this I began to make an important observation. At each large spiritual gathering everyone on the stage and at the podium was male. In the spiritual communities the leadership was always in the hands of men. I began to wonder, could this be the reason I was having difficulty relating?

It was during this time, in the early and middle seventies, that I began to sit in circles with women. I joined a small consciousness-raising group where we explored and shared ways we had been used, abused, deceived, undermined and misunderstood. The anger was necessary, but for me it was also important to move through it and use it as a catalyst. Because of these circles miraculous changes began to occur. I began to see women as beautiful sisters to be loved and trusted, and slowly, I began to see myself in the same way.

There were many women's gatherings in those days, usually in the form of circles. Slowly, out of all this sharing and focusing on problems, usually with political solutions, women's spirituality emerged. I'm happy to report that I have been privileged to meet and work with many fine teachers along the way these past years—women who are calling and leading circles, women whose commitment is deep and whose visions are strong.

Beverly: Do you believe that women play a special role in the circle movement?

Sedonia: Absolutely. The current round of the circle movement had its genesis in those early women's consciousness groups. I definitely see women in the forefront. I believe women are more interested in change and community building than men are. Circling comes easily to women, so easily that men often express envy about the work we do in circles. It is natural for women to not have a leader. When men are around, women are horrifyingly willing to give power to them. Women are almost always willing to share power. The circle is all about shared power. When men do meet in circle they are sitting in a feminine field and have essentially become part of the feminine force.

Beverly: Can you describe the special energy the circle can create?

Sedonia: I have a story to tell about that. Fourteen years ago I was living in a little redwood house in Bodega, California. Some women asked if they could use my house for a circle. One of the women who came was blind. During the circle she asked if the house was circular, which it was. She could feel the circular energy of the house.

The special energy of the circle has to do with how energy is moved. Energy gets moved around very easily in circle.

Beverly: What are some of the benefits of meeting in circle that you have experienced?

Sedonia: There is a safety in circle. I always say the circle is "a safe place to do unsafe things." It is a place to push your edges and be witnessed. I think it is because everyone in the circle has equal access to the center.

Circles can be demanding. There's a lot expected of you. If there wasn't I wouldn't be interested. First of all, you have to show up. If someone doesn't show up it's noticed by everyone. It creates an energy leak. Second, you have to be present in the circle. Third, you need to recognize that every person in the circle is a mirror for you.

Beverly: How important is circling in your life?

Sedonia: Circling is my spiritual practice. I am a creator and participant of circles. Circles of all kinds. The circle of my women's lodge that meets every full moon and new moon. The circle of prayer and gratefulness that I share with those with whom I break bread. The teaching and praying circles I conduct in conjunction with the vision quests I lead. Circles with women my age who are dedicated to becoming wise elders together.

Circles of exploration with others determined to understand ourselves more deeply and fully. Circles of women and men daring to speak the truth to one another. Circles in settings such as corporations and large hospitals. Circles of music making and dancing co-created with friends. Circles to honor birth and death, marriage and separation, coming of age and other important rites of passage. Talking staff circles with peers to resolve issues or define and refine our perceptions and values. Prayer lodge circles and all night drumming and praying circles. Large ceremonial circles that I lead or ones that are led by women shamans. Circles and more circles. Thus the circle grows.

Beverly: What changes have you seen in participants of your circles or circles you've been part of?

Sedonia: I have seen so many changes. I have been meeting in one circle for fifteen years. People grow and become more and more themselves. They heal. They find more effective ways to be in the world. In one of the circles I am involved with we go away together for four days and nights. I've seen some very deep changes in myself and these women.

The level of healing is boundless. Sometimes it is just from being witnessed—our need to be seen is as deep as our need for food and shelter. It is very hard to be witnessed without interpretation, judgment or fixing. It is very hard to get someone to hear, really hear. Once I've told a story and have really been heard I am through with the story. It has been heard. It is so magical. But most people have to learn to do it. That is one of the many benefits of circles that teach witnessing.

Beverly: How do you see circle work benefiting the world at large?

Sedonia: Circles create energy that radiates out into the world. They slowly break down hierarchical patterns. Circles help women to find their voice. I am particularly interested in helping older women find their voices. They have things to say that the world needs to hear.

Beverly: Do you see a benefit in women and men having separate circles?

Sedonia: Definitely. For both it is a place to find out who you are as a woman or man. There is a certain comfort in being with other women in circle. Mixed gender circles are difficult; women and men talk about very difficult things. If they haven't met first in their same sex circles, they can't open up in the same way.

Beverly: What is some of the feedback you get from women in your circles?

Sedonia: The feedback I always get from women when they attend their first circle is, "I feel like I've come home." Personally, I am most at home in a circle. If I have to stand on a stage I feel very uncomfortable.

More than anything, circles are a place to develop compassion. To discover we are all one. We must develop compassion in order to discover this.

Beverly: Do you plan on writing any more books about circles?

Sedonia: Yes, I have written a new book with my coauthor, Susanne Peterman, entitled, *Living from the Inside Out.*

Beverly: In 1990 you were part of a group of thirteen alternative healers who were invited to teach in the Soviet Union. As part of your work there you had the privilege of leading some very large circles. What was that experience like?

Sedonia: I was delighted at how quickly the women there took to the circle. They loved it. The Russian women really touched my heart, they were so sweet. It was especially sweet when we would sing songs to them in English and they would sing back their songs in Russian. There was a special poignancy in this for me and a very deep gratitude that the cold war had ended—that we could join our voices over all the miles and the politics, that we were so much more similar than different. We left a drum, rattles, a shell, feather and sage with a woman in each city who was interested in keeping the circle going.

The Russian women had been through a difficult time and knew they were facing still more difficulties. It was a very big thing for most of them to be able to speak out, but it was very beneficial for them to be able to do so.

Beverly: Do you feel there is a commonality between all women, all cultures?

Sedonia: Yes. It touches me how easily women reach out to one another. How we feel connected to how another woman feels. Perhaps it is because we all share the experience of having children or being able to have them—our nurturing instincts.

Kay Pranis

Kay Pranis has recently been honored by the Make the Peace Campaign for her efforts in peacemaking. Kay's life is a "woman's story" and a metaphor for the circle. She became a community activist through her role as a mother and her commitment to parenting. After sixteen years at home, with no formal training and no credentials in the field, she took the only job offered to her. It just happened to be in the criminal justice system. Suddenly she went from being home-centered to being nationally recognized and in the forefront of restorative justice in Minnesota.

Kay came to her work with circles in a very roundabout way (no pun intended). As a restorative justice planner her job is to promote restorative approaches within the criminal justice system. Shortly after beginning her job she was introduced to the process known as Family Group Conferencing, an alternative to court for juvenile offenders based on the Maori tradition of allowing family members to determine the appropriate way for offenders to make restitutions for their crimes. Kay was instrumental in setting up the first program of this type at the Woodbury police department.

Fifteen months later she met a judge from Yukon, Canada, who taught her the method of circling being used by aboriginal people. Kay facilitated getting trainers and looking for sites in urban areas. (One such site is an African-American neighborhood in Northern Minneapolis.) She has now helped develop circle trainings and circle programs in dozens of settings.

While Kay's job usually involves community organizing and the training support and coaching of others, she found she was drawn to getting personally involved with conducting and participating in circles:

Circles seemed to be organically part of who I am. I went to work eleven years ago after raising my kids. Though often asked to facilitate discussions I always felt inadequate as a facilitator since most facilitators are expected to guide a group toward a particular goal. But with the circle process the facilitator only needs to create a safe space and encourage the best out of everyone else there. I'm also very interested in the healing power of narrative, the opportunity for people to tell their stories. Circles provide the space for personal narrative.

I began to see my work as about empowerment, and the circle as the most fundamental form of grassroots democracy. This touched me profoundly. I saw how people were able to draw things out of themselves they didn't know they had, and I found this fascinating and wanted to work with the process hands-on. I was also drawn to the very conscious spirituality (although without any special structure).

The outcome is consistently good but not through efforts to control. I've learned from aboriginal people that my responsibility is to stay clear, not to understand, but to let the good of creation come through me.

Kay, like so many of the women committed to circles, was called to her work. Circles have become her passion. Although most of her work centers around the Restorative Justice Movement, Kay is an advocate for circles of all kinds. She now provides trainings (along with Barry Stuart, her Yukon mentor) for people in many different settings, including schools. "Our entire training is done in the circle," Kay comments. "We use the process to teach the process."

During our interview Kay summed up her work and her life this way: "My work is about creating spaces where people can be in loving connection with one another."

Sandra Ingerman

Sandra teaches workshops on shamanism around the world. She has conducted workshops in Australia, New Zealand, Austria, Switzerland and throughout the United States.

Beverly: Could you tell me what significance the symbol of the circle has for you personally and in your work?

Sandra: The circle is incredibly important for me. My work is my spiritual path and so there is no distinction between how the circle affects me and my work—they are one and the same. In shamanism the circle represents power. Years ago I met a physicist who told me that the true definition of power from a physics point of view is the ability to use energy.

To me the circle also represents unity, wholeness and love. It represents protection so that when we do our spiritual work in my workshops, people can feel free to go as far into the spiritual realms as they want to, knowing that the circle is there holding the space. So I view the circle as the container. In all my workshops, especially the longer residential ones where more personal stories come up and personal sharing occurs, the container can keep expanding to hold all the emotions and everything else that comes up.

There's always a place for any person in any circle I create. I never say it's not okay to be a certain way in a circle. The circle, as long as I create the space with the group correctly, can hold anything that comes up. When we come together in a circle to do spiritual work, keeping in mind the definition of power being the ability to use energy, it is always amazing to me—the magic that happens and how much more energy there is available for all of us to do our own spiritual work and spiritual healing.

One of the constant complaints I get from people who take workshops with the Foundation of Shamanic Studies is that I have such strong workshops. I'm sorry I have such strong shamanic experiences in the workshops since this bothers some people. Ironically, my own experience—when I'm home doing this work by myself—is dull compared to what I have in the workshops. I really feel that the powerful experiences in workshops are because of all the energy that's available and how much heart is present there.

Beverly: How do you feel your workshops benefit participants?

Sandra: I teach various types of workshops. I teach people shamanic journeying in order to learn how to access information for themselves so they can take back their spiritual authority in life. I don't think I have to explain to anyone in our culture that it's essential for our survival and for the survival of our planet that we all have direct revelation right now, that we create our own spiritual connections and that we take back our own spiritual authority. We need to learn how to live our lives in harmony and in balance again. That's the main thing I'm trying to bring forth in my workshops: How do we get back into harmony again? How do we bring our lives back into balance again? Where is the meaning in life?

I think that life without meaning equals despair, and when I look around at our culture I see a tremendous number of people in despair. So my main goal in all of my shamanic teaching is to try and help people find deeper meaning in life and make their own spiritual connections. That's been my obsession since writing *Welcome Home* and *A Fall to Grace.*

I also teach workshops on healing—on how to use different shamanic healing methods to deal with the spiritual aspect of illness. Yet, even though we look at how to heal individuals, how to heal the planet, the focus of the workshop for me is always how to develop your spiritual connection so that you are your own spiritual authority. What I feel I have learned from—or been given by—clients and the Spirit is that one of the reasons there's so much disease on the planet today is that other life forms want to live more than we do. We've lost our passion for life.

Beverly: What changes have you seen in the participants of your workshops?

Sandra: To experience the love of the spirits, the unconditional love that comes from nonordinary reality, is such a wonderful gift for participants. This is especially important since we don't get the love we need as human beings. The excitement of being able to make one's own spiritual connections and reconnect with nature again is another gift. Because of modern technology we've become so disconnected from nature. In shamanism, everything has a life, everything has a spirit. Being able to communicate this message to people, having them go back to the community, able to see how the souls of other things are affected by human actions is so gratifying. People also begin to feel more in harmony with the elements, the river of life, everything that's around us. Then they go back to their own communities and share what they've learned. I think that is really beautiful.

One of the things that happens for participants in my workshops, especially in residential workshops where we're living and working together for a week, is that for the first time in their lives they experience what true community is. They say, "I want this in my life. How do I get it?" My response to them is, "Now that you know what you're seeking, now that you know what you're trying to create, and now that you are able to set your own intention, life is going to be a lot easier for you. Now you can start to create community around you, because you know what community means."

In my soul retrieval workshops—where we're looking at bringing back lost vitality, lost essence, lost life force—one of the sessions is spent looking at how the soul of a place, the land, the

Earth, can actually be traumatized by certain events. I teach people how to perform rituals in community to help to bring back the soul of that traumatized place. People begin to realize that the Earth has a soul, nature has a soul, everything has soul. And that soul can become damaged, unhealthy. But every time a community ritual is created to help heal a city, a community, a piece of land, there is a change in consciousness and this keeps spreading as more people are educated in this way.

Beverly: Do you feel it's ironic that you teach ancient rituals and traditions to the very groups of people who first practiced them?

Sandra: Of course. But evolution is a circular spiral. There's a real ebb and flow in evolution and yes, certain traditions are returning. The spiral takes on a different shape and moves and grows and then it comes back again to other people who carry it forth for awhile. Then the wisdom is handed on to still other people. Today we're coming back to embrace the feminine principle of wholeness and for now it is women who hold this wisdom and who are sharing this wisdom.

Beverly: What have you learned from your travels?

Sandra: I've learned that if you don't know your past you don't know your future. The youth of today in this country don't believe there's even going to be a future because they don't know their past. Those in other countries have more of a sense of history than we do. Most of us know very little about our ancestors or the countries our ancestors came from. And so I've learned to appreciate the ancientness in other countries. The power that has been there and will continue to be there.

Also, I see a common bond among women in all countries. One of the things that we have forgotten through what we call the evolutionary process and through socialization is that we are part of nature. And as part of nature, all women embrace the goddess. All women are nurturers, all women embrace the receptive principle of life. Basically, we're all beautiful flowers in our own way. We all bloom differently, but we all have the same source. And so when I travel to different countries and I think I'm going to meet different kinds of people, what has always blown me away is that no matter where I go, no matter what circle I sit in, I find that all of us are truly the same.

Beverly: What role do you feel the circle plays in bringing peace, understanding and harmony to the world?

Sandra: This goes back to what I said earlier, that when you come into the circle you see that we're all the same. This breaks down the feeling of separateness. The feeling of separateness from others is where that whole territorial stuff comes in, which is the cause of war. But as people sit in circle together and see how people are so much the same—how we have the same fears and hopes and desires in life, how we all want to be loved, healed and nurtured—the circle starts to naturally create peace. Also, as we sit in circle we see that we are not separate, we get more of an understanding that we're part of life, we're part of something much greater than ourselves.

Ellie Mercer

You met Ellie Mercer earlier in the book discussing the need for women to have a safe, respectful place in which to honor the true nature of their spiritual journeys. She has created such a place within the form of circle. Ellie is an ordained minister in the liberal Protestant tradition and has co-lead workshops with Meredith Jordan in a variety of different settings, including one at the

University of New England on the effects of abuse on spiritual development.

> **Beverly:** I understand that the circle work you were doing was instrumental in your giving up part of your church ministry.
>
> **Ellie:** Yes. The circles Meredith and I offered were so exciting to me, and filled such an important need, that I decided to give up part of my time in church ministry. This was a difficult decision with profound consequences for me as well as for my family. I gave up an identity with which I had become comfortable and I gave up any sense of financial security. A minister is in a position of power. In the churches I used to serve, I found that people projected all kinds of positive things onto me. There were times when I would revel in the delight of such projections. It felt so good. And then I would remember who I really was, and I would find myself wanting to say, "You don't know the real me. You don't know how I, too, struggle with questions of faith. Do you want to know who I *really* am? Would you be surprised if you knew about my fear, my doubt etc.?"
>
> I like the equality I experience in a circle. Both power and responsibility are shared by all. There's an honesty and authenticity that the circle requires of us which works better for me than the traditional models of ministry.
>
> Now I offer circles both outside the church and within the church. There's still a lot of resistance on the parts of people in the church who want their ministers to be placed on a pedestal. But slowly, people are coming to understand the value of a new way to gather and share their spiritual lives, hopes, and dreams.
>
> Meredith and I also conduct circles on issues of "shadow and projection," which we believe exist at the root of all harm human beings cause one another. I have learned things about myself that I would never have learned if it were not for the circle. I'll watch my own shadow material leak out onto a group, usually

through humor, and I'll see the group grow silent. I see when I've breached the safety of the group. This is something I would never have learned about myself in traditional kinds of gatherings.

Beverly: I am sure there are some people who think you've gone off the deep end, or that you are no longer doing God's work.

Ellie: In my ministry in a previous church, I was often belittled and diminished because of my great interest in the creation-centered spirituality of such people as Matthew Fox. I was labeled a heretic. And even though it was often said in a joking way, it was nevertheless shaming.

When I have confined my work to the church, I have experienced a constant struggle with the structure. Through circles, I've found a way to express missing parts of my experience. I've found freedom and authenticity to be in full expression of my own faith life.

Our signature work is a depth-level program of multi-faith spiritual direction which we call "Building Our Spirits to be Strong." We live in tenuous times, which call for all of us to stand in full responsible stewardship for the Earth and all its creatures, including the human family. To do this, we need people of strong spirit, people who can withstand the demands of a profit-driven, consumerist culture. We need people to build a world where every member of the human family has a place in the circle.

Most people who attend conventional churches have not done the kind of inner work that allows them to stand up against the culture as people who are strong in spirit. They attend church hoping the minister will be the one to tell them how to live their lives. These people have a difficult time understanding that each of us is personally responsible for our relationship with God—no minister can mediate that for us—and to be that responsible, we must do the deep inner work that builds this relationship. This is what we mean by the term "doing your inner work."

People who have been in Twelve-Step programs or therapy

have often done a great deal of "inner work," and are looking for communities of faith where they can gather with like-minded others. Unfortunately, they don't often find that when they attend church.

For this reason, Meredith and I have created "Building our Spirits to Be Strong" as a program of spiritual direction, or a tutorial, which people attend twice a month. We ask them to commit to the following requirements: to develop and follow a consistent spiritual practice, to study contemporary and ancient wisdom literature for guidance, and to participate in a project of service to others.

This entire group meets together in a circle of ritual and worship once a month. In the circle, they gather with others who are devoting a period of their lives to deepening their inner work. This combination of individual and circle work is a powerful spiritual model for personal and collective maturation and transformation. We hope churches will one day see the value of building authentic spiritual community in this way.

Carol Proudfoot-Edgar

Carol Proudfoot-Edgar has traveled to Ireland, Finland, the Netherlands and Israel in her work and shamanic explorations. Her hope is to spend more time in other countries—weaving webs of connection with the people of other places and the spirits of their homelands. Most of the requests she receives for working abroad are made by women who come to the United States to learn from her. Subsequently, she travels to their country to teach and assist in the formation of an ongoing circle there. She has also helped to form a Ring of Circles through the Internet that offers journeys, healing, and ongoing conversations about the power of circling and supporting the linking of circles worldwide.

Beverly: Could you talk a little about how your circles are organized?

Carol: First, to be a circle is to recognize that every person matters or else there is no circle—there is a leak in the vessel. In addition, every person's perspective matters because, depending where you are in circle, you perceive differently. All these different perspectives constitute the circle. In my circle work, we each bring some object representing either the theme upon which we are focused or some aspect of our spiritual awareness at this point in our lives. These objects, together on the altar, represent our beginning place as a group of individuals forming a circle to learn together. I can learn more about me, as well as you, if I extend my perceptions to include the world as you experience it. On a simple level this can be done by paying attention to the sacred object you brought to the circle.

I recommend that individuals shift where they sit in circle to get different perspectives. In many circles there is a tendency to sit in the same place each session, somewhat like making one's nest or creating a safe place. However, if you want to learn about changing yourself and get support as you change, then it helps to shift where you are in circle—literally. By shifting one comes to embody the understanding that circle, and we ourselves as circle, are motion, change—not static or stagnant.

Currently, my work is focused on helping people learn how to create, participate in and sustain shamanic circles. Over the years I have taught circles with specific themes—the medicine wheel, divination, death and dying, spring renewal rites—but underlying all these themes is the principle of creating sacred circles.

I teach retreats focused on the "Spirits of Place, of Homeland." With these retreats I am teaching how to know and attend to our interrelatedness with one another and with all beings with whom we share a place, an ecosystem. I think it is important to be specific in our attention. Then our effects will accumulate into global transformations. For example, I do circle retreats in various ecosystems—the Pacific Northwest coast, the Southeast, the desert and the Midwest areas of North America—as well as in specific countries in Europe—Ireland and Holland. These retreats are for both men and women.

In addition, I've developed a special interest in women practicing shamanism. I lead various women's circles, and I am also beginning my second, three-year program in "Women, Shamanism and Bear Medicine."

Beverly: How are your circles structured?

Carol: My workshops are primarily experiential although I bring written material, tell stories and have discussions about the nature of our activities together. This includes talks about how to create circles, how to speak one's self in circle, and how to create a safe and compassionate environment. About half of our time is spent outdoors since I think some of our healing and our greatest teachers are found within the natural world.

Although I have well-designed plans for the workshops, I listen to the issues being raised within the circle, listen to the dreams arising and the messages that come from shamanic journeys. After the first or second circle session, I put aside my plans and allow the organicity of the circle to emerge. It's not that I don't use my plans, it's just that new activities may be called for or my plans will unfold in a different way than I thought previous to the actual gathering.

Beverly: How do you see your circles benefiting the world at large?

Carol: Since the circles which I teach include people from around the world, I am privileged to have continuing conversations about how this work influences them when they return to their homelands. I hear of their renewed focus on their natural world, healing activities and work for peace, and I hear how they establish circles to help them sustain their spiritual practice and transformations. Many of us maintain our circle support through e-mail. Through this process we can do shamanic work on behalf of one another and keep the global connections lively.

I don't have much hope for real change nor for the future of our planet unless we come to know our profound oneness with all other beings, unless we return "home" and know ourselves as embodied spirit, sharing this universe with other embodied spirits. I don't think one "understands" or has this knowing except through direct experience. Once one has such experiences, it is impossible to return to the old way of separation. Once the thirst for true relationship is slaked, even temporarily, the knowing this is possible becomes part of one's memory. It is the beginning point of change. My hope is that the work I do at least provides opportunity for individuals to experience this "beginning."

Beverly: Do you agree that women's circles play a significant role in helping to heal the Earth and bring needed change to our consciousness, and that there is value in women and men having separate circles?

Carol: When I originally began offering workshops they were always mixed groups—men and women. Then several years ago, I was invited to help lead a large women's gathering outside Tucson, Arizona. From that gathering, women began requesting that I come work with them. Over time I found myself discovering the value in groups for women only.

Since my teaching is based on shamanic principles and methods, some of my male colleagues were concerned about me teaching shamanic circles for women only. So I began

studying this issue of separate shamanic circles, both historically and through my direct experiences with both types of
circles. What has evolved is a real commitment to women studying and practicing shamanism together. I think that women's
ways of knowing and being in the world are quite different from
men's. The difference is to be honored, not to be a source of
conflict.

I've come to see how women know more about joining,
putting together; men about separating, taking apart. Women
know more about the power of fusion; men know the power of
fission. Both powers are part of creation and of spiritual development. But we've been suffering an imbalance which has been
written about for many years now. I'm not interested in arguing
this topic, and I wouldn't want to teach only women's groups.
However, whatever new way is coming, whatever new myth is
emerging, I tend to think the impregnation has already occurred
and women are now carrying special seeds, special potential
that needs to be tapped for the birthing to occur.

As women, we carry in our bones the wisdom that has to do
with the great regenerative powers: with mothering, birthing,
rebirthing and protecting the young. I think we live in a time
when these particular women's ways of knowing are needed.

I also think there's a real place for shamanic men's circles, but
the men who will do this need to step forward. So far I don't see
this happening in the larger shamanic community so I'm assum-
ing the time is not quite right. Meanwhile, I treasure the gifts men
bring to the mixed shamanic circles I teach.

Beverly: How would you suggest implementing the concepts
of circle into family, business and community settings?

Carol: I'm interested in shamanic circles. That means circles
which have as their goal the continued strengthening of each
participant's spiritual life and the manifesting of this through
assisting other beings—all other beings.

The problem I encounter with some people who wish to implement this concept of circle into their lives is that they think it has to be some grand change, some large intervention. I'm inclined towards the simple path. One can begin in one's family, for example, by holding hands before eating, giving thanks for all the creatures who have sacrificed their lives so the family might have this food and giving thanks for all the humans who have worked so that this food might be available. When you pay attention to what you're eating—carrots, lettuce, meat, fish—you start paying attention to the cycle of giving and taking, of gratitude. Thanksgiving can be done in the simple way of "rattling" over your food together, thanking the invisible Spirit who provides for all and asking that you may also participate in providing for others.

Whether in families, business or community settings, one can call people together for certain occasions: bring drums, rattles and flutes; celebrate the changing of the seasons; bless a newborn creature; gather around someone ill or dying; honor the beginning of a project, the hiring or retiring of someone in business. In this respect, I think each time we gather in circle and honor the cyclical nature of our world or the rites of passage in people's lives, we contribute to the health of the whole planet.

But the above is different from the concept of circle as a form without a spiritual focus. Indeed, I think the circle as a form is invaluable for changing our customary linear, hierarchical, bureaucratic ways of doing business and practicing politics. Many years ago I helped to create a college (Kresge) at the University of Southern California. One of the guiding principles was to live, learn and govern ourselves through the circle form. So I am well acquainted with the powerful influence circle form can have in political, social and interpersonal dynamics.

Beverly: Are there any messages you would like to give women who are being introduced to circles for the first time?

> **Carol:** My special message is to see this as an opportunity for voicing one's self, for knowing one's connectedness with others, for joining hands and providing with others the safe vessel or container within which alchemical changes may occur and bring long desired transformations for yourself or for another. Remember to draw upon the circle's power to assist in healing for other beings. And remember there's a simple yet real potential for learning in shifting where you sit or stand in a circle. Different perspectives provide much opportunity for new wisdom.

Mary Elizabeth Thunder

Mary Elizabeth Thunder has traveled and lectured extensively in Australia, Mexico, Yucatan, Egypt, Germany, India, Italy and France. In 1994 she was invited to the United Nations in Geneva, Switzerland, as a delegate speaking to women about women's issues. Her work is dedicated to personal and community healing, living in peace within and with one another.

Her vision, entitled "Wolf Song," came as she explains from "The Voice That Echoes on the Wind" and the being of Yehwehnode or Grandmother Twylah Nitsch. Her vision was to bring elders together for laughter, stories, music, celebration and entertainment. They would be called peace elders and would represent all races: a mixture of colors to support the rainbow dreaming and to make a rainbow hoop in a sacred circle. It is her feeling that shoulder to shoulder we stand as one body, one heart, one mind, one spirit under one law, and that is the "Law of the Earth Mother." With events such as Wolf Song, we guarantee future generations the wisdom, prophecy and philosophy of the indigenous peoples.

Beverly: How did you come to the knowledge that you were to become a "Woman Circling the Earth"?

Thunder: I am part Cheyenne, Mohawk, adopted Lakota and Irish. As a sun dancer and a member-teacher of the Seneca Wolf Clan Teaching Society, my Elders feel that my being so many nationalities is a bonus, for I can move among all worlds—white, red, yellow, black.

I spent the first half of my life as a working mother, an administrator and an alcohol/drug specialist for American Indian service organizations. In 1981 I suffered a heart attack and had an afterlife experience. In response to this trauma and at the bidding of my Elders—Leonard Crow Dog, Wallace Black Elk, Grace Spotted Eagle and Rolling Thunder—I left my job at the Dallas Inter-Tribal Center to begin life on the road as a teacher.

Beverly: So it sounds as if you have a mission, a calling.

Thunder: My work is my passion and my passion is being in service to humanity and the world by answering the call of the Great Spirit, listening with respect and honor to my Elders, then "walking my talk" in integrity and truth. My name, Thunder, means truth. Many have called me a guide who gently helps each person take responsibility for her or his own expression of divinity.

Beverly: Do you primarily follow and teach Native American spirituality?

Thunder: I honor all traditions and all ways. As long as they are dedicated to the principle of "creation." I have been blessed by the Dalai Lama, and I have been honored to meet and be blessed for my work by many Eastern masters. I feel all paths lead to the Creator.

Beverly: Do you believe women have a special role in creating positive change in the world and in healing Mother Earth?

Thunder: I remember Grandma Grace Spotted Eagle saying if the world would start thinking like a woman again, if a woman ran this government, well, we would not have any war. I feel that now more than ever is the time for healing the separation: for the male to rebuild the female sides of himself and the female to rebuild the male sides of herself. I feel this is needed to counterbalance a world that is on a linear and violent tangent. Perhaps we need to go a little circular (female) instead of all linear (male) in our whole thinking process. Maybe if more people thought like mothers, they would not send their children to war!

Beverly: Although you want to help all people, it seems you have a special need to connect with and provide guidance for women.

Thunder: My adopted mother, Grace Spotted Eagle, had me promise before her death to write a book about my experiences on this path as a woman, to give other women hope that they, too, could find and actualize spirituality. I have now completed that book. It is entitled *Thunder's Grace* and is the fulfillment of that promise.

Beverly: What difference have circles made in your life?

Thunder: Circles, especially women's circles, have shown me a reflection of who I am. I feel as human beings we can't really see ourselves. I see you and I see your pain but it doesn't have anything to do with me. I have found in the world of illusions the only teachers we have about being human are other human beings. My people call the Spirit "Great Mystery," and I call us the "great mysterious." I feel that by sitting in circle, hearing people's thoughts and beliefs, and getting feedback from others, I get to see my reflection multiplied by however many people are in the circle. If there are twelve women, then that is twelve pieces of myself.

I live my life in circles. Whenever I lecture I have the room set up in a circle. When we make a family decision, it is done in a circle. We live at a ranch with all kinds of people living together. In order to get along with one another we meet in circle to discuss problems and create solutions. It feels so good—no denial, no guilt, no bad words between people, no hurt feelings—just truth and understanding.

Beverly: Are you continuing to "circle the Earth"?

Thunder: Yes. But after nine years of being on the road without a home or base, my husband, Jeff "White Horse" Hubbell, and I have founded a spiritual university where we now live. We are dedicated to maintaining a spiritual center where people of all four races and all religions are honored, where we live our life in a spiritual way and provide ceremonial land for Elders to revive themselves, and teach and meet the people. Where "special" children can come, run and play, enjoy the land or watch the antics of our buffaloes, "Starkeeper" and "Starshine," who are brand-new parents of a baby buffalo named "Rosebud." The ranch is spiritual, sacred land where people can come and take a drink of spirituality and become one with the land.

The women you have read about in this chapter have taken on the circle as their life's work. They are committed to widening the circle through their actions, workshops, trainings, books—and through their very being. I hope you have been touched and inspired by their words as much as I have. If you would like to know more about a particular woman, her work or how to structure your circle in the format that she espouses, please refer to the Appendices in the back of the book.

In the next chapter you will learn more about how you, too, can join the ever-widening circle; how you can help bring the circle to more people and bring more people to the circle.

THIRTEEN

Becoming Part of the Circle

We ourselves feel that what we are
doing is just a drop in the ocean. But if that
drop was not in the ocean, I think the ocean would
be less because of that missing drop. . . .

MOTHER TERESA

Never doubt that a small group of thoughtful,
committed citizens can change the world.
Indeed, it is the only thing that ever has.

MARGARET MEAD

We are stewards, temporarily here to
take care of our own bodies and the Earth Mother
we live on. We are here to fulfill our vision and

*individual destinies in harmony with one another
and in balance with nature. The time of the gun
and the rifle are over. The time of the Medicine
Power is here. This is the time of great
accountability and consequences for our actions.*

Scout Cloud Lee
The Circle Is Sacred

N ow that you have read the first twelve chapters of this
book many of you may feel eager to become one of
the women circling the Earth. In this chapter I will outline
what you, as an individual, can do to become part of the
circle and create change on this planet. While it may seem
to you that some of the suggestions I make are far more significant than others, please do not minimize any of them.
They are all powerful tools for changing the world. Together,
they create an energy so potent it is unfathomable.

We have already begun to see the positive energy the
circle creates. Today there are many more circles than there
were five years ago, and there are more active circles in more
nations of the world than there have been since ancient
times. On any given night, all around the world, women's
circles are meeting—in homes, backyards, community centers, churches and synagogues. Circles are commonly used
to open most spiritual and many psychological conferences
and even some business conventions.

Since I first began to write this book several years ago, a lot has happened in the circle movement. Through the years the benefits of meeting in circle have become more and more known and appreciated by a growing number of people. More circles have been formed, many in segments of the population I would never have imagined would welcome the circle. For example, this past summer I was surprised and pleased to discover that two women, Berma Bushie and Kay Pranis, have been instrumental in bringing the circle into the criminal justice system.

Circles have been introduced to almost every area of the population, including churches, small businesses, major corporations, and colleges and universities.

When the University of North Carolina decided to open its Race and Gender Institute they called upon Christina Baldwin and Ann Linnea to teach them how to have meaningful conversations and design a group covenant. Christina and Ann have also been asked to present workshops at the Lucent Technologies women's conference entitled "Women and Leadership."

The Far-Reaching Effects of the Circle

Circles are having a profoundly positive effect on the world in the following ways:

• As we learn and practice the values of collaboration

and respect for diversity, we are helping to redefine the concept of community.

- As we meet to discuss the need for meaningful work that satisfies our souls, we are creating jobs that contribute to the welfare of others and the healing of the planet.

- As we meet in circles to reconnect with nature, we are facilitating a worldwide increase in people's awareness about the effects we humans have on all of nature.

- As women like Christina Baldwin and Ann Linnea bring PeerSpirit Circles to business environments, board meetings and conferences are becoming far more democratic. This in turn creates healthier and more exciting work environments and improves work relationships between coworkers, bosses and employees.

- As women like Cindy Spring and Sedonia Cahill, cofounders of Wisdom Circles, teach us to listen and speak from the heart, we find that people are better able to resolve their differences based on race, gender, ethnicity, religion, class, political ideology or sexual orientation.

- As women like Sedonia Cahill and Carol Proudfoot-Edgar call circles during their vision quest workshops, more and more women are bringing the values of respect, cooperation and compassion back into their communities.

- As women like Sandra Ingerman help bring us home to circle in her soul retrieval workshops, we rediscover how to bring magic, creativity and passion back into our lives.

- As women like Cecile Andrews bring us Simplicity Circles, we are shifting our consciousness from consumerism and narrowly defined personal goals, and learning such "eco" values as voluntary simplicity, respect for diversity and collaboration.

- As women like Kay Pranis bring circles into the criminal justice system, we find we are focusing more on repairing the harm caused by a crime instead of merely punishing the offender. We are providing an opportunity for all those impacted by a crime to talk about their concerns, and we are finding better ways to provide emotional support to victims. We are bringing community members together in a forum that allows exploration of the underlying causes of crime, and we are encouraging them to offer their gifts and capacities to the process of finding solutions and implementing them.

There are at least four ways that you can join the circle and begin making significant changes in your family, in your community and in the world. They include:

1. Creating or joining a circle
2. Widening the circle by bringing circle and circle principles into other aspects of your life
3. Conducting your life according to circle principles

4. Dedicating your energy and resources to organizations and causes that advocate circle principles

Creating or Joining a Circle

The most obvious place to begin is to become part of an existing circle or to create one of your own. We all have the power to call a circle. We all have the power to transform and heal the horrible predicament we are in.

This book has given you only the bare essentials concerning how to create a circle, so once you have decided what your intention is and what type of circle you wish to create, please see the References and Recommended Reading for reference books on particular types of circles. Depending on the type of circle you are interested in forming, you may choose to read:

- *The Ceremonial Circle: Practice, Ritual and Renewal for Personal and Community Healing,* by Sedonia Cahill and Joshua Halpern
- *Calling the Circle: The First and Future Culture,* by Christina Baldwin
- *Wisdom Circles: A Guide to Self-Discovery and Community Building in Small Groups,* by Charles Garfield, Cindy Spring and Sedonia Cahill
- *Sacred Circles: A Guide to Creating Your Own Women's Spirituality Group,* by Robin Deen Carnes and Sally Craig (goddess-centered)

• *Dreaming the Dark,* by Starhawk (wicca)

Many of these books have more specific details on how to start a circle and how to keep it functioning in a productive way.

Not everyone is in the place to create a circle and yet they would like to become a part of one. If this is your situation, many of these books also have information on how you can contact existing circles. I also include some contact information at the back of this book.

Widening the Circle by Bringing Circles and Circle Principles into Other Aspects of Your Life

The paddler, the mountain climber,
the cancer survivor—each comes back into
the framework of our lives charged with the
responsibility to hold onto our spiritual awakenings.
As life returns to its ordinary patterns, we are
faced with countless decisions about how
to sustain connection and change.

ANN LINNEA
DEEP WATER PASSAGE

*Once a circle is formed and functioning
effectively it is natural to begin to reach out to join
with other circles. This is, after all, what must
happen if we are to survive—we must expand our
tribal identification to include everyone. Every man,
woman and child from every nation is, after all,
a part of the great circle of life.*

SEDONIA CAHILL AND JOSHUA HALPERN
THE CEREMONIAL CIRCLE

Before we can actualize the global healing potential of
the circle, we must integrate circle into our daily lives. The
circle form can be used effectively in many different settings, making whatever is occurring more conscious.

Share what you have learned with your friends, family
and coworkers. Initiate a family night when all family
members sit in a circle, and openly share their feelings and
dreams. Allow your children to take part in family decision-
making.

Show others, by example, how to live their life in a different way. If two friends complain to you about one
another suggest that you meet together in a circle to air
differences and mediate solutions.

Suggest the circle as a format for the social or political
meetings that you attend instead of sitting in rows of
chairs facing a speaker.

Bring the circle to your child's school. Suggest that

teachers sometimes place chairs in a circle or that students be allowed to participate in some decisions about class functions. Many schools teach a section on Native Americans and this is a perfect time to introduce the circle and the talking stick.

Business communities are constantly looking for ways to improve employee relations and to mediate employee conflicts. Circles can be utilized to help achieve consensus, to resolve conflicts and to bring harmony to work relationships. You can begin by simply suggesting that you sit in a circle at your next business meeting.

You can even bring the circle into your church. Christina Baldwin told me about an ordained clergywoman whose goal was to help church committees become church councils. They do this by opening their meetings sitting on the floor around a coffee table, lighting a candle and saying a prayer. They then conduct what Christina calls a "deep check-in," which is possible because agreements such as confidentiality are in place. While the council may move to a higher table to conduct their work, before adjourning they come back to the floor. These simple, yet profound, steps have led to a major difference in the level of cooperation among members.

Bring the circle to your neighborhood or community organizations. Angie Ober, a volunteer victim/offender mediator at a community mediation center, creates what she calls "a circle of understanding" as part of her work.

For example, Angie recently organized a circle of seventeen people who met to discuss the problems of a nine-year-old boy who had gotten into trouble. She wanted to create a community safety net—to provide services before he got into the system.

The circle included the boy, his grandmother, a family friend, his school counselor, the police officer, a scout master, someone from Foster Grandparents, a representative of the YMCA and the circle keeper. By including all these people from the community, Angie said that she proved that "people in the community can step up to the plate—get involved."

At the beginning of the circle the family was told, "We're here to support you in any way we can." They were also told that the group wanted to understand the family issues and dynamics. Although the mother of the boy initially felt bad about the fact that so many people were involved and that her boy had caused so much trouble, she came to appreciate the group's concern. She was told, "We're here to repair the harm, not to judge you."

Angie's "circle of understanding" was structured as follows:

1. Everyone in the circle introduced themselves.
2. The charges against the boy were listed and then the boy was given a chance to tell his side of the story. As Angie explains it, "We said something like, 'Will you

talk to us about the kinds of things you are doing?'"

3. Everyone in the circle was asked to talk about the things they loved to do when they were nine.

4. All members of the circle were asked to make suggestions about how to help the boy and encourage him to stay out of trouble.

5. Utilizing everyone's suggestions, the group set up a plan that included:

- providing the boy with a foster grandparent four hours a week
- getting the boy into the Boy Scouts
- getting the boy a pen pal
- getting the boy a library card
- getting the boy a fishing pole and taking him fishing
- having a school counselor arrange for tutoring

When Angie asked the circle members, "Where do we go from here?" everyone decided to have a follow-up circle.

I've recently begun using the circle format when working with victims of childhood abuse and their families, and have included information on family circles in the revised addition of my book *Families in Recovery.* Family circles offer each family member the opportunity to say what they need to say and be heard by other members without being interrupted. Cross talk, criticism, blaming and judgment are forbidden. Instead, the focus is on each family member getting a chance to talk about how the abuse or the disclosure of the abuse has affected them; each member experiencing empathy for the pain and struggles of other family members; and on healing the damage caused by the abuse.

Bringing the Circle and Circle Principles to the Men in Your Life

A woman's sense of self tends to come from her relatedness to the people around her, whereas a man's sense of self tends to come from pitting himself against others in a process of individuation. While this self-focus often enables a man to act more decisively and with more self-confidence in the world, it presents a tremendous obstacle to his ability to form and maintain intimate relationships. Being primarily self-focused may help a man to stay more in touch with his own needs, but it gets in his way when it comes to discerning the needs of others.

In many ways it is women's strength that we place such importance on relationships. We know how important relationships are in terms of healing both individual and universal wounds. We know that connection is as important as autonomy.

To create a healthy, meaningful relationship with someone else, there must be a connection. True connection requires the capacity to empathize with the other person.

It requires the ability to truly listen to the other person, to learn his or her language, and understand his or her point of view. This is what men can learn from women and from circle.

But women need to be careful that they don't fall into the trap of trying to change men or teach them. This is what codependency is all about. The best we can do is show men, by example, how to be more vulnerable, trusting and empathetic.

Bring men into circling by sharing your experiences with those men you love and trust. Suggest they start their own men's circle, or start a circle for both men and women. As art therapist, Patricia Waters, shared with me:

I have worked with more women than men, but men who come to the groups or classes have been very receptive to the work. For instance, one young man came to an empowering the feminine workshop because he had an athletic injury and couldn't do what he usually did. He wanted to try something he knew nothing about. He was the only man in the class and struggled with the art and the sharing, but by the end he was an accepted part of the group and said he had learned for the first time what was meant by "feminine" and saw that it was very different from how he approached life. Another man who attended my workshop taught kindergarten and said he would never teach it the same way again.

By being positive role models to men concerning the importance of connection, as they have been to us concerning the importance of individuation, we can help create the kind of balance we are all striving for.

If we as women want to be positive role models for the importance of connection we need to continue practicing the ethic of care ourselves. Women need to band together not only for support but in order to reinforce feminine values. Meeting with other women in circle can help us connect further with our capacity for compassion and empathy, intuition and inner wisdom.

Conduct Your Life According to Circle Principles

Perhaps most important, becoming part of the circle means conducting our lives according to circle principles, consciously integrating the lessons we have learned from circle into our daily lives. Every day we make choices that affect the quality of our own lives as well as the lives of others. Paying attention to these choices on a daily basis and then determining to make those choices that reflect our belief systems is a giant step in the direction we need to be headed.

For example, in our circles we encourage diversity and everyone's right to speak their mind without being judged or silenced. We have learned how empowering it is to realize that we are being listened to and that our truths are being honored. Now we need to follow the same principles in other areas of our lives. When someone at work disagrees with something we've said, instead of becoming defensive we can choose to listen to his or her point of view openly and without judgment, remembering from our experience in circle that much can be learned from those with conflicting viewpoints and that everyone has a truth to speak.

Earlier in the book we discussed the various elements that should make up every circle—intention, sacredness, commitment, equality, heart consciousness and gratitude. You will find that by translating these elements of circle into principles for conducting your life you will be able to bring the positive benefits of circle into your everyday life as well as into the larger circle of life.

Intention

It is very important to be clear about your intention, whether it is determining the reason for creating a circle or determining how you wish to widen the circle. This will require time and quiet contemplation since your intention needs to be specific enough to hold power. General intentions, such as "My intention is to encourage all women to become empowered," or "I want to be a better person," or "I want to help change the world," can work to some degree.

More specific intentions, however, such as, "I intend to live my life with honor and by so doing encourage others to do the same," or "I intend to make the practice of gratitude a part of my everyday existence," or "I dedicate myself to being empathetic and compassionate toward all beings," will have far more power and keep you more on track.

Next, you need to live your life with this intention clearly in your mind and heart on a daily basis. While no one is perfect, if it is your *intention* to live an honorable life, to treat all of life with respect and consideration, and to live a spiritual life, you must keep this goal foremost in your mind and heart. Try not to be distracted by other, less meaningful goals such as economic security, success, fame or adoration.

For example, conducting your life with honor means more than not lying, cheating or stealing. It means living your life with integrity and character. The following suggestions for conducting your life with honor at work will give you an idea of what I mean. Although your work day may not begin until 8:00 A.M., you are ethically bound to behave in such a manner prior to going to work so that you will be able to perform optimally. This means getting to bed early enough to get a good night's rest, instead of staying up so late that the next day your energy is depleted, you cannot perform your duties, and you cannot meet your obligations. Even though no one seems to be paying attention to how long a lunch hour or coffee break you take, if you extend them beyond what is reasonable, you are being derelict in the performance of your work and are not conducting yourself in an honorable way.

Sacredness

Once we have created a sacred center at the core of our lives we can begin to move outward, carrying our centeredness into the world. To live a Spirit-based life, to maintain our connection to Spirit on a daily basis, is a tremendous challenge but one well worth the effort. As Christina Baldwin so eloquently states:

> To claim our connection to Spirit on a daily basis is a radical act in our secular culture. It is an act that both liberates us to live in dramatically new and creative ways and pushes us to find like-minded companions. Circle itself becomes a spiritual practice—a celebration with others of the beauty and wisdom of living the sacred life. And as we remember that in each of us resides direct connection to spiritual guidance, we can claim our personal authority to serve as coleaders on the rim of the circle.

In *Calling the Circle,* Christina outlines the following suggestions for bringing and keeping Spirit in our lives:

- We consistently practice spiritual gesture or ritual in order to honor and reopen our relationship with Spirit.

- We slow down our pace in life in an attempt to connect with the pace and vibration of nature.
- We use silence as a way to connect with Spirit, to make a mental transition from home to work and back, and as a way of centering ourselves in times of confusion, conflict and chaos.
- We recognize that each thought we have, each action we take, has the power to create connection, peace and harmony, or separation, disruption and chaos.
- We choose what carries energy in our lives. We make a conscious choice about the kinds of music we listen to, the programs we watch on television, the movies we see, the books we read.

These are wonderful suggestions, and I would add the following: We recognize the sacred in everything. Every person is sacred. Every moment is sacred. Every inch of the earth is sacred. If we live our lives honoring these truths it will have a global effect. Let's look at these sacred dimensions of life more closely.

Every Person Is Sacred

You have within your power the ability to change the world simply by the way you conduct your life, by the way you treat each person you meet. If you honor and respect each person you relate to every day you will become a changed person, and those you honor will become transformed as well.

Each time you meet new people, look them in the eye and consciously welcome them into the circle. Ask their name and remember it. Ask them about their life and truly listen. Look for the common bond that lies between you, even with those who appear to be extremely different from you.

When you disagree with others, look for the truth in what they are saying instead of trying to make them change their mind. When someone angers or upsets you, remember that we can learn the most from those who disagree with us or upset us.

When others disgust or repel you, remember that they are mirrors of your own dark side, projections of those aspects of yourself you have rejected, ignored or denied.

All these actions on your part will have a ripple effect, creating ever-widening circles of compassion, empathy, gratitude and love. All people you meet will feel your compassion and be positively affected by it. Perhaps they haven't experienced the wonderful healing benefits of acceptance for a long time, and your compassion will feel like a wonderful gift. Perhaps it will soften their defenses just enough for them to be less critical or impatient toward their loved ones. Perhaps they will even be more compassionate toward the next stranger they meet.

Every Moment Is Sacred

Circles teach us to value the moment. Through the practice of ritual we learn to stay in the present. Through the practice of quiet contemplation we learn the power of silence.

We can then take these abilities and apply them to other aspects of our lives. Instead of constantly worrying about the future or ruminating about the past, we can instead focus on the present. When each moment is fully experienced and appreciated, we come to know that each moment can be a lifetime and we achieve a sense of acceptance and gratitude for every moment we are alive. This will, in turn, further our understanding that life is a precious gift.

This understanding will encourage us to use our time more wisely. We will become keenly aware that watching mindless television, gossiping about others, or focusing on the accumulation of material goods are all a terrible waste of precious time, and so we will choose to spend our free time focusing on more positive directions, such as creating art, helping others and recycling the material goods we already own.

The Land Is Sacred

Although we may feel that certain places on Earth evoke a sense of sacredness more than others, the truth is that every inch of the Earth is sacred. Its sacredness is present if we only recognize it.

Most of us have great concern for our planet. It is distressing to watch as our Earth and environment are so casually polluted. But over the past few years we've learned that a few voices standing up for what is right can make a difference.

Becoming involved in some of the Earth-positive organizations and causes listed at the back of the book is certainly an important way of showing your commitment to healing Mother Earth. But there are things you can do every day that are equally important.

Each of us can play an important role in cleaning up our environment. A good place to start is in our own homes. The average American home contains three to four gallons of hazardous materials that are defined by the Environmental Protection Agency as corrosive, flammable, reactive or toxic. The chemicals and pollutants in conventional cleaners can make the air in our homes more toxic than the air in our most polluted cities. The toll on our health and the environment can be enormous. Many health food stores and natural food markets carry a variety of ecologically safe, nontoxic cleaners, detergents and environmentally friendly products.

Practicing voluntary simplicity, conserving energy and natural resources, recycling and picking up litter are just a few of the ways we can honor Mother Earth on a daily basis.

All Life Is Sacred

Not only is all human life sacred, but all life—including animals, birds, reptiles and insects—is sacred.

One way that some people have chosen to honor the sacredness of animals is to become vegetarians. In addition to the health risks of eating meat (heart disease, diabetes, osteoporosis and various cancers), raising animals for food is extremely destructive to the environment since it is a leading cause of soil erosion, water pollution and depletion of natural resources. Farm animals are fed more than 75 percent of the grain, corn and soybeans grown in our country while millions of people around the world die of hunger each year.

Those of us concerned about the wild animals of the world need to be reminded that whole species are becoming extinct daily. The rain forests of the world are cut down to make grazing land for cattle. Millions of wild animals in our country are killed because they are a threat to livestock, or because they compete for grass with cattle on public lands used for grazing. (The federal government kills close to two million wild animals every year as a service to ranchers, and ranchers kill many more.)

Commitment

Being committed to your intention means you have made a promise to yourself to be dedicated and faithful to your intention. It also means you make certain agreements or take specific actions to show and reinforce your commitment.

For example, you can both show and exercise your commitment to honor the sacredness of all life by doing the following on a daily basis:

1. Find those places that evoke sacredness or hold spiritual power for you and visit them regularly to engage in some kind of ritual, to offer prayers of gratitude or to meditate.

2. Create an altar in your home where you place special artifacts or sacred objects. Meditate or pray there on a regular basis.

3. Remind yourself of your commitment periodically in order to keep it strong. Some people do this by writing out their commitment and reading it aloud every day. Others say it as an affirmation or include it in their daily prayers. Poems, like the one below, can also serve as a statement of commitment. I suggest you change the "we" to "I" in order to make it more personally powerful.

We join with the earth and with each other

To bring new life to the land
To restore the waters
To refresh the air

We join with the earth and with each other

To renew the forests
To care for the plants
To protect the creatures

We join with the earth and with each other

To celebrate the seas
To rejoice in the sunlight
To sing the song of the stars

We join with the earth and with each other

To recreate the human community
To promote justice and peace
To remember our children
We join with the earth and with each other

We join together as many and diverse expressions
of one loving memory: for the healing of the
earth and the renewal of all life.

United Nations Environmental Sabbath Program

Equality

In circle we learn to share leadership, to view each person in the circle as our equal and our teacher. We need to work to maintain this sense of equality outside of our circles as well. We do this by remembering that we have something to learn from each and every person we meet. Those who seem to us to be the least "evolved" may be our greatest teachers. And those people who disturb or anger us are most certainly our mirrors, reflecting our own behavior.

We need to constantly work toward achieving equal relationships, instead of relationships characterized by dominance or submission. Healthy relationships are based on equality, meaning that each person is seen as an equal in the other's eyes. Unfortunately, most people tend to see themselves as either better than or less than others and this leads to problems.

When we believe we are better than someone else—because we think we are more intelligent, more spiritual, more powerful, more successful, more attractive, more wealthy—we also begin to believe that we have more rights than others do, that we are entitled to better treatment from others, and that we don't have to treat others with honor and respect. This in turn leads to the tendency to control others.

Tyranny always has a price, either because the person we tyrannize eventually rebels and retaliates, or because we soon come to hate ourselves for using our power over someone.

On the other hand, when we become involved with someone we perceive as being "better" than we are, in some way we are setting ourselves up to be controlled by that person. Allowing someone to dominate us is just as destructive both to ourselves and our relationships as is being the one who is domineering.

There is a tyranny in constantly viewing oneself as "less than." It keeps us in a subservient position, robbing us of our personal power and preventing us from recognizing the power we have.

When we are put in a position of power, whether at work or elsewhere, we must fight the temptation to abuse that power and to remember that no matter how much power we wield, we are in fact all equal. You've probably heard the saying, "Power corrupts." We must not allow ourselves to be corrupted by power or allow it to make us lose touch with reality.

Working toward equality versus dominance may even help us to heal the environment. As Cecile Andrews wrote in *The Circle of Simplicity:*

> It's easy to see that inequality hurts people, but perhaps it is the system of hierarchy and dominance that is the root of our environmental problems—when dominance over people is acceptable, we feel it's acceptable to dominate and exploit the planet.

Heart Consciousness

Living our life with heart consciousness means we greet the world with an open heart, as opposed to a cynical, judgmental or self-protective one. This includes listening openly and without judgment to what others have to say. It means constantly reminding ourselves that others have a right to their truths, opinions and beliefs, and that we shouldn't impose our truths onto others.

It means treating others with empathy and compassion, putting ourselves in the other person's place whenever we catch ourselves judging them. We tend to be judgmental and critical of others because we lack empathy for their position. When we judge others we, in essence, put ourselves in a position *above* them. When we have empathy, however, we put ourselves in *their place.* Judging is a position of *superiority.* Empathy is a position of *equality.*

Heart consciousness means we listen from the heart to find our common experiences so we can move beyond the judgments and assumptions that clutter up our minds.

It also means we practice speaking from the heart—that is, speaking our truths without censoring ourselves or trying to impress others. It means we find a way to communicate to others in a way that can be heard.

Finally, living our lives in heart consciousness means discovering the power of silence to help us connect with our inner wisdom. Instead of speaking or acting impulsively, we take the time to connect with our deepest truths for guidance. We practice quiet contemplation on a daily basis in order to allow new insights, feelings and inspiration to enter. We sit in silence as a way of connecting with the sacred within.

Gratitude

The way to bring gratitude into our daily lives is to practice gratitude not only in our circles—in statements, prayers and mindfulness—but as a way of life. If we embrace the belief that gratitude is an attitude more than anything else, this will not be difficult to do. If our attitude is one of gratefulness, then throughout the day we will look at the world with appreciative, thankful eyes. We will notice the beauty all around us and be in a constant state of gratefulness for what we see. We will look at the people in our lives who provide us companionship, support and lessons, and we will be in a constant state of gratitude for them. We will appreciate the beauty of nature all around us. We will appreciate our bodies for their strength and mobility, and for the pleasure they provide. We will look at what we possess—home, car, clothes—and will be in a constant state of gratitude for what they provide us—shelter, freedom, comfort. We will even look at adversity and be grateful for the lessons it brings.

In his book, *Gratefulness: The Heart of Prayer,* Brother David Steindl-Rast talks about living one's life in a constant state of prayer. In Bhakta Yoga, practitioners repeatedly whisper God's name in a prayer form known as japa or japam. "Keep the name of the Lord spinning in the midst of all your activities" is a favorite bhakti maxim. Whether they are washing, planting or shopping, these sacred words penetrate the subconscious mind to infuse it with gratitude.

Among indigenous people, from the Arctic circle to the Australian outback, the common element of life is a daily relationship to sacred center. For Native Americans, gratitude is a natural and necessary part of worship. It is believed that each individual prayer reinforces the bond between the human being and the great powers. Worship is a personal commitment to the sources of life and is a way of giving thanks and centering oneself in the world. What is missing for most of us in the modern world is an understanding of how to live as an act of worship. We don't know what to revere, or how to experience or show reverence.

Native peoples, in general, perceive "the environment" as a sensate, conscious entity suffused with spiritual powers. Hence their interactions are a respectful and spiritual exchange. "Everything we do is a prayer. Our religion is a way of life," an Absaroke (Crow) woman, Vera Jane He Did It Half, once explained. In fact, there is no word in Indian languages for "religion," the closest concept usually being "the way you live."

As Brother David Steindl-Rast explains, within our human impulse to be grateful flows the vast cycles of universal reciprocity—for everything that is taken, something has to be given in return. If we merely take in a breath and stop there, we will die. Likewise, if we merely breathe out, life is not giving or taking, but give and take.

Native Americans, like the poet Delores La Chapelle, understand this law of universal reciprocity and our interdependence with all life:

> We give-away our thanks to the earth
> which gives us our home.
> We give-away our thanks to the rivers and lakes
> which give-away their water.
> We give-away our thanks to the trees
> which give-away fruit and nuts.
> We give-away our thanks to the wind
> which brings rain to water the plants.
> We give-away our thanks to the sun
> who gives-away warmth and light.
> All beings on earth: the trees, the animals, the wind and
> the rivers give-away to one another so all is in balance.
> We give-away our promise to begin to learn
> how to stay in balance with all the earth.

Our praise and thanksgiving are as essential a part of life's give and take as are the cycles of oxygen and water—

or any other nourishment flowing through the biosphere. Perhaps the greatest gift we humans have to offer the rest of creation is our heartfelt appreciation. The ability to receive in thankfulness the blessings of life is an awe-inspiring quality.

Dedicating Your Energy and Resources to Organizations and Causes That Advocate Circle Principles

There are many, many organizations and causes already in existence that are diligently working toward solving world problems such as hunger, violence and ecology. In Appendix II I have listed a few organizations that espouse circle principles. If you are interested in becoming an active member in an organization or in joining a cause, I urge you to act on that desire instead of putting it off and telling yourself you are too busy or you don't have enough money.

There is so much to be done that we can become over-whelmed and, consequently, become disillusioned. There-fore, it is usually best to focus on one aspect of the world's problems and to begin with small, manageable increments. You don't have to donate a huge amount of money or com-mit yourself to so many meetings that you don't have time for anything else. You just need to do your part.

One such place to start would be to investigate whether

or not there is a Restorative Justice program in your community. Many Peacemaking and Sentencing Circles are made up of volunteers from the community. See Appendix VI for more information.

It is equally important that we begin using circle principles in our own backyards, so to speak. If our focus is on cleaning up the environment, we need to begin by cleaning up our own yards, our own neighborhoods and our own towns. If our focus is on encouraging diversity and equality, we need to start with our own households before moving outward to our schools, churches and business environments.

We truly can change the world one circle at a time. By following the suggestions outlined in this chapter, you can become part of the circle—part of the solution instead of part of the problem.

CONCLUSION

This book has been about the importance of creating circles for women and about women's role in changing the earth. This may, to some, contradict the entire concept of circle since the very idea of circle is to be all-inclusive. But as Sedonia Cahill and Joshua Halpern state at the end of *The Ceremonial Circle*, "Before people are able to step back into oneness they have to feel a sense of worth and pride in themselves." Women's circles need to be seen as a necessary, yet transitional step to bring us into greater unification.

Ancient stories from all traditions have prophesized a time when people from all over the world will come together in peace—a time when sacred balance and harmony will be restored. We are at the beginning of that time.

In order to restore balance on Earth we need to recognize that our concept of being separate is just an illusion—

that we are all part of the whole. All our prejudices, judgments and feelings of separateness must be resolved in order for us to find our way back into wholeness.

The circle is not complete unless all things and all people are part of it. Therefore, we must open our arms to include every race, class and gender. In order for the women's circle movement to be truly successful we must all reach out to others and bring them into the circle. We do this by bringing more people into our circles and by forming new circles. We do this by showing others the benefits of living in the circle. We do it by honoring every person, place and thing as sacred. Most importantly, we do it by living our life by circle principles.

We must begin to live our lives with the awareness that every choice we make, no matter how small, affects everyone and everything within the great circle of life. The foods we eat, how we earn and spend our money, whether we conserve energy or waste it, whether we are compassionate and kind to those around us—all these little decisions are powerful choices that lead us back to wholeness.

Ultimately, *Women Circling the Earth* is about finding the most honorable ways to conduct our lives on a daily basis: the most honorable way to treat one another, the most honorable way to make decisions involving others, the most honorable way to heal the damage we have done to Mother Earth, and the most honorable way to treat Mother Earth and all her living creatures today.

Conducting our life with honorable intention can be a heavy burden. We all need help carrying the burden. The circle provides us with the support, strength and renewal we need to carry the load. It creates the energy needed to empower and motivate us. It is a constant reminder that we are all interrelated and need one another in order to survive. It provides us the grounding and focus we need when we get off-center and lose our way. Finally, the circle continually provides us lessons about ourselves—lessons about forgiveness and compassion, about judgment and projection, about envy and acceptance. As we all strive to become the best we can be, as we all strive to lay aside our pettiness and open our arms to the important things in life, the circle is there to remind us of what is real, meaningful, enriching and fulfilling. The circle is there to remind us of who we really are.

REFERENCES

ONE: The Quiet Power of Women's Circles

Baldwin, Christina. 1998. *Calling the Circle: The First and Future Culture.* New York: Bantam Books.

Campbell, Joseph, ed. 1971, 1976. *The Portable Jung.* New York: Penguin Books.

Gilligan, Carol. 1993. *In A Different Voice: Psychological Theory and Women's Development.* Cambridge, Mass.: Harvard University Press.

Hillel, Rachel. 1998. *The Redemption of the Feminine Erotic Soul.* York Beach, Maine: Nicholas-Hays.

Redmond, Layne. 1997. *When the Drummers Were Women: A Spiritual History of Rhythm.* New York: Crown Publishing.

Walker, Barbara. 1988. *The Women's Dictionary of Symbols and Sacred Objects.* San Francisco: HarperSanFrancisco.

TWO: Changing the World, One Circle at a Time—The Women's Circle Movement

Fox-Genovese, Elizabeth. 1999. *Feminism Is Not the Story of My Life.* New York: Anchor Books.

Lee, Scout Cloud. 1995. *The Circle Is Sacred: A Medicine Book for Women.* Tulsa, Okla.: Council Oak Books.

Lawlor, Robert. 1991. *Voices of the First Day: Awakening in the Aboriginal Dreamtime.* Rochester, Vt.: Inner Traditions.

Medicine Eagle Brooke. 1991. *Buffalo Woman Comes Singing.* New York: Ballantine Books.

THREE: Circle as Community

Cahill, Sedonia, and Joshua Halpern. 1990. *The Ceremonial Circle: Practice, Ritual and Renewal for Personal and Community Healing.* San Francisco: HarperSanFrancisco.

Ingerman, Sandra. 1991. *Soul Retrieval: Mending the Fragmented Self.* San Francisco: HarperSanFrancisco.

FIVE: Consensus and Mediation

Baldwin, *Calling the Circle.*

Cahill and Halpern, *The Ceremonial Circle.*

SIX: Our Hunger for the Sacred

Cunningham, Nancy Brady. 1995. *I Am Woman by Rite: A Book of Women's Rituals.* York Beach, Maine: Samuel Weiser, Inc.

Northup, Leslie A. 1997. *Ritualizing Women: Patterns of Spirituality.* Cleveland, Ohio: The Pilgrim Press.

SEVEN: Circle as Empowerment

Baldwin, *Calling the Circle.*

Ingerman, *Soul Retrieval.*

Sered, Susan Starr. 1994. *Priestess, Mother, Sacred Sister: Religions Dominated by Women.* Oxford, England: Oxford University Press.

EIGHT: Choosing a Women's Circle to Create— An Overview

Andrews, Cecile. 1997. *The Circle of Simplicity: Return to the Good Life.* New York: HarperCollins.

Baldwin, *Calling the Circle.*

Cahill and Halpern. *The Ceremonial Circle.*

Garfield, Charles, Cindy Spring and Sedonia Cahill. 1998. *Wisdom Circles: A Guide to Self-Discovery and Community Building in Small Groups.* New York: Hyperion.

Walker, Barbara. *The Woman's Dictionary of Symbols and Sacred Objects.*

NINE: The Structure of Circle, the Circle as Structure

Cahill and Halpern, *The Ceremonial Circle.*

Roberts, Elizabeth. 1991. *Earth Prayers from Around the World.* San Francisco: HarperSanFrancisco.

TEN: Creating Council Circles

Andrews, *The Circle of Simplicity.*

Cahill and Halpern, *The Ceremonial Circle.*

Garfield, Spring and Cahill, *Wisdom Circles.*

Pranis, Kay. "Peacemaking Circles," *Corrections Today.* Dec. 1977.

ELEVEN: Creating Ceremonial and Sacred Circles

Northrup, *Ritualizing Women.*

Cahill and Halpern, *The Ceremonial Circle.*

Ardinger, Barbara. 1992. *A Woman's Book of Rituals and Celebrations.* San Rafael, Calif.: New World Library.

THIRTEEN: Becoming Part of the Circle

Baldwin, *Calling the Circle.*

Andrews, *The Circle of Simplicity.*

Steindl-Rast, David. 1990. *Gratefulness: The Heart of Prayer.* Mahwah, N.J.: Paulist Press.

BIBLIOGRAPHY AND RECOMMENDED READING

Circle Formats and Circle Skills

Andrews, Cecile. *The Circle of Simplicity: Return to the Good Life.* New York: HarperCollins, 1997.

An excellent book on simplifying one's life and creating learning communities.

Baldwin, Christina. *Calling the Circle: The First and Future Culture.* New York: Bantam Books, 1998.

A book that has now become a classic. Christina's philosophical beliefs have inspired many in the circle movement.

Carnes, Robin Deen, and Sally Craig. *Sacred Circles: A Guide to Creating Your Own Women's Spirituality Group.* San Francisco: HarperSanFrancisco, 1998.

Garfield, Charles, Cindy Spring, and Sedonia Cahill. *Wisdom Circles: A Guide to Self-Discovery and Community Building in Small Groups.* New York: Hyperion, 1998.

Starhawk. *Dreaming the Dark.* 15th ed. Boston: Beacon Press, 1989, 1997.

Starhawk was one of the first people to write about the

circle and for this we owe her a great deal. This is a ground-breaking book on the structure, dynamics and spirituality of the circle.

Zimmerman, Jack, and Virginia Coyle. *The Way of Council.* Las Vegas, Nevada: Bramble Books, 1996.

Provides a method of training for both professionals and nonprofessionals in basic communication skills using the council model.

Cultural Perspectives

Lawlor, Robert. *Voices of the First Day: Awakening in the Aboriginal Dreamtime.* Rochester, Vt.: Inner Traditions, 1991.

A comprehensive study of the indigenous people of Australia and an important spiritual document.

Sheeran, Michael J. *Beyond the Majority Rule.* Philadelphia: Religious Society of Friends, 1993.

Quakers have been meeting in circles and governing by consensus since the 1600s. The author traces the Quaker tradition of religious decision-making and how it can be applied to contemporary society.

Thunder, Mary Elizabeth. *Thunder's Grace: Walking the Road of Visions with My Lakota Grandmother.* Barrytown, N.Y.: Station Hill Press, 1995.

The author takes us through her experiences with Grandma Grace Spotted Eagle, a remarkable elder, and other legendary elders such as Wallace Black Elk, Rolling Thunder and Chief Leonard Crow Dog. She describes her inclusion in the Sun Dance, one of the world's oldest and most venerable of sacred initiations.

Underwood, Paula. *The Walking People: A Native American Oral*

History. San Anselmo: A Tribe of Two Press, Institute of Noetic Sciences, 1993.

Ywahoo, Dhyani. *Voices of Our Ancestors: Cherokee Teachings from the Wisdom Fire*. Boston: Shambhala, 1987.

According to the ancient Native American calendar, we have entered a new cycle of Thirteen Heavens, a new age in which we have the opportunity to let go of aggression and fear and begin to live a life of enlightened consciousness. With a voice that is powerful and compassionate, the author calls us to become "peacekeepers" in our hearts and in the world.

Women's Spirituality

Anderson, Sherry, and Patricia Hopkins. *The Feminine Face of God*. New York: Bantam Books, 1991.

A classic book on the different manifestations of women's spirituality.

Duerk, Judith. *A Circle of Stones: Woman's Journey to Herself*. San Diego: LuraMedia, 1989.

A self-guided journey to the archetypal feminine written from a Jungian perspective.

Eller, Cynthia. *Living in the Lap of the Goddess: The Feminine Spirituality Movement in America*. New York: Crossroad Publishing Co., 1993.

Eller explores what women who worship the goddess believe through interviews, participant observation and analysis of movement literature.

Gimbutas, Marija. *The Language of the Goddess*. San Francisco: HarperSanFrancisco, 1989.

A classic by a pioneering archaeologist who presents abundant evidence of the prepatriarchal cultures in Europe and Asia who worshipped God in female forms.

Hillel, Rachel. *The Redemption of the Feminine Erotic Soul.* York Beach, Maine: Nicolas-Hays, 1998.

RavenWing, Josie. *The Return of Spirit: A Woman's Call to Spiritual Action.* Deerfield Beach, Fla.: Health Communications, Inc., 1996.

A visionary guidebook for the new millennium that weaves spiritual practices and healing rituals together with stories and insights for the redemption of our personal power and compassion.

Reilly, Patricia Lynn. *A God Who Looks Like Me: Discovering a Woman-Affirming Spirituality.* New York: Ballantine Books, 1995.

An excellent guide to reframing Christian theology in a way that honors women. Especially helpful for those women who are emerging from negative experiences with harsh religious traditions.

Spretnak, Charlene. *The Politics of Women's Spirituality.* New York: Doubleday/Anchor, 1982.

An important collection of essays on the rise of spiritual power within the feminist movement.

Steinem, Gloria. *Revolution from Within.* Boston: Little, Brown, 1992.

Argues for the necessity of spiritual development as a basis for political and social change.

Umansky, Ellen, and Dianne Ashton. *Four Centuries of Jewish Women's Spirituality.* Boston: Beacon Press, 1992.

Jewish women, from ancient times to the present, speak about spirituality. Very inspiring no matter what your religious background.

Earth-Based Spirituality/Shamanism

Allen, Paula Gunn. *The Sacred Hoop: Recovering the Feminine in American Indian Traditions.* Boston: Beacon Press, 1986.

A collection of essays reclaiming the contributions, traditions, values and vision of Native American foremothers. Written by one of our Native elders and a University of California professor.

Arrien, Angeles. *The Four-Fold Way.* San Francisco: HarperSanFrancisco, 1993.

An accessible book on earth-based spirituality across many cultures.

Harner, Michael. *The Way of the Shaman.* San Francisco: HarperSanFrancisco, 1980, 1990.

This classic on shamanism pioneered the modern shamanic renaissance and is considered by many to be the foremost resource and reference on shamanism.

Ingerman, Sandra. *Soul Retrieval: Mending the Fragmented Self.* San Francisco: HarperSanFrancisco, 1991.

Through the age-old shamanic technique of soul retrieval, Ingerman has enabled thousands of individuals to overcome traumatic dissociation, memory repression and other problems. With warmth and compassion, Sandra describes in this book the dramatic results of combining soul retrieval with contemporary psychological concepts.

RavenWing, Josie. *A Season of Eagles.* New York: Writer's Showcase/Writer's Digest, 2000.

RavenWing's personal journey of wild and soaring shamanic initiations that include contact with a mysterious teacher, a Navajo woman dreamer, and a case of other human and non-human forces bring us face to face with the great mystery we call life. Josie's love of nature and her desire to empower not only herself but other women through her story is especially moving.

Paganism and Witchcraft

Adler, Margot. *Drawing Down the Moon*. Boston: Beacon Press, 1979.

A colorful description of paganism in America.

Libera, Caitlin. *Creating Circles of Power and Magic: A Woman's Guide to Sacred Community*. Freedom, CA: Crossing Press, 1994.

In the pagan/wiccan tradition, this book tells the story of a particular group, describes its processes and rituals, and asks thought-provoking questions to help readers in creating their own circles.

Ceremonies and Rituals

Ardinger, Barbara. *A Woman's Book of Rituals and Celebrations*. San Rafael, CA: New World Library, 1992.

Cahill, Sedonia, and Joshua Halpern. *The Ceremonial Circle: Practice, Ritual and Renewal for Personal and Community Healing*. San Francisco: HarperSanFrancisco, 1992.

I consider this inspirational guide the most important source book you can find for creating ritual and ceremony. This wonderful book also includes interviews with well-known ceremonialists, such as Starhawk and Vicki Noble.

Cunningham, Nancy Brady. *I Am Woman by Rite: A Book of Women's Rituals*. York Beach, Maine: Samuel Weiser, Inc., 1995.

By sharing spiritual insights, Cunningham invites us to create unique rituals that enhance the pride and pleasure of being women.

Lee, Scout Cloud. *The Circle Is Sacred: A Medicine Book for Women*. Tulsa, Okla.: Council Oak Books, 1995.

This excellent book provides a host of resources. Included are chapters on honoring the circle, making drums and rattles, ritual cleansing, music, dance, creating altars and other sacred spaces, women's moon cycles, dream stalking and vision questing. The text is augmented with words of wisdom from medicine women such as Alinta, an Australian aboriginal woman; Princess Moon Feathers, a 100-year-old Cherokee; Mahisha, a Hawaiian elder; and Spider Red-Gold of the Celtic tradition.

Northup, Lesley. *Ritualizing Women: Patterns of Spirituality*. Cleveland, Ohio: The Pilgrim Press, 1997.

Northup searches out distinct but common patterns of ritual and worship among women in Christian, Jewish, neopagan, feminist and traditional contexts.

Redmond, Layne. *When the Drummers Were Women: A Spiritual History of Rhythm*. Pittsburgh: Three Rivers Press, 1998.

Layne Redmond is an acknowledged expert on the ancient history of women in music. In this book she chronicles the story of women as drummers and leaders of ritual. She demonstrates that women today can reclaim drumming as a sacred technology that celebrates the unifying cycles of the earth, cosmos and human body.

Starhawk. *The Spiral Dance*. New York: HarperCollins, 1989.

This classic book explores the goddess religion and offers a wealth of information on ritual and ceremony.

_____. *Truth or Dare*. San Francisco: HarperSanFrancisco, 1989.

In this book Starhawk examines the nature of power—how to exercise "power with" instead of "power over."

Stein, Diane. *Casting the Circle.* Freedom, Calif.: Crossing Press, 1990.

Walker, Barbara. *Women's Rituals.* San Francisco: HarperSanFrancisco, 1990.

Creating Community

Peck, M. Scott. *The Different Drum: Community Making and Peace.* New York: Simon & Schuster, 1987.
  Fascinating observations on the stages of spiritual development in individuals and groups.

Eisler, Riane, and David Loye. *The Partnership Way.* San Francisco: HarperSanFrancisco, 1990.
  A practical workbook for understanding how to move into a partnership way of viewing the world. Designed for group study, it provides a way for a circle to gather, educate itself, and decide what functions it would like to have.

Connecting with and Healing the Earth

Earth Works Group. *50 Simple Things You Can Do to Save the Earth.* Berkeley, Calif.: The Earth Works Group, 1989.
  By making their suggestions simple and accessible, the authors hope to make it easier for you to get involved. Great list of existing organizations at the back of the book.

Halifax, Joan. *The Fruitful Darkness.* San Francisco: HarperSanFrancisco, 1993.
  A personal account of Halifax's spiritual journey and reconnection to the Earth.

Hynes, Patricia. *Earth Right.* Rocklin, Calif.: Prima Publishing, 1990.

The author offers creative ideas for how to take action that will help us reclaim our Earth.

Lappé, Frances Moore. *Diet for a Small Planet*. New York: Ballantine Books, 1971, 1982.
    This classic book taught America about the social and personal significance of what foods we choose to eat, and offers a fascinating philosophy for changing yourself—and the world—by changing the way you eat.

Roberts, Elizabeth, and Elias Amidon. *Earth Prayers*. San Francisco: HarperSanFrancisco, 1991.
    Prayers, poems and invocations from around the world focusing on Mother Earth and all her inhabitants.

Seed John, et al. *Thinking Like a Mountain*. Santa Cruz, Calif.: New Society Publishers, 1988.
    A collection of writings to help people connect with the earth and establish a council of all beings.

Crones and Midlife

Linnea, Ann. *Deep Water Passage: A Spiritual Journey at Midlife*. New York: Pocket Books, 1998.
    The author's reflections on her literal and metaphoric kayaking journey help both women and men look at the heroic aspects of all life passages.

Walker, Barbara. *The Crone: Woman of Age, Wisdom and Power*. San Francisco: Harper & Row, 1985.

Bringing the Circle into the Workplace

Fox, Matthew. *The Reinvention of Work: A New Vision of Livelihood for Our Time.* San Francisco: HarperSanFrancisco, 1994.
Shows how we can bring a spiritual consciousness into our work lives.

Montuori, Alfonso, and Isabella Conti. *From Power to Partnership.* San Francisco: HarperSanFrancisco, 1993.
Using Eisler's *The Chalice and the Blade* as a guide, the authors explore other ways to work and learn cooperatively.

Circling with Children

Milford, Susan. *Hands Across the World.* Charlotte, Vt.: Williamson Publishing, 1992.
365 ways for children to learn about other cultures and connect with other children around the world.

Schimpf, Ann [Ann Linnea], et al. *Teaching Kids to Love the Earth.* Duluth: Pfeifer-Hamilton, 1991.
An award-winning educational tool for teachers, parents and others working with children.

Connecting with Your Shadow

Johnson, Robert A. *Owning Your Own Shadow.* San Francisco: HarperSanFrancisco, 1991.
Owning one's shadow is a necessary step in healing ourselves so we can, in turn, begin to heal our world. This book is a classic on the subject.

Zweig, Connie, and Jeremiah Abrams, eds. *Meeting the Shadow: The Hidden Power of the Dark Side of Human Nature.* Los

Angeles, Calif.: Jeremy Tarcher, Inc., 1991.

In this wonderful collection of sixty-five articles written by such people as Robert Bly, Kim Chermin, Maggie Scarf, Marsha Sinetar, Brother David Steindl-Rast, Ernest Becker, Audre Lorde, James Hillman, Joseph Campbell and Deena Metzger, an overview of the shadow as it appears in families, intimate relationships, sexuality, work, spirituality, politics, psychotherapy and creativity is presented. It also teaches what is called "shadow-work"—tools that help us recognize the projections that color our opinions of others.

Miller, William A. *Your Golden Shadow: Discovering and Fulfilling Your Undeveloped Self.* San Francisco: HarperSanFrancisco, 1989.

An articulate and easy-to-understand book on the shadow that will encourage you to risk mining your shadow in search of the gold hidden there.

Creativity and Journaling

Baldwin, Christina. *Life's Companion: Journal Writing as a Spiritual Quest.* New York: Bantam, 1990.

Cameron, Julia. *The Artist's Way.* New York: J. P. Tarcher, 1992.

Capacchione, Lucia. *The Creative Journal: The Art of Finding Yourself.* North Hollywood, Calif.: Newcastle, 1979.

Goldberg, Natalie. *Writing Down the Bones: Freeing the Writer Within.* Boston: Shambhala, 1986.

Metzger, Deena. *Writing for Your Life: A Guide and Companion to the Inner Worlds.* San Francisco: HarperSanFrancisco, 1992.

Fiction that Inspires and Points the Way

LeGuin, Ursula. *Always Coming Home.* New York: Harper Collins, 1985.

In this archeology of the future, LeGuin creates an entire culture for us to consider, including mythology, a history, maps and songs.

Starhawk. *The Fifth Sacred Thing.* New York: Bantam, 1994.

A tremendous amount of teaching is interwoven into this story set in the early years of the twenty-first century where the circle is used as the governing body.

Ingerman, Sandra. *A Fall to Grace.* Sante Fe, N.M.: Blessingway Books, 1997.

A rich source of conversations with wise and ancient teachers, this novel will inspire your search for meaning in life and teach you learn important truths about your spiritual path.

APPENDIX I:
WOMEN CIRCLING
THE EARTH

Carol Proudfoot-Edgar

Carol makes herself available for gathering with people in various ways to assist them in learning the practices of shamanism and creating circles that endure over time.

She has developed a Web site, *www.shamanicvisions.com* that addressses various aspects of applied shamanism. The Web site includes a schedule of her retreats including full descriptions of the focus for each retreat. If you are interested in contacting her about her work, you can write or e-mail her at:

Carol Proudfoot-Edgar

275 Rabbits Run Road

Santa Cruz, CA 95060

E-mail: *CedgarBear@aol.com*

www.shamanicvisions.com

If you are interested in joining with other circles in the world for seasonal celebrations, healing and tending our planet, you can join by signing up at the Web site or by contacting Carol directly.

Sandra Ingerman

As the leading practitioner of soul retrieval work, Sandra conducts both private workshops and workshops in conjunction with the International Faculty of the Foundation of Shamanic Studies, where she is the educational director. She is currently working on a book entitled, *Let There Be Light: Healing The Earth Through Transmutation* (Harmony Books 2001).

Her three books, *Soul Retrieval: Mending the Fragmented Self; Welcome Home: Following Your Soul's Journey Home;* and *A Fall to Grace,* can be purchased at your local bookstore or you can order them by calling the number below.

Contact:

Sandra Ingerman

P.O. Box 4757

Santa Fe, NM 87502

505-820-7957

Kay Pranis

Kay is a Restorative Justice Planner for the Minnesota Department of Corrections and an advocate of Peacemaking Circles.

Contact:

Kay Pranis
Minnesota Dept. of Corrections
1450 Energy Park Drive
St. Paul, MN 55108
651-642-0329

Mary Elizabeth Thunder

Mary is a well-known speaker, human rights advocate, sun dancer and peace Elder. She travels globally to share the message of Earth Mother's peace and healing through the healing of oneself. She and her husband, Jeffrey "White Horse" Hubbell, live and maintain a ranch in West Point, Texas, which is considered a spiritual university.

Contact:

Mary Elizabeth Thunder
Thunder Horse Ranch Woman's Dance
2041 Makinson Road
Route 1, Box 87C
West Point, TX 78963
409-242-5247
E-mail: *thunder@cvtv.net*

Mary K. Sandford

Mary K. Sandford is the associate dean, College of Arts and Sciences at the University of North Carolina at Greensboro. She utilizes circles in her classrooms and has introduced circle councils to other staff members. Contact her for more information on how she uses circle in her work with students and faculty.

Contact:

Mary K. Sandford
University of North Carolina at Greensboro
College of Arts and Sciences
100 Foust Bldg.
Greensboro, NC 27402

Patricia Waters

Patricia Waters, MA, ATR, REAT, is cofounder of The Creative Arts Studio in Santa Rosa, California, where she conducts creative circles in art process for healing and self-empowerment. She is on the faculty of The Person-Centered Expressive Therapy Institute, Center for Creative Arts Therapy, and adjunct faculty at Sonoma State University's Department of Extended Education. She has produced the video "Transformation Through Art, A Personal Mythic Journey," based on over fifty years of her artwork.

Contact:

Patricia Waters
P.O. Box 184
Cotari, CA 94931

Angeles Arrien

Angeles' work with the Fourfold Way is widely known and respected. She offers seminars and training, and many teachers have respectfully incorporated her work into their understanding of circle.

Contact:

Angeles Arrien
P.O. Box 2077
Sausalito, CA 94966

Josie RavenWing

Josie is a workshop facilitator, songwriter, healer and author of *The Return of Spirit: A Woman's Call to Spiritual Action* and *A Season of Eagles*.

Contact:

Josie RavenWing
1535 B. Jackson St.
Hollywood, FL 33020
www.healingjourney.net

APPENDIX II: CIRCLING ORGANIZATIONS

PeerSpirit Circling

PeerSpirit, Inc. and Calling the Circle Foundation, founded by Christina Baldwin and Ann Linnea, are the business manifestations of the PeerSpirit Circle movement which is dedicated to bringing the circle into mainstream culture. Services include: training in circle facilitation called The Circle Practicum; client-tailored business consulting to introduce PeerSpirit Council Management into corporate and organizational environments; and creative seminars and wilderness adventures which use the circle as the container for experience.

Contact:

PeerSpirit, Inc.
P. O. Box 550
Langley, WA 98260
360-331-3580
Fax: 360-331-3580
Web site: *www.peerspirit.com*

Tenfold PeerSpirit Circles for Women

Tenfold is a facilitated weekend that leads to ongoing peer circles using PeerSpirit structure. Harriet Peterson and Sarah MacDougal were in the first Tenfold conducted by Christina Baldwin and Ann Linnea in March 1993, and they have become the primary facilitators of this seminar.

Contact:

Tenfold
P.O. Box 83
Taylor Falls, MN 55084
650-465-4902
Fax: 650-465-3104
E-mail: *tenfold@gte.net*

Wisdom Circles

Wisdom Circles is an association formed to encourage people to meet in small circles in order to listen and speak from the heart.

Contact them if you would like to know more about the activities of other wisdom circles, or to share your experiences with the format and what adaptations or innovations you've made.

They also offer a sixty-minute CD, *The Ceremonial*

Circle: Invoking an Earth-Centered Wisdom Circle, with Sedonia Cahill, consisting of ten tracks of spoken word with music, drumming and invocations.

Contact:

Wisdom Circles
3756 Grand Ave., Suite 405
Oakland, CA 94610
510-272-9540
E-mail: *cindy@wisdomcircle.org*
Web site: *www.wisdomcircle.org*

The Council Process

Jack Zimmerman and Virginia Coyle at the Ojai Foundation offer introductory training for prospective council leaders combining Native American practices with Buddhist wisdom teachings. They also offer intermediate training and a semiannual "Gathering of Council Leaders."

Contact:

Jack Zimmerman/Virginia Coyle
9739 Ojai-Santa Paula Rd.
Ojai, CA 93023

The Grandmothers' Circle

Based on the work of Mary Diamond, Kit Wilson and Jo Harris, this organization helps older women create circles in order to experience the spirituality and empowerment of aging. They also offer assistance to others who wish to create Grandmother Circles in various locations and offer a newsletter for $10.00 a year.

Contact:

The Grandmothers' Circle
3907 E. Campbell Ave.
Phoenix, AZ 85018
602-955-6818
Fax: 602-957-6328
E-mail: *kitw@home.com*

Rogers-McKay

This non-profit organization was founded in 1996 by Meredith Jordan and Eleanor Mercer and was named after their mothers, who were their first spiritual teachers. These women introduce circle (shared) leadership models in churches, schools, health and mental health care settings, and community service organizations. They also conduct ongoing depth-level psychospiritual study and direction for individuals and groups, dream study circles, and spiritual retreats, using circle as the primary teaching tool.

Contact:
>
> Rogers-McKay
> P.O. Box 1725
> Saco, ME 04072
> 207-284-1034
> Web site: *www.rogersmckay.org*

Earth Drum Council

Earth Drum Council was founded in 1990 by Morwen and Jimi Two Feathers to provide opportunities to drum and dance in community. They offer an annual gathering in western Massachusetts and one-day gatherings in Cambridge.

Contact:
>
> Earth Drum Council
> P.O. Box 1284
> Concord, MA 01742
> E-mail: *earthdrum@earthdrum.com*
> Web site: *www.earthdrum.com*

Tribes: A New Way of Learning Together

Since 1987, when Jeanne Gibbs originated this process for social development and cooperative learning, tribal circles have been flourishing in classrooms. Her books and curriculum training apply the circle in school settings.

Contact:

> Interactive Learning Systems
> 1505 Bridgeway, Suite 121
> Sausalito, CA 94965

The Council Circle Foundation— Dennie LaTourelle

Dennie provides experiences in council and council teacher training, and works extensively to create a circle-based community that can impact the spiritual environment in her city.

Contact:

> Dennie LaTourelle
> The Center for the Study of Sacred Psychology
> 823 Summit Rd.
> Santa Barbara, CA 93108

Tending Sacred Circles (TSC)

TSC is a nonprofit organization dedicated to creating and sustaining global shamanic community.

Contact:

> Tending Sacred Circles
> P.O. Box 66816
> Scotts Valley, CA 95067
> Web site: *www.shamaniccircles.org*

APPENDIX III: MEETING CENTERS AND RETREATS

Women's BearMedicine Circles

These retreats are held by Carol Proudfoot-Edgar, a walker and teacher of the shaman's path. In Carol's words:

I am not interested in "experiences" for themselves alone, but rather in discovering the patterns beneath many spiritual experiences which culminate in profound transformation for the individual. For this reason I invite women to join in a shamanic circle whose continuity spans the next three years: gathering five days in fall and five days in the spring. These are the seasons in which occur the fundamental dynamics of death and rebirth, preparing for hibernation and bringing forth the flowering from our wintering time.

The governing principles of our circles are to address the spiritual evolution of each woman and to learn shamanic practices that assist in serving the larger whole beyond our circle.

In addition to learning how to be a shamanic circle, we learn healing ways such as soul retrieval, assisting souls both entering and leaving this world, various methods of divination and rituals of transformation. We learn and do dances, songs and ceremonies that the spirits teach us and those based on ancient ways, still known, yet for many of us deeply lost to our conscious awareness.

In each gathering of our circle we manifest the "invoking image-making" of the shaman, knowing this can take many forms. We will allow the images that arise from trances and merge with spirits to find their form through our crafting, singing, painting, writing and other creative manifestations.

The reason I require a commitment of three years is that the ways of shamanism are most deeply learned and remembered when experienced again and again. That is why shamanism flourishes in communities. Within circles, actual opportunities are presented both by events arising within the circle and by the intervention of spirits.

By making covenant to gather for three years we also reap the blessings that come from such commitments. It is important to know that each of us is making this covenant to gather in circle for three years—aware always that powers beyond our present knowing can alter our lives. In such cases, the circle still holds those not present—in prayer, in spiritual work on their behalf, in love.

Contact:

Carol Proudfoot-Edgar
275 Rabbits Run Road
Santa Cruz, CA 95060
E-mail: *CedgarBear@aol.com*
Web site: *www.shamanicvisions.com*

The Ranch

The Ranch is a retreat, conference and training center on forty acres of beautiful rolling Oklahoma hills. It exists to provide a sacred ceremonial playground and can be used for group, personal and corporate retreats, sacred ceremonies, meetings, conferences and trainings.

The Circle Is Sacred medicine camps for women were created at the ranch in response to requests received from women around the world to spend focused ritual time together. In the words of Scout Cloud Lee:

Spirit's longing for us is as intense as our longing for Spirit. We must bridge the gap between our longing and the sacredness of all-that-is. Through sacred practices we learn the language of our dreams, and through rituals we reconnect with Spirit and community. Our time together will inspire, instruct and involve us all in ritual space, celebration, ceremonies and games that honor our passage as women leading the way into the twenty-first century.

The encampment includes ritual acts such as the:

- Pipe Ceremony
- Sweat Lodge
- Ava Ava Cava Seeing Ceremony
- Opening the Eagle Bundle
- Making of Medicine
- Fire-Women Ceremony

Contact:

The Ranch

6409 N. Country Club Rd.

Stillwater, OK 74075

405-377-2201

Web sites: *scoudcloudlee.com*

magicalchildfoundation.com

visionus.com

APPENDIX IV: OTHER ORGANIZATIONS OF INTEREST

The Institute of Noetic Sciences (IONS)
475 Gate Five Rd. #300
Sausalito, CA 94965
415-331-5650
Web site: *www.noetic.org*

Offers leading edge research in consciousness. Many IONS chapters in the United States conduct wisdom circles for members.

New Dimensions Radio
P.O. Box 569
Ukiah, CA 95482
Web site: *www.newdimensions.org*

Offers a diversity of views from many traditions and cultures which help foster positive personal and planetary development through its broadcasts on National Public Radio (NPR) stations and its large selection of audiotapes.

All One Tribe Foundation
P.O. Drawer N
Taos, NM 87571
E-mail: *year2000@allonetribedrum.com.*
Web site: *www.allonetribedrum.com.*

Disseminates research on the physical, psychological and spiritual benefits of drumming. The foundation donates half its profits to indigenous world causes.

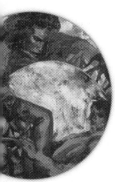

APPENDIX V: OTHER OPPORTUNITIES TO CONTRIBUTE

Talking Circle: Native American-Based Attack on Diabetes

Talking Circles are places for people to come together and talk about "Our Health, Our Solution." This includes taking control of their eating habits, exercise and other factors that will help stem the epidemic of diabetes in their communities. Participation involves providing help with child care and gas for transportation.

Your $30 Gift of Service will buy two gallons of gasoline that cover two round-trips to a Talking Circle on a reservation. (Gift #NA1)

Your $50 Gift of Service will pay for child care for thirty children at one day-long Talking Circle. (Gift #NA2)

By interviewing and recording local native nutritional experts in food gathering, storage and meal preparation, traditional knowledge can be preserved on tape for generations to come.

Your $250 Gift of Service will purchase audio recording equipment and supplies to interview native experts and to preserve their knowledge. The tapes and transcripts will be housed and used for curriculum development at local native community colleges. (Gift #NA3)

Contact:

The SEVA Foundation
1786 5th Street
Berkeley, CA 94710
1-800-223-7382
Web site: *www.seva.org*

The Heifer Project International (HPI)

HPI is a nonprofit organization that helps hungry people feed themselves, earn income and care for the environment. HPI has more than 300 projects in over forty countries. For over half a century, HPI has provided livestock and training to more than four million families around the world.

One of HPI's most important commitments is care of the earth. HPI believes development must be sustainable—that projects should be long-term investments in the future of people and, ultimately, the planet. That's why HPI provides hungry families with a source of food and income, rather than short-term relief. And that's why HPI teaches partners environmentally-sound farming methods. Through HPI training, families learn how to keep their small plots of land healthy and renew the soil for future generations by planting trees, using natural fertilizer and limiting grazing. By helping families raise their animals in harmony with nature, HPI works to ensure a healthy, productive future for us all.

You can help families around the world become self-reliant by purchasing a gift animal or tree seedlings. For example, for $500 you can give the gift of a heifer, for $50 a share of a heifer. The gift of a goat or sheep is $120, and the share of a goat or sheep is $10. The gift of a llama is $150, the share of a llama is $20. The gift of honeybees is $30. Tree seedlings are $60, and the share of seedlings is $10.

You can also download free educational materials on saving lives and the environment from their Web site. You can share this information with your circle, group, congregation or local school.

Contact:

Heifer Project International
P.O. Box 98175
Washington, DC 20090-8175
800-422-0755
Web site: *www.heifer.org*

The Council of All Beings

This is a deep ecology experimental process organized by John Seed and offered by a number of facilitators throughout the world. A newsletter, facilitator list and more information can be obtained directly from the Council.

Contact:

John Seed and Eshana
Rainforest Information Centre
Box 368
Lismore NSW 2480 Australia
Phone: 61-0-66218505
E-mail: *jseed@peg.apc.org.*

Other Environmental Agencies

Greenpeace
1436 "U" St., NW
Washington, D.C. 20009

National Audubon Society
645 Pennsylvania Ave., SE
Washington, D.C. 20003

National Coalition Against the Misuse of Pesticides
530 7th St., SE
Washington, D.C. 20003

National Wildlife Federation
1412 16th St., NW
Washington, D.C. 20036

Natural Resources Defense Council
40 West 20th St.
New York, NY 10011

Oceanic Society
218 "D" St., SE
Washington, D.C. 20003

Rainforest Action Network
300 Broadway, Suite 28
San Francisco, CA 94133

World Wildlife Fund
1250 24th St., NW
Washington, D.C. 20037

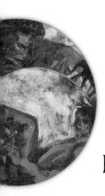

APPENDIX VI: RESTORATIVE JUSTICE

Family Group Conferencing and Sentencing Circles

We tend to be a nation of whiners, blamers and buck passers. Yet at the same time we insist that our criminals take full responsibility for their actions even when it means they will be punished by incarceration if they do so. Fortunately, there is a new movement called "restorative justice" that takes the focus off punishment and instead emphasizes repairing the harm by addressing the emotional and material needs of victims. This includes a strategy called "conferencing" in which the offender and victim meet face-to-face, along with their supporters, to discuss the crime and set up a plan for restitution. The conference begins with the offender taking responsibility for his actions. Then the victim and his or her family tell the offender how the crime affected them.

This may be the first time an offender is ever confronted with the results of his or her actions.

In 1989 New Zealand served as a beacon around the globe by legislating family group conferencing as an alternative to imprisonment for first-time offenders. Based on the Maori tradition of allowing family members to determine the appropriate way for offenders to make restitution for their crimes, family group conferencing has been utilized by many members of the justice system and by school disciplinary boards throughout Australia, the United Kingdom and the United States. In fact, several states, including North Carolina and Minnesota, have made family group conferencing a statewide policy.

Our current criminal justice systems and school disciplinary systems focus on guilt and establishing blame. Family group conferencing focuses on solving problems and repairing the harm. Currently we define accountability as punishment, but restorative justice defines accountability as demonstrating empathy and helping to repair the harm.

As opposed to the current court system, conferencing provides the following benefits:

1. It meets the needs of individuals and the community as a whole more than it meets the needs of the court.
2. It provides the offender an opportunity to apologize for his wrongdoing. Even those offenders who

would like to apologize to their victims are discouraged from doing so by our current court system since to apologize is to admit wrongdoing and to admit wrongdoing usually means either jail time or, in civil actions, a hefty financial settlement.

3. It separates the person from the wrongdoing. The behavior is bad, not the person.

4. Remorse and apology are more effective in healing the damage than material reparation or punishment.

5. It empowers victims versus reinforcing the victim role.

6. It helps the offender to connect with other people's feelings and encourages/teaches empathy.

7. If we isolate and stigmatize the offender it doesn't help them look at their actions. As opposed to shaming and making the offender feel like a horrible monster, conferencing teaches responsibility and empathy. For example, at the beginning of a conference the facilitator states that they are not there to decide whether the offender is a good or bad person.

8. It focuses on problem solving versus placing blame.

9. It provides an opportunity for all involved to repair the damage that's been done. For example, accountability is defined as empathy and reparation versus punishment.

10. It advocates the idea that the stigma is removable; repentance is encouraged and forgiveness is possible.

According to a poll conducted by the Real Justice organization, victims of minor crimes stated they most needed the following in order to heal from the crime:

- An opportunity to express their emotions concerning the crime
- An acknowledgment from loved ones concerning how the crime affected them
- Assurance that what happened was unfair and undeserved
- Holding the offender accountable
- Financial restitution
- Contact with the offender, including an opportunity to receive an apology, to ask questions and to get an assurance of safety in the future

Many family group conferences include volunteers from the community. If you would like to get involved, please contact:

Real Justice
P.O. Box 229
Bethlehem, PA 18016-0229
Web site: *www.realjustice.org.*

or

Kay Pranis
Minnesota Dept. of Corrections
1450 Energy Park Drive
St. Paul, MN 55108
651-642-0329
E-mail: *Kpranis@co.doc.state.mn.u.s.*

For more information about discussion of peacemaking or sentencing circles, see *Building Community Justice Partnerships: Community Peacemaking Circles,* by Barry Stuart, available from:

Aboriginal Justice Section
Department of Justice of Canada
Ottawa, Ontario, K1A0H8
Fax: 613-957-4697
Attention: Learning Network

ABOUT THE AUTHOR

 Beverly Engel, M.F.T. has been a marriage, family and child therapist for over twenty-five years. For most of those years she specialized in working with adult survivors of childhood abuse (physical, emotional and sexual), victims of domestic violence and emotionally abused women. Always interested in helping women in particular, she has conducted hundreds of groups for female survivors of sexual abuse as well as groups for women who are physically or emotionally abused in their adult relationships with men.

This work, plus her growing personal need to connect with spirituality, is what led her to women's circles. There she found both personal and professional fulfillment and learned that by joining hands and joining hearts women can overcome even the greatest obstacles.

She lives in the central coast of California where she divides her time between writing books, conducting and attending women's circles and practicing psychotherapy.

Beverly welcomes your comments concerning the book and is available for presentations on women's circles. You can contact Beverly by e-mail at:

beverly@beverlyengel.com
or by mail at:
P.O. Box 6412
Los Osos, CA 93412 or
visit her at her Web site at *www.beverlyengel.com*

ABOUT THE ARTIST
GAIL LAPINS

I was very honored to have Beverly Engel choose my painting *Souls Connected* for the cover of *Women Circling the Earth*. Beverly asked me to share my thoughts and feelings regarding my art with you, her readers.

My paintings are explorations of an internal world where characters, events and scenes mirror reality, but are not restricted by logic or structure. Separate images are thus assembled to convey a variety of corporeal and psychological sensations inherent to the narrative. My paint surfaces build a bridge to the past as well as to the future, with the complex compositions breaking down time and space. I challenge viewers through the narrative fragments to create their personal interpretations.

It is the journey, the wondering spirit on its quest for the sacred rather than the destination itself, which I depict in my paintings. As I have grown artistically and matured as a woman, my paintings have become more authentic and sure. I come to my paintings with joy, anger, pain and sorrow. It is imperative for me to keep that creative passion alive and not let it become tamed with habit. Courage is the foundation of integrity and with it you dare to take risks.

Above all, my paintings celebrate women and their strength to endure and flourish. Women walk the Earth with the beauty of their souls. Many of the exhibitions I have been part of honor women: Heritage Museum, Royal Birmington Society of Artists, Museum of Arts Downtown Los Angeles, Women's Caucus for Art, Coos Bay Art Museum, Woman Made Galleries, to name a few.

I would love to share my art with you. You can see more art on my Web site *http://gaillapinsartist.com*. Or contact me through e-mail at *info@gaillapinsartist.com*.

Also by Beverly Engel

The Right to Innocence
Divorcing a Parent
The Emotionally Abused Woman
Encouragements for the Emotionally Abused Woman
Partners in Recovery
Families in Recovery
Raising Your Sexual Self-Esteem
Beyond the Birds and the Bees
The Parenthood Decision
Blessings from the Fall

Also by Beverly Engel

Blessings from the Fall

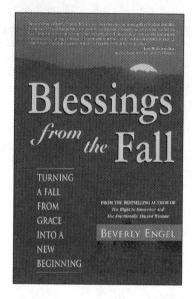

Code # 4568 • Quality Paperback • $10.95

For anyone who has fallen into shame, this book will help you accept it and move forward to a new life of promise. Instead of yielding to the temptation to run away and hide, you will learn what it takes to face things head-on. You will learn how to transform your life from shame and denial to recognition and self-awareness, and finally to acceptance and gratitude. You will understand how powerful and life-changing—and positive—a fall from grace can be.

Books for Redemption and Healing

The Evolving Woman

In her latest book, bestselling novelist Catherine Lanigan brings you true stories from real heroines. These are candid stories from women of all races, religions and walks of life, who drew upon their resilience, faith and strength of character to overcome abusive relationships that had left them shattered in mind and spirit. *The Evolving Woman* is an inspiration and lifeline for any woman living the misery of domestic abuse.

Code # 7591 • Quality Paperback • $11.95

Only When I Sleep

This touching true story of a young woman's battle to overcome Hodgkin's disease and give birth to the child of her dreams will bring tears to your eyes and joy to your heart. In vivid prose, she invites you into her family's home, into their hearts, and into the battle of their lives.

Lisa Shaw-Brawley
Foreword by Robert Urich

Code #7745 • Quality Paperback • $10.95

More of the Inspiration
You've Been Waiting For

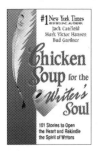

Chicken Soup for the Writer's Soul
Whether you're a beginning writer, seasoned pro
or a writer at heart, the stories of purpose, passion,
endurance and success contained in this volume will
inform, entertain, uplift and inspire you.

Code # 7699 • Quality Paperback • $12.95

**Chicken Soup for the
Golden Soul**
Celebrating the myriad joys of living and the wisdom
that comes from having lived, this collection offers
loving insights and wisdom—all centering on
the prime of life.

Code # 7257 • Quality Paperback • $12.95

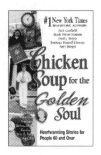

**Chicken Soup for the
Teenage Soul III**
The third volume for teens is here, offering more stories
on love, friendship, family, tough stuff, growing up,
kindness, learning lessons and making a difference.

Code # 7613 • Quality Paperback • $12.95

**Chicken Soup for the
Christian Family Soul**
The stories in this collection will deepen your faith and
expand your awareness of how to practice Christian values
in your daily life—at home, at work and in the community.

Code # 7141 • Quality Paperback • $12.95

Selected titles are also available in large print, hardcover, audiocassette and CD.

Available wherever books are sold.
To order direct: Phone — **800.441.5569** • Online — **www.hci-online.com**
Prices do not include shipping and handling. Your response code is **BKS**.